CW01360241

FAMILY SAILING IN
EUROPEAN WATERS

FAMILY SAILING IN EUROPEAN WATERS

Derek Phillips

Book Guild Publishing
Sussex, England

First published in Great Britain in 2010 by
The Book Guild Ltd
Pavilion View
19 New Road
Brighton, BN1 1UF

Copyright © Derek Phillips 2010

The right of Derek Phillips to be identified as the author of this work has been asserted by him in accordance with the Copyright, Designs and Patents Act 1988.

All rights reserved. No part of this publication may be reproduced, transmitted, or stored in a retrieval system, in any form or by any means, without permission in writing from the publisher, nor be otherwise circulated in any form of binding or cover other than that in which it is published and without a similar condition being imposed on the subsequent purchaser.

Typesetting in Times by
Keyboard Services, Luton, Bedfordshire

Printed in Thailand under the supervision of
MRM Graphics Ltd, Winslow, Bucks

A catalogue record for this book is available from
The British Library

ISBN 978 1 84624 374 5

Contents

Preface		vii
Introduction		ix
Preparation		1
1	The First Voyage: Holland 1982	7
2	Exploring the UK: Cornwall 1984	17
3	France 1986	23
4	Brittany 1987	37
5	Holland	63
6	Ireland 1988	73
7	Passage to the Sun: Spain 1989	101
8	Around the Ferry Ports of France and England 1991	139
9	'A Porto too Far': Portugal 1994	165
10	The Halcyon Cruise: The Netherlands 1995	195
11	Cruise to the Sun: Brittany 1996, July – August	231
12	Not so Much a Cruise – More a Doddle: Holland 1997	263
13	Passage to the Mediterranean I: Rye – St Jean de Losne 1999	285
14	Passage to the Mediterranean II: St Jean de Losne – Port St Louis 2000	309
15	Barcelona – Marseilles 2003	327
Glossary		347

Preface

On completion of my autobiography *Five Careers and Dog* (Book Guild 2007) in 2006, I cast around for a subject for a new book, which had nothing to do with work and everything to do with pleasure ... also something with which I had been involved for a large number of years.

The subject which presented itself was sailing, and this had the advantage that, over a period of some 20 years, I had completed an illustrated log of each of our annual voyages to give to all the crew on our return; allowing a fairly accurate record of events when accompanied by the more formal ship's log of dates, winds, tides and journeys.

Our first boat was a Cornish Crabber 24 purchased from a farmer who farmed sheep on Romney Marsh. He had been given the boat by his wife to take his mind off farming ... it hadn't worked! Our nautical advisor, Patrick Benson, suggested that we should take a look at this boat, the *Midley Belle*, at her home in the boatyard in Rye, very convenient for us. This done, it was all agreed, so that suddenly we found ourselves the proud owners of our own sailing boat, a decision we never regretted.

A Cornish Crabber 24 is a 24-foot gaff-rigged dayboat, a safe boat ideal for family sailing, and for learning the ropes. Then after some six years we moved on to a larger version, the 30-foot Pilot Cutter.

For 20 years we sailed in European waters towards Holland and the Friesian Islands, down the French coast to the Morbihan; across Biscay to Spain and Portugal, with a few final years to the Mediterranean.

One reads of people with no experience who go to sea and get into trouble, and we had our share of this ... but if we have learned anything, it is a very healthy respect for the sea, and to ensure that at no time do you put your crew or your boat into avoidable danger.

Finally I want to emphasise the joy of sailing, something which can be enjoyed by the whole family, which doesn't cost an arm and a leg, and becomes the basis of family holidays over the years.

Introduction

It is nearly 30 years ago since the idea of owning our own boat started to form and some years after that before the idea became reality. When in the early 2000s our eldest son Starkie was living in Singapore, he asked me to let him have a list of all the family holidays since he had been born in 1954. I did this, and looking back at it now has helped me together with my diaries and sailing logs to form a fairly accurate record of our life on the water ... in the same way that my flying logs (held at the FAA Museum, Yeovilton) enabled me to record life in the Royal Navy Fleet Air Arm during the war, for my autobiography.

These records together with my office diaries starting in 1975 have allowed me to compile a fairly accurate record of our boating activities until my retirement in 1993. These are associated with the more detailed sailing logs of each of our voyages in both *Midley Belle* and *Emma* over the years.

We compiled two types of log, the formal sailing log completed on a day-to-day basis recording the distances sailed, courses made good, the wind speed and direction, barometer readings and remarks, then there are the more informal diaries written on our return containing photographs, crew lists and stories, a copy of which is given to each member of the crew as a memento of the trip.

On occasions my wife Diana has done a separate log, the skipper's mate's story ... she tells me this is 'the real log'.

All of these bits and pieces have been useful in helping me to write this book, together with the delightful sketches provided by Wolfgang Manner, an important member of the crew.

Preparation

It was difficult to know where to start to write a book about sailing when I have for some years since retirement written books about my profession as an architect, very different to my 20 years of recreational sailing.

To start with I wrote down a few thoughts, as guidance: school … the Royal Navy … the RYA and exams … Dacorum College, Hemel Hempstead … purchase of house at Rye … *Midley Belle*, the River Rother and *Emma* … Holland … France, the Morbihan … Southern Ireland … Spain … Biscay … the Mediterranean … handover of boat to my son Adam in 2003 … This gave a framework with which to start, although I expected there to be many variations as time went by.

I should explain at the outset that there was no tradition of sailing in my family, my father had been a banker in India, whose great love was golf, and his father had been a stained glass window designer, so no tradition of sailing there. My first experience had been at school, when at Haileybury the art master, a Mr Delmar-Morgan, had started a sailing club, which allowed me to exchange a love of art for a love of the water. But I suspect that this was more because of the great teas he used to provide after sailing!

My next experience was at the end of the war in Australia. When serving in the aircraft carrier *Implacable* to show the flag in Sydney and Melbourne, we were allowed to take out the ship's boats when anchored offshore in the evenings. I remember one occasion when sailing in Sydney Harbour the wind died completely when we were a mile or so away from the ship. The officer of the watch, seeing our plight, offered by radio to send us a tow, but as a crew we decided to row back – very gung-ho! What idiots we were! But this was about the only experience of sailing until years later when I could afford my own boat. This was where it really all began.

Having said this, there were moments when the idea of sailing did arise, one such being when on holiday in 1962 in Tobermorey in Mull I would gaze enviously at a yacht parked along the pier, thinking that perhaps one day, maybe... But it took some years before this became a reality.

It all started to become more than a gleam in the eye when we acquired our holiday home in Rye with its harbour, and a dream became more than a possibility, although even then it took some years before it took shape in the form of a Cornish Crabber called *Midley Belle*.

Having acquired our boat, it was then necesssary to learn to sail it, and this is where the the Royal Yachting Association (RYA) is invaluable in providing a programme of study to enable one to master the art. Courses in sailing are available throughout the country, and we were particularly lucky in that they were available at the Dacorum College in Hemel Hempstead. So for some years I attended the courses, enabling me to a pass the exams for Competent Crew and Dayskipper/Watch Leader in June 1982, and the Coastal Skipper and Yachtmaster Offshore Shore-Based Course in July 1985. At the same time I took the exam for Radio Operator,

PREPARATION

Midley Belle being craned into the water

so that I felt able to act as skipper of *Midley Belle* in our trips across the Channel to France and Holland.

Our first skipper was a friend, Chris Oakley, and I see from the ship's log that our first trip was made on 3rd April 1981, recorded as 'An experimental trip to try out the motor'. The following day was described as the first day's 'real sailing', where we raised the mainsail and jib, and as recorded in the log we broke out the bottle of champagne kindly provided by John Payne, the farmer who sold me the boat.

Chris Oakley remained the skipper until Pat Benson took over in July 1982, and then I took over from August onwards when we made our first foreign voyage to the Netherlands. My sailing days had begun.

Our first sails were mainly exploratory, taking place in April and May 1981, checking the sails and gear, and correcting any minor faults.

There was one occasion when Chris Oakley was skipper, and the engine failed. He decided to beach *Midley Belle* on Camber Sands, in the end having to get the harbour-master to tow the boat back to Rye when the tide had allowed sufficient water to

...can be a source of embarrassment!

float her off. Another and rather more serious occasion was when we got into difficulties (failed engine again) outside Rye Harbour and had to be rescued by the Dungeness Lifeboat. The lifeboat took all the crew off, except for the skipper, a friend of Starkie's called Chris Wallace, and myself; and then towed the boat, leaving her anchored offshore at Dungeness. *Midley Belle* was brought back to her moorings in Rye by Bob Read the following weekend, when I was away in Hong Kong.

Whilst Cornish Crabbers have their moments, they are not the most comfortable, being designed as a daybook. The layout, which in the after cabin allows for a portaloo placed between the two bunks, can be a source of embarrassment!

The Skipper's Wife's Story

3rd October 1981

In the early days of our sailing, before Derek had done the RYA exams and felt competent to skipper Midley Belle, *a friend of Starkie's, who had once entered the Fastnet Race, came to Rye with Starkie and offered to skipper the boat for a day sail. So, together with Amelia and her boyfriend at the time (known as Womble), we set out. It was not a nice day, very blowy and the sea was rough, but our advisor said it would be OK.*

We left our berth and went down the channel, and out to sea, in order to go round Rye Buoy and back. But very soon it was clear that this was not a good idea and we tried to return, but in turning we started to take in water, faster than we could bail it out, and the engine stopped ... We called the lifeguards, who must have seen our plight as they arrived very fast.

The first thing they said was, 'Have you got your life belts?'
'Oh yes!' we said.
'Then why the hell haven't you got them on?' We quickly did!
They then said, 'Throw your line,' but we knew all about this and said, 'No! You throw us yours,' and they did.
The theory is that if a rescue boat accepts your lifeline then

they have the right to claim salvage ... not that I think the RNLI ever do!

The result was that they took Amelia, me and Womble off in the inflatable ... whilst they towed Midley Belle *around to Dungeness.*

They took us 'frails' back to their station and gave us blankets, so we could take off our wet clothes, and cocoa with rum. Then took us back to our house. Unfortunately Derek had the key in his pocket ... but the bread shop next door had a key but the baker had gone into town, so we had to wait while the key was fetched. By now we were holding up a wedding party on their way to church. As we climbed out of the van, both Amelia and I let our blankets fall, to the amusement of the wedding party.

The lifeboatmen put Womble in a tepid bath, as he was suffering from hypothermia, and he recovered. Later Derek rang and asked if I could collect them, but he had the keys of the car in his pocket ... so they had to get a taxi. A bottle of whisky later and all restored.

1

The First Voyage: Holland 1982

Although purchased in 1981 and used for offshore sailing from her moorings in Rye, it was not until August 1982 that we sailed *Midley Belle* to Holland, with a determined crew consisting of family joined by Jonathan Woodhouse and Chris Oakley, not forgetting Wolfgang.

The boat's log was completed, giving details of winds, tides and courses but this was in the days before I would write an illustrated history of the voyages, to give to each member of the crew something to keep as a reminder. However Jonathan is a keen photographer, and he acted as the 'official' photographer, so I am writing this with the assistance of the boat's log and the pictures provided by Jonathan, and some sketches provided by Wolfgang.

Leaving Haynes Yard at Rye in the early morning, we sailed towards Dungeness and then crossed the Channel to Calais, leaving *Midley Belle* overnight, before carrying on to Ostend the following day.

The decision was made to enter the canal system at Flushing and to stop at Middleburg; this was completed, allowing us to carry on to Veere, a delightful spot. Chris Oakley had to leave for home, but we carried on to Zierikzee, spending the night there before reaching Bruinisse the following day.

Bruinisse is a very smart marina, full of expensive boats We had to spend a weekend here on another occasion, and on the Friday evening a lot of people arrived with provisions, so we thought that there would be much activity the following day . Wrong! Not a boat moved. It's a bit like a caravan park – nothing to do with sailing.

The following day, on to Wilhamstad; this was one of the highlights of the voyage, a beautiful walled town, and if you are moored in the centre of town there is no charge. We spent two nights there, before continuing on to Hellevoetsluis, with a good chandler and restaurant.

From Hellevoetsluis, back to Bruinisse and the homeward journey via Veere, then on down the Channel and out at Flushing with a night in Zeebrugge.

In Zeebrugge we experienced a little difficulty, as we arrived rather late at night due to bad weather, and were accosted by harbour officials and police who seemed to think that we were coming to join an anti-nuclear demonstration and wanted us to leave. But they relented when I said that I would not leave the harbour because of the bad weather outside, and in any case I did not even know there was a demonstration! So a night in Zeebrugge, leaving the following day for Ostend, but returning as the weather outside was still unpleasant.

It was not until the following day that we set off for Ostend, but this was not to be as we made a mess of shaking out the reefed sail, tearing it, so that we decided to dive into Blankenburg where the sail could repaired. Due to this hang-up it was necessary to leave *Midley Belle* there and carry on home by ferry from Ostend with Patrick Benson in charge of bringing *Midley Belle* back to Rye two weeks later.

Pat with a new crew visited Blankenburg on 13th September, getting the boat home safely via Dunkirk and Calais. The entry in their log for 14th September goes as follows:

Distress signal observed ... we went to assistance of a wind surfer, but were joined by other vessels heading in the right direction.

Due to lack of wind it was necessary to motor most of the following day, then stocking up with wine and cheese in Calais.

We shared a buoy in the outer harbour with a yacht full of drunken Belgians singing dirty French songs.

A good trip goose-winging across the Channel the following day in poor visibility, all in all an eventful trip back to Rye, but a safe one.

This was the end of sailing in 1982. *Midley Belle* was taken out of the water by Bob Read, who removed the mast and standing rigging, storing all in his sail loft. Work during the winter consisted of antifouling the bottom, and work on the mast and superstructure. Diana says: 'Antifouling is a filthy job, done by the skipper's wife as she is small and can get under the boat!'

From Chris

The engine on Midley Belle *never seemed to work properly. In 1981 – the early days, when sailing trips consisted of zigzagging around Rye bay for an hour or two before the tide forced us to return – the engine (a Yanmar) conked out in a bumpy sea, just as we were trying to return after one such trip. I remember that look of blind panic in Derek's eyes – a look that, I have to say, was soon to become quite familiar, with me, as skipper, trying to work out what to do next. It did not look good. Rye was very, very tidal. The boat would sit on the mud most of the time; only for about four hours around high water was it possible to move, and then, on the two-mile trip down to the sea, one was fighting a flood tide; a few hours later, after sailing in circles in the bay, one would then have to fight the ebb to get home.*

I suppose we could have sailed back up the river, and if I was in the same situation now, that is certainly what I would have done. The reason I did not was that getting back into the narrow berth, which was at right angles to the river, with a two-knot ebb tide, was like a game of Russian roulette: if the boat got caught halfway into the berth, then the tide would pivot it so that the bow crashed into the neighbour. And, given the Belle*'s seven-foot bowsprit, this particular game of Russian roulette was being played with a Magnum. I might as well admit it – I had already bent a stanchion post on the neighbouring boat by just such a misjudged manoeuvre. This was manoeuvring under power ... as* *for trying to get into the berth under sail – well, that would be Russian roulette with a Magnum and two bullets in the magazine. Also, I was taking the attitude that everything had to either be done perfectly or not at all. Derek fully sympathised with this. He had been in the Fleet Air Arm, and knew that Jerry or Jap was always there, ready to punish the most trivial mistakes.*

If I had to do the same thing now, it would be different. I would have everyone ready to fend off, including someone sitting on the bowsprit, and if we did not make it on the third attempt we would just sail round to Strand quay or the fuelling berth, where we could lay alongside until the engine was fixed. If we screwed up a few times in the process then, hey, provided that no one died, that was part of the fun, and something to talk about in the pub later. But that was then. Going back up that narrow river just did not look like an option, and there were no nearby ports to sail to either. So I decided to pull up the centreboard and just beach the boat on Camber Sands. From every point of view, I could not have timed it better, which is to say, I could not have timed it worse. It was a warm, sunny, but blustery Saturday afternoon in May, and with a crowded beach, our audience was in the hundreds. I had been feeling a bit seasick, and was just beginning to recover, thinking, no problem, just mend the engine and float the boat off at the next high tide and we will be fine, when the RNLI launch appeared out of nowhere, with the crew attired as though they were performing a rescue at night, in mid-ocean, in a force 11 storm. I have to be careful in choosing words to describe the Rye Harbour RNLI as just a few months later they pretty much saved the Phillips' lives, but in retrospect, they could possibly have done more that was useful on this occasion, such as towing us to a mooring. Instead of this, though, they insisted on taking us on board and dragging us to their clubhouse where they fed us with coffee laced with rum. It was here that the real reason for their interest – Amelia, Diana and Jemima wearing not very much – emerged.

Luckily, others were on our side, in particular an old-timer from the boatyard who I will call Bob, even though that may not have actually been his name. Bob's prognosis was not good. I had managed to beach at the top of a spring tide, and if we could not float the boat off at the next high water, which was at about 2 a.m., then we would not get the opportunity again for another fortnight. To cheer us up, Bob then started telling us stories about what happens to boats that get left on Camber Sands. Again, not good. To further complicate the issue, the slope of the beach is so gentle that the towing boat, in order not to be aground, was going to have to be about 400 metres away. So on top of everything else we had to find 400 metres of tow rope. But even at the top of the tide that night the boat hardly moved. The others (Bob, Derek and Simon, Jemima's boyfriend at the time) then made the long journey back to Rye on foot, but I stayed on the boat, unable to sleep, and when a JCB drove by at first light I then tried, unsuccessfully, to persuade the driver to dig a trench to help ease the boat out, which gives you an idea how desperate I was getting.

The next spring tide, in a fortnight, brought me right up to my exams at Cambridge. If I could have my time over, this would not have stopped me coming down to help get the boat off, especially as I did not do especially well in these exams anyway, but as it was I did not even dare call the Phillipses to find out if they still had a boat, and if so, whether it was still in one piece. Luckily, I need not have worried. When I finally plucked up courage to call, Solly (Rebecca's boyfriend at the time) answered, and could not have been more reassuring. No damage, boat towed off fine, everything OK again. So I could relax. Of course the 'sand yachting' episode (as Richard Jones called it) was tame compared to their adventures the following September, with someone else called Chris skippering, where the wind freshened to an onshore gale, and they nearly lost their lives, but it was plenty enough excitement for me.

My next involvement with Midley Belle worthy of a Salty Dog Yarn was a year and a half later. Derek had left the boat in Middelburg, in south-west Holland, and my job was to bring it back to Rye. I arrived with two chums from the Physics department in Oxford, according to the log, on 30 September 1983. We had taken the overnight ferry from Sheerness to Flushing, and arrived fairly tired, not having been able to afford cabins and *just dossing down in sleeping bags. I seem to remember seeing* The Count of Monte Cristo *in the cinema, and talking about the MIT mathematicians who had a formula for Blackjack and were getting banned from casinos with Jo Zuk, a story which became the film* 21 *25 years later, but other than that, I do not remember much other than that it was misty, and that the sea was very calm.*

We got to Midley Belle *quite early, and left Middelburg in the boat at 1020, and were at the sea lock at Flushing at 1225, where we managed to rip out one of Derek's cleats following an unexpectedly rapid fall in the water level. We then motored in a southwesterly direction through the haze. There was hardly any wind until quite late that day, giving us about 2 hours of actual sailing, and we arrived at the entrance to Ostend (a busy one with, amongst other things, a ferry the size of a block of flats plying in and out) – according to the log – at about 7pm. We were about to hand the sails, when Steve Wilkinson turned the ignition key on the engine, and nothing happened. Another case of the Yanmar choosing its moment perfectly. Luckily, Steve is smarter than the average bear, and after a few abortive attempts to crank the engine, figured out that the problem was in the ignition relay, and that if one shorted the bolts on the back of the solenoid with a screwdriver, then one could get the starter motor to turn regardless. This caused an impressive display of sparks, but worked a treat, and I notice a log entry I made about the 'new, improved' starting handle consisting of a screwdriver. We were forced to use this technique anyway, as we managed to lose the real starting handle that day (Derek later found it in the bilges). So there was some feeling of achievement when, about an hour later, we rolled up at the North Sea Yacht Club in Ostend in search of food, even though this ended up being a bit like the Monty Python 'Cheese Shop' sketch, as despite the extensive menu it turned out that we could have anything we liked – provided it was steak and salad. But that was just fine.*

The next day we did not leave until midday – I am not sure why. Maybe we were trying (unsuccessfully) to fix the engine; maybe we were waiting for the tide – I cannot remember. The

THE FIRST VOYAGE: HOLLAND 1982

wind was much the same. What little there was was in exactly the wrong direction, so we motored most of the way, finally finding a mooring buoy next to the lock at Calais at 2am. Not leaving the boat, we then departed at 9am for Folkestone. The log says that we ran out of fuel the previous day; I guess that we must have found an extra can somewhere as we did two hours of motoring, anchoring in Folkestone harbour at 9pm. Again, we did not leave the boat, and were off at 7am to catch the tide to get to Rye, finally arriving at 11am.

Although not directly related to any sailing, this otherwise unexciting story has an epilogue which is directly related to the fact that we had had only one decent night's sleep in four days, and were knackered. *Diana had given me the key to the house in Rye, and it would have made sense to stay a night before travelling, but I did nothing so sensible. I took the London train shortly after the others, arriving at Sheerness, where I had left my car, after dark. Driving back to Hemel, it was only possible to stay awake by having the windows fully wound down and* Ride of the Valkyries *playing at maximum volume on the car stereo. I must have got home about midnight, but had to be up early for the start of term in Oxford the following day.*

Here I met up with Jo and Steve again at the introductory party at the Department of Theoretical Physics that evening. At these events one is required to make polite conversation with the dons, and drinking one or, at most, two glasses of cheap wine is part of the ritual. Having a bottle *of wine or two, though, is simply unheard of, although not, apparently, for our esteemed colleague Guy Coughlan, who got paralytic, and, having a car, I seemed to be the one responsible for getting him home. Then, on the landing outside his flat, it turned out that he did not have his keys. Apart from a question about my sexual orientation, searching his pockets produced no result (he was otherwise more or less unable to speak), so I went back to search our office and sure enough, his keys were there on the desk. When I got back, though, he had already been sick on the carpet. Guess who had to clear it up? Yup – you got it. We left him clinging to the toilet bowl in his flat (or 'Calling up God on the Great White Telephone' as it is picturesquely known) and then went to Brown's Restaurant, where we had arranged to meet a few others earlier. We were standing, waiting for a table when I blacked out. All I remember is being on the floor, thinking, 'Why am I on the floor?' Luckily I lived only a few yards away. 'If I go directly back to my room, and go directly to bed, and sleep for a long time,' I told the others, 'I will be all right.' So I did, and I was.*

Patrick Benson letter

Sir,

I have the honour to present a report on the latest voyage of the gaff-sloop Midley Belle *on manoeuvres in the Royal Sovereign area of the Eastern Channel between the 18th and 20th inst. of September, 1981.*

As requested and required by verbal order I did take command and put to sea, however, the weather being foul, the voyage terminated shortly after leaving the harbour entrance and returned. The wind was a 7, gusting 8, and the seas heavy and spraying. I have the pleasure to report no hands lost.

After a night spent in the fleshpots of the port, the crew (now supplemented by a new midshipman, S. Phillips, and a rare and wise master mariner, Mr Christopher Wallace, such a man whose ancestors could have sailed with St Brendan, and whose tales of eastern voyages, deprivation, dusky maidens and strange customs among the heathen did make our blood warm and run cold, turn and turn about) did put to sea again into shorter seas and slightly kinder winds, enjoying a trip of duration, 3 hours.

The crew proved willing and strong although one came down with an unidentified disease, but as it was found to be incommunicable, the quarantine flag was not hoisted, indeed it is curable with hot food and ardent spirits, these were therefore administered as a preventative measure.

The pressed crew had been loyal for the first two voyages but on rumours of the good life among the savages of Wales they deserted the ship on our Lord's day.

THE FIRST VOYAGE: HOLLAND 1982

I did therefore put to sea with Masters Phillips and Wallace, and a most exciting voyage was made.
I have the favour of being your obdt. servt.
Patrick Benson, Skipper (acting)

Crew Roster:
Tony Ponsford MRGC MPT (run)
Kim Carter RN (run)
Chris Wallace
Katherine Hardwicke (run)
Gary Tudor 2MFG
P. Benson
S. Phillips

2

Exploring the UK: Cornwall 1984

In 1983 we made a second visit to Holland which confirmed our love of sailing in the canals, and up the Nordsee to Amsterdam, but we felt the following year that we should try waters closer to home. This, coupled with with an invitation from Peter Keeling, the director of Cornish Crabbers, to join a regatta of likeminded boat owners in Falmouth, ended with the family enjoying the delights of Mousehole, Mevagissey and Polperro, and much more: the charm of Cornwall.

We left Rye on 5th August, stopping at Brighton, Cowes, Dartmouth and Fowey, ending up in Falmouth a week later. We had hit a squall off St Aldhem's Head, where Adam and Jonathan managed to set two reefs in the mainsail which, with the engine running, enabled us to keep head to wind until the squall passed. So around Portland Bill and on toward the Dart.

This entailed a night sail, and Adam worked out a clever compass light using a reostat, enabling us to set the level of light low enough to read the compass course, without causing glare. As there were three of us, we organised a watch system, working three hours on and one and a half hours off, enabling there always to be two on deck with one sleeping below. This worked well.

This being our first night sail, we were quite relieved when by 0230 we spotted the Berry Head light dead ahead, allowing us to round Scabbacombe Head for the Mewstone, with entry to the Dart by 4 a.m. – a magic moment.

We spent a 'make and mend' day in Dartmouth sorting out the alternator fan belt which had been slipping.

The following day a north-easterly gave us a good sail south from Dartmouth to Start Point, but less good when turning westerly past Prawle Point, Bolt Head and across Bigbury Bay toward Plymouth. The poor wind provided Adam with the opportunity for some fishing, and he caught six mackerel for dinner.

Having cooked our mackerel, we decided to walk into town. This proved to be even less pleasant than the red-light district of Amsterdam, as it is necessary to walk through the Stonehouse district of Plymouth – not a pretty sight!

As we had not planned to arrive in Falmouth until Saturday we decided to make a detour to visit Fowey, a little harbour that Diana and I had visited before we were married. No wind, and so motoring all the way for nearly five hours, but allowing us to pick up Marie who had arrived by train.

As planned, we arrived in Falmouth Marina by the afternoon of the Saturday, finding that there was a party for all the Crabbers at the Royal Cornwall Yacht Club. Peter Keeling made a speech of welcome, and explained about the racing for the following week.

The truth is that we don't do racing, and this was a humiliating experience, in that of the four days' racing we ended up last on two occasions and second to last on the other two. The winner, as on most occasions, was Ken Patterson (he is said to bring his own wind with him). He had given me good advice by telephone before we came, and on arrival we found that we had both been in the Fleet Air Arm during the war at the same time, but not in the same squadron.

As we didn't feel like cooking after the racing, we went out for a typical Cornish meal – a Chinese. But perhaps the most important aspect of the trip was the realisation that we needed to acquire alternative transport.

During the week's racing we increasingly felt the need for a small tender to enable us to get from *Midley Belle* to the shore and this was solved by the purchase of a Bombard inflatable, which was small enough to deflate and stow on board. We did a deal with Penryn Marine close to the marina, to combine the Bombard with a small Marina outboard, all for under £100 – the best buy of the trip.

Cornish Crabbers had organised several social events, one of the most memorable being a night barbeque at Turnaware Point, allowing a visit to Trelissick House.

Diana had arrived, bringing Jemima; Adam had brought son Ben and, a great surprise, Michael Farr arrived, a friend from Hong Kong, with his son. It all made quite a party, with gourmet cook Jemima cooking a splendid meal in the evening. But all good things have to end, and eventually we left for a voyage around the Cornish coast with a first stop at Mousehole.

The ship's log is a different matter to the personal log, and this page is included to emphasise the importance of keeping the ship's log up to date, written on the day – the personal log later!

From Mousehole on to Penzance, then on to the delightful port of Mevagissey. The harbour dries, so it is essential to time your entrance and exits right. This was a delightful part of the cruise, visiting Fowey and Polperro and finally on to Plymouth, where we moored at Sutton Harbour Marina.

Jonathan tested the ability of the crew to deal with a man

overboard, by suddenly getting up and jumping into the sea. I am glad to say that we coped rather well coming up on him on the lee side – textbook stuff. He had checked on the tide and wind before he jumped: he's not stupid!

From Plymouth on to Salcombe, where with the arrival of new crew there were too many to sleep on board, and so Diana and Jemima slept in a tent on the shore.

From Salcombe on to Dartmouth: despite this having been one of the most expensive stopovers of the whole trip, we had so enjoyed it that we decided to visit it again.

From Dartmouth it was a long old haul, sailing all the way with strong south-westerlies, around Portland Bill and into Weymouth, taking 12 hours in all.

That night the skipper and Diana chickened out of sleeping on board and found a B&B in the town.

It was at this point that there was a general exodus, as people had to get on with their lives, leaving the skipper and Adam to bring *Midley Belle* home.

We left Weymouth early, sailing well as far as St Aldhelm's Head by 11 a.m., and it was soon after this that we had a little excitment. The chart marks 'overfalls', and you better believe it. We saw what appeared to be a 7-foot wall of surf ahead. As there seemed nothing else to do but go for it, we went ahead, and after a couple of hundred yards it subsided. As we left it behind, we noticed another yacht going in the opposite direction which appeared stationary, just going up and down.

At this point the visibility was poor and we lost contact with the shore, so it was with some relief that two hours later, with a break in the mist, we saw the Needles half a mile dead ahead.

By this time the tide had turned foul, and it was a long haul up the Solent towards Beaulieu and Buckler's Hard.

The following day we had a magic sail with south-westerlies all the way to take us eastwards towards Rye. Passing Worthing it was easy to spot The Towers, the large and ugly block where my parents used to rent a flat when my father was in England. Then it was on to Brighton Marina. From Brighton onwards it was perfect weather, enabling a final day's sail past Beachy Head, sailing into the River Rother on the top of the tide right down to our berth by 1610. The end of a memorable holiday, to which six members of the family contributed, together with assorted mates.

A Cornish Disaster

Long before the idea of a boat was even a gleam in the eye, we had an experience of a wreck. We had hired a house in the Cornish fishing village of Porthguarra, close to Newlyn, and, after a first night's sleep, we woke to see out of the window a yacht lying on its side at the entrance to the port.

The boat was made of concrete and skippered by a Mexican who, with his Danish wife, had sailed across the Atlantic on the way to Denmark. The couple had a small baby, who was teething and had kept them awake. In entering the English Channel off Cornwall, they had felt it was safe to put the yacht on 'autopilot' and gone to sleep ... big mistake! They woke to find their boat wrecked on the Cornish shore with a large hole in its side and blocking the exit for the fishing boats to leave the harbour.

That day the rescue teams arrived, attaching ropes and pulleys to attempt to rescue ... all to no avail ... it was like a constant TV programme for those of us on the shore, with the news hitting the headlines, and the police stopping "sightseers" from entering the village.

After a few days the local fishermen got fed up with having their port blocked and organised their own rescue operation by hiring a 'polystyrene machine', with all the locals bringing plastic bottles which were then filled and the yacht filled with them. To a great cry from the surrounding locals the yacht lifted off at the next high tide and was towed around to Newlyn, where the hole in the side was mended. We never heard the end of the story, but believe that a local bookbinder offered to skipper the boat to Denmark. We hope it all worked out!

3

France 1986

Our first voyage to France did not take place until 1986, but was followed by further trips in subsequent years – in 1987, 1992 and 1998 – until we finally reached the Mediterranean in 2003.

The gallant crew at the start of the voyage

But 1986 is perhaps the most memorable, the visit being organised by Martin Tregonin, the harbour-master in Penzance, to persuade owners of Cornish Crabbers and Pilot Cutters to join a fleet of Crabbers to sail to Concarneau on the Brittany coast, where they would be hosted by the town, and join in the Vieilles Coques race. It is necessary to explain that although Crabbers are not in fact 'old gaffers', to all intents and purposes they were to be considered as such by the town and would join in the annual race.

So it was that *Midley Belle* set off from Falmouth on 9th July in company with *Melloney*, Martin Tregonnin's boat, and *Gallatea*, a beautiful two-masted gaffer, thought to be the original wooden boat from which the modern version had been designed, together with a number of others, to make the crossing to L'Aber Wrac'h.

L'Aber Wrac'h is the first port in Brittany, to which boats sailing from the UK will generally make to gain entrance to the Chenal du Four, and on to the Raz de Sein and the south.

The crew consisted of Adam and wife Marie, with Jonathan Woodhouse and skipper Derek, *Midley Belle* having been brought around from Rye without the skipper. It was not a propitious start as there was little wind, and our engine was only giving 3.5 knots in calm water, so that we were taken in tow by *Melloney* until the wind picked up and we could sail. As it was we missed the tide to take us round the Raz, having to spend the night in the Bay of the Graves. Here we were introduced to Jean Pierre, the local dolphin, who played around the boat. The following morning we negotiated the Raz, sailing all the way to Audierne, mooring with all the other cutters for the night.

Picnic in Concarneau

FRANCE 1986

Due to our slow progress we proceeded independently the following morning, arriving at Concarneau, where we were greeted by Jean Jacque the harbour-master in a dory shouting 'Boisson ce soir!' and *boisson* it certainly was, coupled with picnics and fireworks all weekend.

Concarneau is itself an historic town, with an old walled city entered across a bridge from the harbour, and this on its own would have made the visit memorable. But the hospitality of the French, with barbeques on the beach where the fires and food were all provided, and parties in the town, made a great start to our holiday.

Diana, Amelia and Jane, a friend, had arrived by car, and the following day we all made a sentimental journey by car to Ile Tudy, where we had spent a holiday with the children some years before. Ile Tudy had hardly changed, although the hotel where we had stayed appeared to have been converted into flats. The quay where we had been horrified at the tidal height – Starkie and Adam at ages six and four had been sitting on the edge with a 30-foot drop to the sea bed below – hadn't changed a bit!

Sunday was the day of the great race, the Vieilles Coques – or

The alternative means of transport

would have been had there been any wind. As it was the Crabbers spent most of the day 'as idle as a painted ship upon a painted ocean' and we finally gave up, although *Annie*, the Pilot Cutter, did finish and win a prize. Diana, Jonathan and Jane had chosen to go to Carnac to see the stones, and had the better day.

The Bastille celebrations the following day took the form of a series of parties on the different boats. I have vivid memories of *Herta*, a large and beautiful gaffer, *Samphire* and others, where the whisky ran free accompanied by great singing. 'The Leaving of Liverpool' is a haunting memory still. Fireworks followed at midnight with many expensive red parachute flares let off, setting alight pools of oil and petrol in the harbour. It was a miracle that nothing else caught fire.

The return journey started with a long day on engine, as there was little wind, arriving at Audierne at 0140 to find Amelia and Jane had arrived by car. An enforced lay day in Audierne followed, where we visited the lovely old town with an evening meal of sardines cooked by Jonathan.

It wasn't until the Wednesday that we set off for Douarnenez via the Raz, in a sea mist leaving harbour. However we held our course, with the coast eventually coming in sight in good time to make the necessary course alterations to go the outside route around the Raz.

After going round the Raz the wind improved, and we were able to have a good beam reach towards Douarnenez, arriving by 1540.

The Concarneau spirit continued with an invitation to visit *Micky Finn*, a racing machine from Cardiff, with a bunch of Welsh sailors afloat with gin singing their hearts out. Yet another great party, and a never-to-be-forgotten rendering of 'Singing in the Rain' with everyone shaking up beer cans, and beer spurting everywhere.

Jonathan was clearly unconscious, as it was not until the next day, when Amelia and the skipper had taken the boat as far as Cap de la Chevre en route to Le Conquet, that he finally emerged from the forward cabin.

After lunch the westerly wind, which had given us a good beat up towards the Cap, strengthened, veering to the north, and making way towards Le Conquet become difficult so we decided to run into Camaret.

Camaret proved to be a long distance for the car (some 60 miles via Brest) whereas on the chart it looked to be only 13 miles which meant the car party didn't arrive until after lunch the following day. However it all worked out well as our communication centre (Judy, Diana's sister in the UK) established that Wolfgang and family were not too far off, so that it was possible to redirect them to Camaret, where they arrived by the evening.

The skipper and Jonathan took up the cockpit floor, and repaired the bilge pump, which had not worked well, also repairing the stern gear grease pipe, enabling the stawfing gland to work properly. This ensured that we had no water in the engine bilge – the enforced lay day had proved useful.

19th July was a general change-round. Wolfgang replaced Jonathan who was taken to Brest by car with Amelia and Jane, departing on the Roscoff ferry for the UK, whilst the skipper, Diana and Wolfgang sailed to Le Conquet with a fair wind.

Diana enjoyed the spectacle of the skipper and Wolfgang making a mess of putting up the jackyard topsail, always put up in the past most expertly by Jonathan; however the expertise was acquired without too many problems for the future.

At Le Conquet we moored to a buoy, so the Bombard was put to good use to get ashore. At this point the skipper decided to turn in but Wolfgang and the girls decided to try out the local disco. Not a good idea; it seems it was for 14-year-olds only.

On the following day: to L'Aber Wrac'h. It was a fast journey due to fair tides, but with problems on entry due to poor visibility. Having established proximity to the correct cardinal buoy, we were aware of being surrounded by rocks on all sides. We were not alone and a large blue catamaran seemed to be having the same problem, but we got it sorted out, following a large sloop in and berthing at 1500. We had averaged over 4 knots berth to berth.

L'Aber Wrac'h was *en fête*, with a circus, street bands, mime artists and an open-air restaurant selling the cool Muscadet – all very entertaining! After this it was on around the Cotes du Nord towards St Malo. Most French marinas have a poster which says 'La Mer, ce n'est pas la Poubelle', which had a marked effect on Amelia. She was appointed as the Pollution Officer, our gashcan renamed 'the Poubelle', all junk to be placed in this, to be emptied into the next marina dustbin – minor infringements by the skipper severely frowned upon.

We reached Roscoff where we had a lay day on the Tuesday; this started badly as the skipper, using the Bombard, tried to climb a metal ladder to reach the shore but in doing so the Bombard shot away, leaving him hanging by his left arm from one of the rungs. Don't let anyone tell you that a pulled muscle is a little thing. I can confirm that it was agony for a week afterwards, giving meaning to the phrase 'it only hurts when I laugh'! The next day, Wednesday, was Royal Wedding day, and Diana joined the crew for the trip around to Perros Guirec; we listened to the ceremony on the radio, drinking a toast to 'the Yorkies'.

But one of the problems we encountered was gulf weed fouling the propeller. This causes loss of power, and black smoke – nothing to be done but stop engine. Wolfgang stripped off and managed to clear the problem by leaning over the side of the Bombard; less hassle than swimming below the boat, which Adam had reported en route to Falmouth.

The next day, Thursday, we made for Treguier, a 26-mile leg with a heavenly wind taking us along the coast. We calculated that there would be a flood tide in the estuary till 2330, which was happily correct, taking us to the cathedral city of Treguier by 2300, where Diana and Amelia were found playing dominoes in a local cafe.

A quick visit to the cathedral, then a hurried meal and bed, knowing that the next day would mean an early start for Paimpol. When a student of architecture at Liverpool, the skipper had visited this town with Philip Dod and Nic Diamantis, and been befriended by Monsieur and Madame Carpentier at their house, the Four a Chaux, and in our 'no-boat' days we had also visited them; so we decided to look them up. But how things change.

We finally found the house, now a part of a new housing estate, in a section of the coast renamed as the Cornice Four a Chaux. We met the new owners of the old house, who are doing great things to it, but they told us that both the Carpentiers were dead. Perhaps it was a mistake to try to recapture our past.

Leaving the following morning we had a broad reach for Binic, taking the inside route through the Rade de Portrieux and arriving at 1530, just too late for the cill, so having to anchor off, taking the ground of fine sand, allowing an easy walk out before floating again by 2000. On Sunday we set off easterly for Cap Frehel: poor wind far as the Cap, but once round it freshened to a south-westerly force 4 giving us a fast run down to St Cast (5 miles in 50 minutes), a great feeling. The skipper misread the *Port Pilot*, parking outside the inner harbour saying, 'It is OK, it never gets less than 1.6. metres', only to find *Midley Belle* firmly on the mud by teatime. All was OK when after dinner we moved the boat to a buoy closer to the harbour mouth, which really didn't dry out.

The final leg to St Malo with Diana aboard on Monday 28th was an excellent morning sail on a beam reach with a south-westerly force 3 taking us towards St Malo.

A quote from the *Shell Pilot* says: 'one look at a chart has made many a cruising yachtsman hesitate before visiting this most agreeable of all Brittany ports', and you better believe it, as the *Cruising Association Handbook*, the *Shell Pilot* and the French chart don't seem to agree on the position of the various buoys. However we made it in, and happily we did not encounter fog.

Once inside the Bassin Vauban we set out to look for Jeremy and Rebecca, who were bringing daughter Florence across by ferry, booking into a B&B for the weekend. The weekend proved to be a great success with swimming and enjoying the old city of St Malo, with a memorable meal out at the little restaurant La Porte St Pierre, set into the walls of the old city. It was a fabulous meal with nine of us, five courses for the 72-franc menu – it would have cost double the price in England.

Michael Janes, our pilot for the Channel Islands, arrived together with Nic Hall. We purchased bonded stores at the yacht club; this

Anthony and Jenny Fanshawe

was remarkably easy, you leave a note of requirements before 11 a.m., the stores being delivered to the boat by 1730. Prices were more competitive than Heathrow for whisky, vodka, brandy and gin.

After the weekend, a poor wind meant engining nearly all the way from St Malo to St Helier in Jersey in the Channel Islands. This was to be Wolfgang's last sail, and Gerti and Danny came over on the ferry and enjoyed a lay day with us, before departing with Wolfgang to start the long drive back to Reichenau. Yet another change of crew, with the arrival of Tony and Jenny Fanshawe. Tony was an old friend from Starkie's days studying Philosophy at Bristol Unversity, Tony had only dinghy-sailed, but was quick to pick up the mysteries of gaff rig.

Next a quick sail from St Helier to St Peter Port in Guernsey, giving Jenny a rosy view of what sailing can be – undermined later when things were not so nice!

The following day being a lay day Michael went off to visit friends and the rest of us hired a car and toured the island, ending with 'English tea' at a little hotel.

From St Peter Port we sailed to Braye on Alderney, a lovely island, almost unspoilt by tourism. Here the skipper excelled himself on arrival when he managed to put that lethal weapon, the bowsprit, through the window of another yacht! The owners of the other boat took it remarkably well: I am far from sure I would have been so charitable, leaving it to insurance companies to sort things out back in England. Peace was restored with drinks of gin and tonics on our boat in the evening, followed by a meal together at a little hotel in St Anne's, the only town on the island.

We had missed a day due to bad weather, so the original plan to go from Braye to Cherbourg was abandoned, and the decision was made to go direct to the UK with landfall in Gosport.

The next day saw lousy weather, with the engine on all day until reaching St Catherine's Point, from where a fair wind took us round Bembridge Ledge, and so into the Camper & Nicholsons Marina in Gosport. The skipper did the right thing flying the yellow, and telephoning Customs & Excise who said that if they had not come in two hours we could take it down. They didn't come but then the skipper did the wrong thing – he didn't take it down. Big mistake ... the following morning a very enthusiastic crew of Customs officers arrived and did us over, and I don't mean maybe! They had everything out of everywhere; mirrors on sticks looking into bilges, and they were so happy when they found our bonded stores bought in France. However as there were so many of us, they finally agreed that we were within our limits, so all was well.

At this point Michael left for home. The forecast suggested a south-westerly force 4, and all seemed to be set for a great sail to Brighton, and in a sense it was – it was quite the fastest passage *Midley Belle* had achieved, a 7.5 log speed at times, but the force 4 became a near gale and Jenny was not happy. The southerly hurled us down the Channel with a double-reefed main, small staysail, and finally with the jib alone. We learnt later that two 12-metre yachts were dismasted in the Solent and yet another sank, so 'we done good'.

Jemima now lives in Brighton and met us, inviting us to stay over, so we had a lay day the next day. As Nic decided to return home it left a place for Jemima the next day to join us on the passage home to Rye. Leaving at 5.30 in the morning, we had a great sail to Rye, catching the flood tide up the Rother, allowing time to tie up at our mooring by 1730. This was the end of the longest cruise we had done, about 1,000 miles. It was Jemima's birthday the following day so a great party was held at 10 Market Street, giving Ben, Adam's son, a chance to see Grandpa's boat, and even to get a short sail the following day, before we all returned to our various destinations, at the end of a great holiday.

Joining the ship (from the Fanshawes)

We were flattered to be invited to go sailing with Derek and Diana on the Midley Belle. *We were friends of the Phillips' eldest son, Starkie, from university, and had been invited to their delightful and ever so slightly eccentric house in Bovingdon, so we had some idea of what to expect. We knew that Diana would be there, the fearless, charismatic, artistic mother who led the family and kept the colourful, bizarre Phillips family show on the road. Diana was small, with a grinning round face, always dressed in bright clothes. She carried a silver tobacco tin embossed with pixie faces and with charms and cigarette-making tools hanging off it, and every now and again she would roll and triumphantly smoke a roll-up fag, before barking out an order or a witticism and then laughing uncontrollably in her surprisingly gruff, low and loud voice.*

Diana is married to Derek, whose retirement project the Midley Belle *was, after a career as an architect. Derek was in many ways Diana's opposite, a sober solid citizen to Diana's hippy chick come Mrs Tiggy-Winkle persona. Diana needed Derek's licence to be as she wanted while Derek needed Diana to amuse and ground him in their large family of five children, plus dogs, donkey and of course a parrot. So it was appropriate that Derek should be Captain Pugwash while Diana naturally took charge of décor. No surprise then that the* Midley Belle *was decked out like a pirate ship with a fabulous, busty naked bowsprit sculpture.*

The first night

We arrived in St Helier, two of us, knowing that Midley Belle *was a small pirate ship with only four bunks, and expecting to go sailing with just Derek and Diana. Imagine our surprise when we found that we were numbers five and six on board (or was it six and seven?). As the last aboard we were shown to our beds, in the open cockpit. After a simple dinner of fish and chips and just a touch of booze we bedded down. We were moored up in a marina so we had a background tune of the slap, slap, slapping of halyards on aluminium masts, interspersed with the roar and whoosh of Diana's nuclear snoring, and at about 3 in the morning, just as we were dropping off to sleep, we realised that the boat outside us was Dutch as its crew came home from a night on the town in their characterful clogs. They settled down with a round of* gutnachts *shouted in Dutch, allowing us to drop off to sleep finally.*

'Sailing' to Guernsey

But it is a given of sailing in Midley Belle *that we had to leave on the tide and the tide was always at 5 or, if we were lucky, maybe 6 in the morning. So we were up before the lark and, feeling pretty bloody, we prepared for a day's sail to Guernsey. Except we didn't sail, we motored. Anyone who has ever motored a sailing yacht will know that it is a pretty compromised activity, because sailing boats carry a keel to keep them upright and frankly are the wrong shape. Somehow* Midley Belle *was more compromised than most. This season, Derek had changed the propeller on the* Midley Belle *and was hoping for great things. But it was not to be.* Midley Belle *could do no more than 2.5 knots on the new propeller and the noise and vibration of the small fishing boat motor dominated one's being after a short while. Arriving in St Peter Port, we booked into a hotel for the night. We have never been so grateful for a shower, a soft bed and no clogs.*

We had a day to spend on Guernsey, and it was a Sunday; in those days, the whole of Guernsey closed down on a Sunday. There was nothing open anywhere in St Peter Port – not a pub, nor a *café, nor a shop. And then, it started to rain, and rain, and rain. We spent a very long, very damp and very dull day, squashed together on the* Midley Belle *– all 6 or 7 of us – waiting for the tide to take us to Alderney (which was anticipated to be ideal, as was Derek's way, at about 5.30 the following morning).*

Alderney

To help give us confidence in his captaincy, Derek had brought along an acquaintance, who thought he was good at navigation, as his Navigational Consultant. Before setting off, the skipper and his consultant would be deep in discussion over the charts, deciding the optimum route to wherever we were going, looking at buoys to avoid to port or starboard and places of interest on the way, not to mention the inevitable discussion of tides and the conclusion that we had to leave at half past five and no later, or some unmentionable and never explained disaster would overcome us.

Like we would be in a better temper.

Anyway, it was on one of our island-hopping trips around the Channel Islands that we went to Alderney. It was an uneventful trip and we arrived in Alderney Harbour, built rather beautifully by Polish slave labour directed by the Nazis in the last war, at about 6 in the evening. There is no marina at Alderney so we had to pick up a mooring. There were quite a few yachts in the harbour. Most had arrived before us (not surprising, even though we had undoubtedly left before them) and after tidying up their boats the crews were enjoying a well deserved drink while planning for the next day's sail.

By this time there was a fair amount of tension between Derek and the NC, having had a few disagreements over tides or rocks or buoys or something during the day. They did, however, agree on the mooring they wanted to go for. But there was one small problem: a neat, pretty, tidy 32-foot yacht was moored between us and the mooring at right angles to our course. The owner was relaxing with a gin and tonic cooled with ice from his freezer down below at his chart table, pondering his route the next day.

It was clear that all was not well at the helm. In fact there was a fight over the tiller between Derek and the NC. The rest of us, not wishing to get drawn into this fight and not sure what we could do to resolve the problem, moved away as far as we could, to the bow of Midley Belle. *The fight was about whether to go round the bow of the 32-footer or the stern. It was resolved, as with all the best disputes, by a compromise, we went through the middle.*

Imagine the surprise of the poor chap planning his next day's sail over a gin and tonic when the bowsprit of the Midley Belle, *followed shortly by a busty naked wooden lady, smashed through the porthole next to his gin and tonic and showered broken glass over his charts. We went into reverse and managed somehow to disentangle ourselves. We had been lucky. There was no serious damage to either boat apart from the smashed porthole. The victim of this adventure was though very shocked. We in* Midley Belle *tried to calm him down in the only way we knew; by offering him another gin and tonic. But while we had the raw materials we had no cut crystal and ice. So we offered this poor, very proper chap a fantastically over-strong drink in our luminous plastic tumblers that were just beginning to glow in the twilight, and drank to his health with the same kit.*

History does not relate what he thought of the peace offering, but Derek put on his sensible hat and sorted out the insurance that evening in the pub. The NC went ashore and wasn't seen again. He either went home, or Derek buried him on Alderney.

At last a real sail

At this point Jenny left us, to take the sensible way across the channel, by ferry with an engine that meant it could do more than 2.5 knots and did not deafen its occupants. We were men of course, and could not take that way out, so we sailed, or rather motored, at 2.5 knots, to Gosport, where we arrived completely deaf and shaken. Jenny came down to join us for the last leg of the trip.

Some things had changed. As well as NC, Diana was not on

board, but Jemima had come to take her place. And we were just four on board so everyone had a bed. This was a memorable event because we finally got a good sail. Midley Belle, *charming though she was, was heavy and much of the weight was too high up to keep her level in a blow. The gaff rig was great downwind but meant that going upwind was a chore as she did not point well. Because of her weight and rig she was slow in a light wind and because of her lack of weight low down she could not handle too much breeze; unless we were going downwind.*

As usual we were going to leave at 5 from Gosport (not everybody's idea of an ideal holiday destination) to sail to Brighton. Now this sounds quite close but when you are going there at 5 miles an hour at best, it's a very long way. But we were lucky; we had a fabulous fresh breeze (some called it a gale) from behind us so we could run all the way, and it was dry. For once Midley Belle *was made for the conditions and she seemed to chortle as she did her top speed the whole way.*

Jemima caught mackerel off the stern and then fried them in butter with a little lemon; unbeatable for all but Jenny who had been asleep in the foc'sle and now woke up feeling a little the worse for wear; but after a hot drink she began to enjoy the show.

The only slight concern was the way that waves were breaking just behind the Midley Belle, *and it was not a good idea to think too hard about what would have happened had one broken over the stern of the boat, particularly when Derek mentioned that she was one of the first production boats and had been built with a non-draining cockpit. The later ones had draining cockpits.*

But we made it in record time (for Midley Belle*) and at last we had had an enjoyable sail in the old girl. We arrived in Brighton invigorated and not a little relieved to be reaching a safe haven. We felt that we had done the equivalent of surfing across the Southern Ocean in a Volvo Open 60, but at a quarter of the speed, of course.*

Antony and Jenny Fanshawe

4

Brittany 1987

At sea in the Channel

The Crew

Coastal Passage to Falmouth

Rye – Poole
8th – 10th May   Derek Phillips (Skipper)
                       Patrick Benson
                       Sue Hall

Poole – Weymouth
5th – 6th June   Derek Phillips (Skipper)
                       Tony Fanshaw
                       Steve Brookson

Weymouth – Dartmouth – Plymouth
20th – 21st June   Derek Phillips (Skipper)
                       Nick Dean
                       Steve Brookson
                       Chris Oakley
                       Jeremy Johnson-Marshall

Plymouth – Falmouth
5th – 6th July   Derek Phillips (Skipper)
                       Jeremy Johnson-Marshall
                       Tony Tatton-Brown

To France and on to Morbihan

Falmouth – Concarneau
7th – 10th July   Derek Phillips (Skipper)
                       Jeremy Johnson-Marshall
                       Tony Tatton-Brown

Concarneau – La Trinite
11th – 16th July   Derek Phillips (Skipper)
                       Diana Phillips
                       Amelia Phillips
                       Wolfgang Manner
                       Tim Wood
                       Jeremy Johnson-Marshall
                       Rebecca Johnson-Marshall

The Return Journey to Roscoff

Morbihan – L'Orient
17th – 21st July   Derek Phillips (Skipper)
                    Diana Phillips
                    Amelia Phillips
                    Wolfgang Manner
                    Tim Wood

L'Orient – Round the Raz to Douarnenez
22nd – 25th July   Derek Phillips (Skipper)
                    Diana Phillips
                    Amelia Phillips
                    Tom Winchester

Roscoff and Home
Roscoff – St Malo – Channel Isles – Gosport – Rye
2nd – 16th August   Adam Phillips (Skipper)
                    Jonathan Woodhouse
                    Marie Phillips
                    Beth

Coastal Passage to Falmouth

The cruise from Rye to Morbihan started in stages as early as May continuing until reaching Falmouth in early July. Sailing in company across the Channel through the Chenal du Four, round the Raz for the Bastille Day celebrations in Concarneau. On to Morbihan and back through a number of different points back to Roscoff where Adam and his wife took over and brought *Midley Belle* safely back to Rye arriving on Sunday 16th August. Total distance 1,175 nautical miles.

8th – 10th May The First Stage

Nearly a disastrous 'non start' when there wasn't enough water below the boat to move; only Patrick's expertise in organizing a 4-ply pulley to the post on the outside enabled us to pull ourselves off and out into the stream.

The first night was spent at Brighton marina where Jemima organized a splendid meal at her flat, but the skipper had butchered his leg and felt sick. OK the next day for the run to Cowes.

Velsheda, the last of the J-Class yachts was moored off Cowes and the following day followed us down the Solent, an impressive sight. Sue took a couple of excellent photos of her.

Very good sail down to the Needles and across to Hand Fast Point and so into Poole where arrangements had been made to leave *Midley Belle* at Dorset Yacht until early June.

The Skipper

5th – 6th June Gales in the Channel

Good sail towards St Alban head with Tony and Steve but was warned to steer six miles off shore due to gunnery practice off Lulworth Cove. This delayed us and despite an early start at 0600 we didn't berth in Weymouth until 1345.

The wind got up during the night and we made good time towards Portland Bill. Radioed coastguards for confirmation of weather conditions and told 'Gale 8' imminent, decided to return to Weymouth. Spent the day in Weymouth in the hope that the weather might improve. Took a bus out to the 'Bill' which looked horrific and only thankful we didn't attempt going round. Bought a lobster from one of the fishermen who had returned with his catch; this had to be murdered by the skipper but it tasted excellent for dinner. Weather still no good the following day, so gave up the attempt to get further west and arranged with the Weymouth harbour-master to leave *Midley Belle* until 19th June. The system at Weymouth is that you have also to pay a 'look see' man who is responsible to the harbour-master for moving the boat if required and to check moorings. The system worked well.

20th – 21st June On to Plymouth with crew problem

Nick Dean from Edgecomb Maine was staying with us while doing research into old wooden boats in Greenwich and Liverpool, he jumped at the chance of a sail and together with Steve and Chris Oakley we set off on the long haul from Weymouth, around the 'Bill' and across Lyme Bay for Dartmouth. This time the 'Bill' was as gentle as a kitten. Unfortunately there was little wind and it meant $15^1/_2$ hours on engine. What wind there was was 'on the nose', a generally unpleasant day. Chris and Steve jumped ship in Dartmouth leaving Nick and the skipper to go it alone or get help. Help came in the form of Jeremy Johnson-Marshall, Rebecca's husband, who nobly travelled through the night from Bristol enabling a start for Plymouth by 1000, arriving at 2215 having been on engine all day.

Renewed my acquaintance with Sutton Marina, my favourite marina along the south-west coast and arranged for *Midley Belle* to remain there for the next two weeks. Returned to Bovingdon by train with Nick.

FAMILY SAILING IN EUROPEAN WATERS

5th – 6th July Finally to Falmouth

Diana had arranged by telephone with the chandlers A.E. Monson and the Plymouth Customs for bonded stores to be available and it was necessary for the skipper to travel down on Friday evening 3rd July to be ready to receive stores on Saturday morning.

We got the following: 6 bottles of whisky
                         6 bottles of 'blue' Smirnof vodka (litres)
                         6 bottles of gin
together with 1,400 Marlborough cigarettes (total cost £90.00).

The wisdom appears to be that these are available if your passage plan takes you north of the Elbe or south of the Brest Peninsular – the latter in our case. But with a bottle of vodka for £1.66 it's got to be worth it.

The delivery was followed by a visitation from the customs, to 'seal up' the stores (not allowed to be drunk inside the 3-mile limit on passage to France). The problem was that in a Crabber there is no lockable cupboard ... so with great forethought the skipper drilled a hole in the 'Oilies' cupboard to enable the

Jeremy and Tony

BRITTANY 1987

Jeremy having a swim

customs (reluctantly) to wire up the bolt and add their lead seal. Honour was satisfied.

The crew in the form of Tony Tatton-Brown and Jeremy Johnson-Marshall arrived later and a start was made at 1400 for Fowey

English coastline

where we berthed at the visitors pontoon at 2115, getting the water taxi in to take us for a meal ashore.

A short journey the following day leaving the berth at 0600 and berthing Falmouth 1330 in time to get all necessary stores for the voyage across. We had caught some mackerel and as the wind died at about 0900 we stopped trying to sail and Jeremy cooked a breakfast of mackerel and rice. Apart from this break we sailed well with only $2^1/_2$ hours on engine in and out of harbours.

In Falmouth we beached *Midley Belle* and hired a pressure hose to clean off the bottom – a lot of barnacles had collected on the passage down the Channel this year.

The cleaning of the mackerel

To France and on to Morbihan

A 'Navstar' Decca navigator had been ordered after seeing the demonstration at the boat show in January and we had almost given up hope of getting it when on the day I was due to leave I was told mine had arrived in London. A quick trip into town on Friday 3rd July, £399.00 poorer, and there it was complete with incomprehensible instructions, in its box waiting to be installed, but not by me!

Fortunately in Jeremy we had an electronics wizard and before arriving in Fowey he had already started to understand the beast, whilst before leaving Falouth it was installed and all initial position data set in. It is a 'Magic Box' and after using it for the whole of this cruise it seems incredible how we ever managed without it.

7th – 10th July *The crossing*

Martin Tregonning in *Melloney* lead the crabber fleet as last year, and apart from our boat there was *Gallatea* from last year, *Sirius*, another wooden crabber and *Viking*, a wooden sloop ... all well matched so there was little problem in keeping together.

Some trouble with their propeller shaft delayed *Melloney* initially but we were all sailing well on a broad reach with a 'fair wind for France' by 0650 on Tuesday.

Watches set of two hours on and two hours off, starting from 10.00 a.m. enabling two people to be on deck at all times. Dark by about 2200 with surprisingly little shipping, making the night sail comparatively easy, arriving at the entrance to the Chenal du Four soon after 0500 on Wednesday.

The fleet kept in touch by radio and a decision was made to motor on to Le Conquet to ensure catching the fair tide. *Midley Belle* continued sailing as the wind was still good and we all arrived Le Conquet together at 0840 – but as the wind was exactly right we decided to wait only for the tide to turn, as it did at 1400, and carry on around the Raz. This proved a good decision as we had some of the best sailing of the cruise, with a dead run

FAMILY SAILING IN EUROPEAN WATERS

Sirius

Gallatea

Viking laid alongside Ile Tudy

down the Chenal du Four with the tide, rounding the Raz at 1800 and mooring Audierne by 2030 after a 6-knot beam reach along the coast. The first time we have 'sailed' all the way.

The next day we decided to call in at Benodet as we were not due at Concarneau until the following Friday; left late, and sighted the rest of the crabber fleet well off the coast sailing east. Considerable excitement when listening out on Channel 16 we heard that *Viking* had hit an uncharted rock off Port de Lesconil and was in danger of sinking ... she was helped by *Melloney* and another yacht *Zulu* transfering crew to bail out, to enable her to limp into Ile Tudy. We abandoned the idea of Benodet to follow *Gallatea* and *Sirius* into Ile Tudy. The owner of *Viking* was fortunately a shipwright and was able to effect necessary cawking and repairs so she could continue the following day to Concarneau.

Friday saw us across the short stretch of water to Concarneau where a fair wind enabled us to sail right up to the marina entrance – we had arrived.

11th – 16th July Concaneau, Bastille Day, and on to La Trinite

Diana, Amelia, Tim and Rebecca with Florence met us in Concarneau having crossed on the St Malo ferry from Portsmouth.

This year much like last year a series of parties, except that all the 'Vieux Coques' were allowed to park in the 'fishermen's' harbour which Jean Jacques thought a great privilege, but we thought a somewhat doubtful honour – as it was right in the centre of the town and very noisy.

The first day, being free, we motored over to the Anse de Kersoz at highwater and let *Midley Belle* take the sand so we could complete the job started in Falmuth, we got the bottom completely free of barnacles this time. Very warm so we all swam.

There were two 'Vieux Coques' races this year, the first on Sunday. So little wind that we chickened out and motored over and swam off Big Meil, very hot and sunny.

Wolfgang and family arrived late p.m. Sadly Tony had a touch of 'Montezuma's Revenge' and retired hurt from the proceedings, having to stay close to 'the facilities', Derek drove him to Quimper to catch a train to Paris and home.

The second day's racing, the wind a little better, and *Midley Belle* completed the course, arriving about 9th from last. At the evening 'prize giving' the skipper was somewhat surprised to be called up to receive a prize – a chart of Concarneau – not understanding 'all that French' we thought it might have been for being the only English boat to 'sail it' all the way from Falmouth ... but we never found out.

Nothing actually happened on Bastille Day itself so we left for the Ile de Groix (port Tudy). Jeremy and Rebecca took the car so Diana and Amelia both able to be on board. This was the first day of using Navstar without Jeremy's expertise, but he had given good instructions and the skipper had no difficulty in setting in the waypoints and we arrived at Pte Tudy at 1800 after a nine hour run, most of which was on engine with nil wind. The following day Amelia and Tim were picked up by the French (very unsmiling) gendarmerie for sleeping on shore in the tent, and we were given a lesson by the French Douane for not displaying 'the yellow'. However all resolved, Amelia and Tim released with a warning that in France you only sleep in tents in official camp sites and it ended up with the magic 'Fiche' to give to any other Customs officers who might ask – unlike UK where

The crew in Concarneau

if no one comes at the first port you don't need to display the yellow again, in France you go on displaying at each port until you have been 'done' ... we had thought by displaying in Audierne we had complied ... one learns the inscrutable ways of customs!

Navstar proved very valuable the following day, very windy, beating against a S.S.E., we had to find the route through the passage de la Teignouse into the Baie de Quiberon. The whole of this long peninsular and its group of islands looks very similar ending with Ile Hoedik and without the certainty of accurate navigation the way through the passage would cause some concern. Diana had reached her 'sell by date' and slept for six hours during this trip.

Arrival at la Trinite sur mer on Friday 15th at 1930, when Wolfgang's family arrived by car, Marina cost FF64.00, the most we paid in France (usually about FF40.00). Jeremy and Rebecca were already set up in a friend's flat and this was lovely as we were able to have a great party in the flat with eleven people and even sleep in beds. Jeremy's friend Nigel Irons is the designer

Tim sailboarding

and maker of large ocean-going racing Trimarans and we visited the factory which he has set up to make two new ones, some 60ft long each ... they are quite spectacular racing machines. Weather unfortunately was deteriorating.

17th – 21st July Morbihan and on to L'Orient

We left La Trinite late on 17th having spent a lazy two days in the luxury of Nigel's flat. As we sailed out a French boat signalled that it was force 8 outside, but we doubted it. We put in two reefs in the main and made the trip round into Morbihan with the tide (you can't make it without it!) berthing at Loc Mariaquer at 1915. Here the weather was foul, with strong winds and rain, we decided to have an involuntary 'lay day'.

Tim and Danny, Wolfgang's son, hired a sailboard for a day, but due to the stormy winds it was difficult for beginners to learn.

On the 18th Tim drove Jeremy, Rebecca and Florence to Roscoff

'The market Auray'

and the ferry, and they returned to Plymouth where Jeremy had left his car at Sutton Marina. On the following day, Sunday, *Midley Belle* with Wolfgang, Amelia and Tim made two attempts to get out of Loc Mariaquer – the first beaten back by the wind, the second successful ending in Auray, a really beautiful old town far into the Morbihan.

The following day we spent the morning looking around the market, one of the best I have found in France, it takes over the whole of the centre of the town. We bought live 'spider' crabs which the skipper had to murder due to his squeamish family ... no trouble with eating them!

In the afternoon we left our mooring on the tide to sail out all the way to Port Croasty, mooring briefly at Gravenis where there is one of the largest Tumuli in France. Diana, Wolfgang, Tim and Eva, the latter on board for the first time, went ashore and inspected, using the bombard ... fine cave carvings.

From Port Croasty the following day, Tuesday, a difficult day's motor sailing against a WNW wind out of the Baie de Quiberon

Diana and spider crabs...

round to L'Orient. We arrived about 1630 and on approaching the harbour entrance we were followed in by a very sinister French submarine, not a smile from the conning tower, although we were so close we could have hit it with an apple.

We found a very useful little berth for the night at Port Louis (turn right on going past the harbour entrance) saving the fag of going all the way up to L'Orient Marina. Met Diana, who was driving.

22nd – 25th July L'Orient round Raz to Douarnenez

Wednesday 22nd saw a nice gentle twelve-hour sail in fair winds from L'Orient (Port Louis) to Benodet, with only a short spell required on engine initially when there was nil wind. We saw a large buoy where one should not have been, and yes it was a 'moving' buoy, in short, another French submarine, but smaller than yesterday's. Benodet a very nice marina and delightful town, decided on a lay day to make and mend.

We removed both fan belts, refixed Navstar with shake proof washers, did all engine checks and replaced a snap shackel on the

BRITTANY 1987

...followed by a French submarine

'Jack Yard'. Wolfgang carved 'Midley Belle' on the tiller beautifully, and Diana carved a head topped off with a 'Turks Head Knot' so we look very smart. In the evening the skipper hosted a splendid meal out at a little restaurant in the town, for all the crew (8). It must be a cliché that the food in France is twice as good and half the price as in England, but it's true.

Tim had to leave on Friday and Amelia drove him to Quimper following the boat to Audierne in the evening – *Midley Belle* had a ten-hour passage, half of which was on engine; so little wind at lunch time we stopped engines and drifted while we ate, to avoid the noise.

The moorings at Audierne are a couple of miles from the lovely old town so Diana and Derek walked in to the centre and played dice in 'The Bikers Bar'. We found a tiny marina had been built right up in the centre of town ... but to get to it you have to catch high water, otherwise very little water in the Channel.

Saturday saw Diana, Amelia and Wolfgang set to go round the Raz. We got the tide just right, but with the wind on the nose it was still quite difficult.

The Navstar was helpful in calculating exactly the bearing on which to turn to round the Raz. Diana, who spent most of the time asleep in the cabin, got up in order to have herself photographed at the tiller rounding the rocks.

Arrived at Douarnenez at 1715 when Tom Winchester met us, having travelled out from England via Paris.

Diana and Wolfgang at the Raz

26th – 30th July Douarnenez to Roscoff

On Sunday morning Wolfgang and family left for the long haul back to Reichenau (1,000 miles) by car, and Tom, Diana and the skipper took the boat to Morgat – not a place to bother with again. There was a festival of dinghys and sailboards with a million visitors, which didn't improve the place, but it was a 'nothing' town.

Diana and Amelia had had enough boats for a while and Tom and the skipper sailed alone down past the Cap de Chevre and around to Le Conquet, the first part was excellent sailing, but it was 'motor sailing' all the rest of the way for the five hours up to Le Conquet where Diana and Amelia were waiting on the quay.

After we got home a letter was forwarded to me by the Rye harbour-master from the skipper of Trenouth who had past us sailing down the Cap and he enclosed a photograph he had taken, which was very kind of him; when you're 'sailing well' you can never photograph yourself.

Midley Belle from Trenouth

Le Conquet is a favourite of mine, a charming little harbour with a town set on a hill and overlooking it; but the skipper distinguished himself by 'falling in' when trying to board the Bombard at the quay. Fortunately the sea was warm and no harm done. 'Moules' for dinner restored the spirits.

The passage from Le Conquet to L'Aber Wrac'h is only 24 miles, so to catch the tide which is strong in the Chenal de Four it was best to leave it till 1300. It started clear but approaching L'Aber Wrac'h the fog came down with a visibility of 400 yards. We had had trouble in similar circumstances last year when we were lucky to follow another boat in safely.

This year we relied on the Decca to come up to the Lebenter buoy, then the Pot de Buerre and finally into the harbour – the first totally blind approach we had achieved, with Amelia on the bows calling out the buoys exactly where they should have been ... it was all a miracle to me. One wonders how one ever did without it.

The following day, being a lay day, we took off by car and checked out the coastline ahead, finding no satisfactory anchorage at Goulven and deciding that although we were a day or two early, having decided to cut out a trip to Ushant (where Nelson always seemed to be blockading the French fleet), we would carry on the following day, Thursday 30th, to Roscoff.

The exit from L'Aber Wrac'h is nearly as hairy as entering, all those rocks and even though the visibility was excellent one still worries about how one ever got in – and you go out a different way.

Uneventful sail to Roscoff passing the middle passage between Ile de Batz. Very necessary to arrive +1 hour HW. Laid *Midley Belle* against the harbour wall as last year, enabling the bottom

Le Conquet

to be inspected – very few barnacles (unlike those that collected in English waters when in Weymouth and Plymouth) and remarkably clear after a month's cruise. Tom and the skipper crewed, Diana a passenger.

This was the end of the cruise for us, with Adam and Marie, Jonathan and Beth taking over. They met us the following day on arrival from England bringing Ben. From there on we looked after Ben and had a few gentle days in France before returning from St Malo to Portsmouth on 7th August. We had a final celebration with a great meal at the Hotel Des Arcades in Roscoff.

BRITTANY 1987

2nd – 16th August   Roscoff – St Malo – Channel Isles – Gosport and home to Rye

We left Ben on Sunday to go with the crew to Primel, a short passage, but not short enough for Ben who didn't enjoy it! We met them at Primel for a splendid barbeque on the beach and afterwards fireworks, as it was a 'festival de la Mer'. Rainy night, so Ben came back with us and took no further part in the 'boating'.

The following day to Tregier stopping at the lovely little port of Lacquirec. Surprised to find *Midley Belle* the following morning parked in the marina, as they had originally planned to get only as far as Perros-Guirec.

We didn't encounter *Midley Belle* again until her return to Rye two weeks later.

We visited Paimpol and Erquy then on to St Malo visiting the Chateau Bienassis and Mont San Michele with a million others. The last time we had seen 'the Mont' was in the depths of winter with hardly a soul, a better way altogether. On Thursday a final visit to the Euromarchie to buy the wine and other goodies –

Restaurant at St Malo

FAMILY SAILING IN EUROPEAN WATERS

Derek cleaning 'the bottom'

Adam and crew leaving Sunday 2nd August

BRITTANY 1987

Ben writing the postcards home – agony

Paddling at Pte Minard

The journey home

coffee and mustard are both much cheaper in France – and took the Portsmouth ferry from St Malo on Friday 7th, after a final memorable meal at the little restaurant we found last year – the Porte St Pierre under the old walls. Just as good only the FF65.00 menu was now FF75.00, still a bargain.

Postscript

We have received an application for next year's crew from a Herr Gnagflow, who appears well acquainted with Wolfgang (see opposite).

Herr Gnagflow, whilst being 'somewhat' inarticulate, sounds a good chap at heart.

Further applications will be considered strictly in order received.

BRITTANY 1987

Hello skipper - here is a foto from me. I am a very good the best fore deck gorilla. I live in Reichenau. 1 week ago a friend (not the best, because basicly he is a showy offer and talkes too much in my oppignon - you should have heard what he told about you and your family) came

back from a sailing in Britta (I don't know) Fran said (he was pissed of course, like always, he was not on your boat he for sure was during the night. And what he spoke about your wife! he said she doesn't like big wind and big water, but am sure she is the best traveller under god and rig n so too) he might not get his job again next y

FAMILY SAILING IN EUROPEAN WATERS

can understand that [illegible] ... & be at the same ship with him. You must be a very generous person and for sure you are the best skipper under god to repair the damages he does. & is totally useless and I admire your personality; and he never has tobacco, doesn't he? You must be a saint. I also never have tobacco. I am big & strong and a clever bugger. (thats how people who know me and whom you would also like and trust call me. Because I am too humble to write about me like that.) I am sure you never had a better foredeckgorilla (FDG, as we sail [illegible]). But I am sure I don't tell you something new because you know everything concerning seamanship. And I am sure that we will make a good team. I like to get up early like all we seamen do. Did my friend (!) try to grab your daughters tits? I would be surprised if he did. I am different. Ships are my women. I like screws. (you understand? Ha...ha..ha). A good joke at the right time makes life on board easier. People find me very entertaining. But if your wife doesn't like those sort of funs I can will be charming or quiet. Here comes my friend Wuifi and I will let him add some lines.

Dear Derek, thank you very much for the lovely trip [illegible] ... I hope the weather there was better than it was here. [illegible] I liked it a lot, although, like always, it seemed [illegible] ... if you really are in need of a crew for next year (where will you go?) [illegible] to be a member again. Thank you again. WUIFI

You see how slimy he is, trying to get my job even in a letter that I wrote. "I wouldn't mind to be a member again". Eh... creepy lounge lizzard he. Anyway. See you next year skipper. I know we speak the same language. Hello your new FDG

GNAGFLOW

5

Holland

We first visited Holland in 1982; it was our first voyage (Chapter 2) and as the skipper had not started doing the personal logs for each year I have to rely on memory together with Jonathan's excellent photographic record. However from 1983 onwards I have the personal logs to assist.

Records show that Patrick Benson skippered *Midley Belle* from Rye, starting in July and taking her as far as Durgerdam by 4th August. There she was left until the skipper with a different crew picked her up for the main cruise, leaving her in Middleburg to be skippered by Chris Oakley and friends in September, to bring her back to Rye. For this reason we had a crew of over 16 overall – not all family, but family friends too.

Part 1: Rye – Durgerdam, 18th July – 30th July

Patrick Benson was in charge with his own crew, Derek only going as far as Dunkirk, leaving Patrick to sail on to Amsterdam.

Using the ship's log, it is clear that the passage was not without incident: fog off Calais delayed entrance onward to Dunkirk. From Dunkirk to Ostend, although only 11 miles, sailing all the way left an exhausted crew; a lay day in Ostend allowed some work to be done on *Midley Belle*, before carrying on to Zeebrugge. The bobstay was shortened by one link in the chain, and the stays tightened.

From Zeebrugge, on to Zieriksee by dark. The following day we crossed the main traffic lanes into Europort, Rotterdam en route to Scheveningen, but due to bad weather forced to go back to Hinder buoy to regain lost ground, losing some five hours. Consulting the *Cruising Association Guide* it mentions weird tides and currents south-west of Europort, which might account for this.

The following day we set off for the beginning of the Nordsee Canal at Ijmuiden, but had to return due to bad weather, so another night in Scheveningen. This was made up for the next day when, having got up for an early start to catch the tide, we had a great day goose-winging up the Nordsee to Amsterdam, where Patrick reported that we were invaded by a drunk from another boat. It took 20 minutes to remove the drunk, who immediately fell off the jetty into the water. Patrick manfully hauled him out and guided him back to his own boat; reported to be all OK the following day!

At Durgerdam Patrick's crew were discharged prior to the skipper and a new crew's arrival to carry on with the main cruise by 7th August.

Large boat on the Nordsee

Part 2: Durgerdam – Middleburg

Our part of the passage as mentioned in the personal log for 1983 starting from Rye saw Diana in Vienna, where she had been attending the seminar in Reichenau; so it was a great gathering of the clans with jetfoils to Ostend, and cars to Amsterdam, catching up with *Midley Belle* in the little marina outside the town at Durgerdam. This was opposite the main railway station where Pat and his crew had left *Midley Belle* on 30th July.

The new crew, consisting of the skipper, Diana, Amelia, Jonathan Woodhouse and Jane Spooner, joined *Midley Belle*. Some maintenance was required, the worst of which was the engine, it being necessary to use the starting handle, the reason thought to be the earthing of the battery. This was not resolved, and the engine had to be started on the handle for the rest of the cruise. However the majority of the maintenance items were resolved.

Leaving Durgerdam on 8th August, we sailed across past Patros Island to Muiden and down the River Vechte to Weespe where we stayed overnight, getting a lot of poor advice from the harbour-master (harbour-masters can generally be relied upon, but this one spent his time looking bronzed and trendy).

The canal at Edam

Following the harbour-master's advice to go direct to Amsterdam by canal, we found that although only 10 feet our mast was too high to go under the bridges along the canal. We had to retrace our steps back through Weespe and Muiden back to the lsselmeer, spending another night in Durgerdam. This gave an opportunity to make a visit to Amsterdam in the evening, to see the extremely seedy red-light canal district.

The following day, a quick sail across the channel to Volendam, then on to Edam. Edam is a beautiful town with its own canal system, and we sat by one of these eating delicious cakes, planning our next few days to leave the southern area of the Isselmeer, and depart through the lock at Enkhuisen for the northern section. A slight hang-up as the girls wanted to visit the little town of Hoorn, so a compromise was reached whereby we went there by car and renewed our acquaintance with the local *klompenmaker* who Diana had met the previous year. His craft was directed to the consumer economy – his clogs were designed to last only three months!

Hoorn, the tower

Hoorn, where Tasman had left for his voyage to Cape Horn, was *en fête* with all sorts of mechanical merry-go-rounds, highly sophisticated hardware right up against the shops and other buildings. We found a restaurant called the Hoofdetooren in an old medieval tower by the harbour, with beautiful food.

Sculpture on harbour wall at Hoorn

Leaving Enkhuisen the following day we sailed north to the ritzy yacht basin of Hindeloopen, where many German families keep their boats, which has excellent facilities. We worked out that *Midley Belle* has a no-go window of 110 degrees into wind which is quite frustrating, but we gain with the wind behind us and sail well on a broad reach, reaching 6 – 7 knots

On the Sunday with Diana on board we sailed in perfect conditions up the east coast of the Isselmeer to Makkum, which proved to be one of our favourite towns. We decided to stay over for a couple of days, it being the town best suited to reach the lock at Kornwederzand, and then out into the Waddensee, and on to the Friesian Islands.

There was a little hang-up on the trip to the Friesians, as we had intended to go to Vlieland, but in the event decided due to the weather conditions to run for Terschelling; this having implications as Diana and Amelia had taken the ferry from Harlingen and were waiting for us in Vlieland. Telegraphic communication broke down, and they were left without accommodation in Vlieland. All was solved by the local bank manager who took pity on them, providing a bed and, as he was told it was our wedding anniversary, a bottle of champagne! (An interesting aside was that he said that this was when he heard that they were English – he would not have offered had they been German, so the war still leaves its mark.)

Parking in Makkum

In the end all was restored with *Midley Belle* back through the lock at Kornwederzand, to Makkum where we met up with the rest. From Makkum to Urk: an interesting town which before the war had been an island, but was later joined up to the mainland. It is still very independent, and the *Cruising Asociation Handbook* describes the natives as unfriendly – not our experience!

On the following day, 19th August, we had a long sail back south down the Isselmeer, making landfall just north of Durgerdam, picking up the line of buoys entering Amsterdam. The evening was for planning the final week of the holiday, going down the Nordsee and out into the North Sea at Ijmuiden and then taking the offshore route past Rotterdam to Stellendam, and back into the inland seas for a final few days to renew our acquaintance with places remembered from the previous year.

We had telephoned our communication centre (Judy in Dulwich) on our arrival, to let Wolfgang and family know, and the following morning woke to find a message stuck in the rigging telling us that they had arrived in the night and were parked in the car park.

So then it was all aboard, en route down the Nordsee. We stopped for lunch at a particular point where the canal takes a turn, where we were hit by a wave from a passing barge which sent us rocking dangerously, and crashing against the pier. We lost a fairlead overboard with other minor damage, and a decision was made to leave immediately and carry on to Ijmuiden, where we moored for the night.

Planning for an early start in the morning we woke at 0500 to find thick fog, so decided to delay until 0900. Leaving then, we followed two large yachts out, which were soon lost in the mist, only to be seen returning a while later. Deciding that 'discretion is the better part of...', we hightailed it back, following a reciprocal course. We were happy to hit right between the two moles, then back through the lock, and into our original mooring.

Since it was clear that it was not to be a day for sailing we decided to visit a town down the coast called Zandvoort for swimming, not realising that this was a topless beach. 'No worries', as our Australian cousins would say!

The evening was rather marred when Amelia got the results of her A levels; these were less than good, and general gloom developed. Jane's on the other hand were excellent, so she cried too, from happiness!

The following day saw an early start for Schevenigen; an excellent chandlers allowed replacement of the cleat, also the gas bottle. On past Europort, weaving a bit to avoid the large neighbours, but eventually got things right to hit the lock at Stellendam, and into the Haringvliet. A brief meeting with the cars, and on to spend the night in Middelharnis, ending with a rather rowdy evening in a local hostelry, where we were invited to drink quantities of beer and Geneva (Dutch gin). One of the participants was the traffic controller for the port of Rotterdam who told us we had been lucky to have chosen a Wednesday to cross Europort, and always to avoid Tuesday and Fridays as these days are more heavily trafficked.

We were joined by Sigi, Wolfgang's daughter, for a gentle sail down to Willemstad, one of our favourite towns, then on to Bruinesse and Zierikzee in the Oosterschelde with a good wind taking us onwards to Veere and Middleburg.

On Sunday 28th August we had agreed with Chris, the new skipper, to leave *Midley Belle* in the yacht harbour in Flushing; but we hadn't reckoned on the bridge in Middleburg, where we waited and waited for it to open, but it didn't, as it was a Sunday. In the end we had to leave *Midley Belle* in Middleburg and make all the necessary arrangements with the harbour-master for Chris to pick the boat up at a later date. So ended for us the longest cruise that we had so far attempted, and we left *Midley Belle* for Chris to bring home.

Part 3: Middleburg – Rye

With Skipper Chris Oakley and crew (Stephen Wilkinson and Jo Zule) I have only the ship's log for guidance. Picking up *Midley Belle* from the centre of Middleburg on 30th September, leaving at 1020 they negotiated the canal system, exiting at Vlissingen, and helped by a mild south wind made way for Ostend, mooring at the North Sea Yacht Club by 1936.

It was the following morning that they were unable to find the starting handle for the engine and had to adopt an ingenious method of starting using a screwdriver. (The starting handle was eventually recovered, together with other missing bits, in the engine bilge.)

From Ostend, on the next day to Calais, using the welcome system of buoys for navigation. After a night in Calais it was back to the UK, spending a night in Folkestone on the Sunday, then a short morning trip along the coast to our mooring at Rye – the end for what was for us a mammoth cruise.

...the lonely life of the skipper

6

Ireland 1988

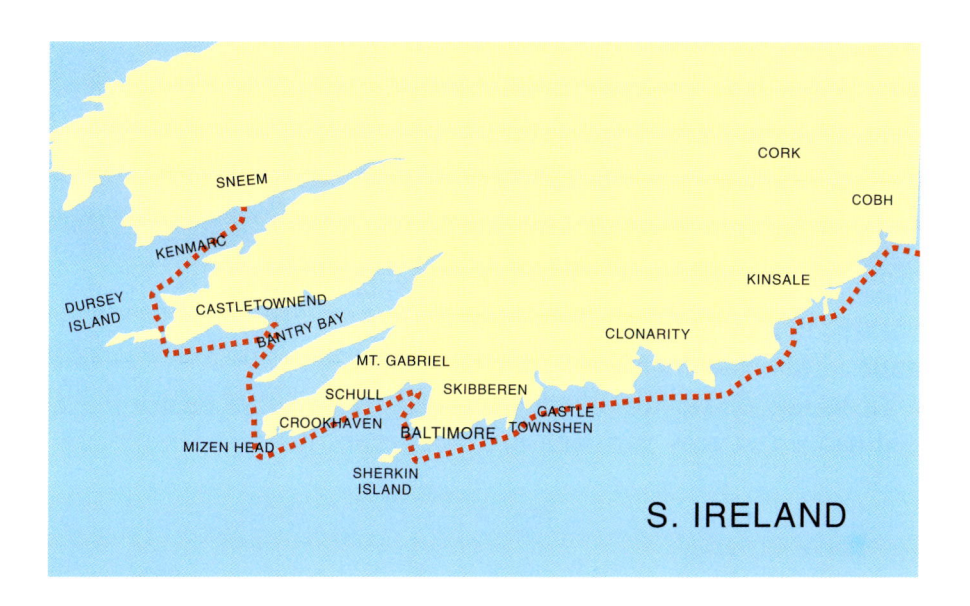

Coastal passage to Falmouth

1988 saw the sale of *Midley Belle* and the purchase of *Emma*, a two-year-old Cornish Crabber Pilot Cutter 30. *Emma* is 6.5 tons with double the sail area of 'the *Belle*', and with many advantages. She has full standing headroom below, and for the skipper the joy of a navigating position separate from the galley. The galley has an oven, allowing the cooking to be more adventurous. With a hot water heater, separate sea loo, wash basins and shower, it seems very luxurious and sleeps six.

The crew at the start

Emma sails well and we were now able to keep up with other vessels instead of seeing everything pass us by, even passing quite large sloops when broad-reaching.

In taking *Emma* to Falmouth we got the weather nearly right, and had a fast easy trip with north-easterlies taking us westward,

En route to Ireland

IRELAND 1988

apart from two days on engine when the wind died. Good reach from Brighton to the Solent, doing so well that we continued on to Yarmouth IOW.

The only snag was that the gaff jaws had distorted badly and Adam had to climb up the mast at Yarmouth and wrestle the gaff downwards. However John Fitzjohn, the first owner, had had the foresight to obtain spare gaff jaws, this time strengthened with quarter-inch plate, and this was soon fitted.

The following two days there was no wind so that it wasn't until Dartmouth that we tried to use the new gaff jaws, to find that nothing would get the gaff up – it was stuck down. Advice sought in Dartmouth from the local rigger suggested 'tallow' was the solution, and this could be found at a boatyard in a creek some distance away. So a taxi ride over and a milk carton of tallow later the gaff jaws were eased, and not a day's trouble since.

Adam, Marie, Tim and Maureen left the following day, but Tony Fanshaw, who had originally agreed to crew for the final two days to Falmouth, couldn't make it. So he was replaced by a lovely builder (female) called Barbara who, with the skipper's partner Nick, arrived at about 10 a.m. and brought *Emma* to Falmouth,

Arrival in the River Dart

sailing most of the way. The reach into Falmouth was only marred by the jib sail not furling on coming up to one of the town quays, but by going alongside the diesel quay this was fixed and we motored on to the pontoon. Here, after spending the night on board, we all left the boat until the main cruise date of 1st July.

To Ireland: Falmouth – Cork (Crosshaven), 2nd – 5th July

The crew asssembled in Falmouth on Friday 1st July with Derek and Andreas (Swarzenegger) Stefferl arriving from Bristol early to obtain delivery of bonded liquor from Monsen's, sealed in by the Customs officer during the afternoon. Last-minute stores were purchased and all checks made before Jonathan Woodhouse and Rebecca's husband Jeremy Johnson-Marshall arrived late, ready for an early-morning departure on the Saturday.

Saturday however saw a tentative departure at noon with gale-force winds forecast, so we only had a proving run as far as the Helford River, a beautiful location, idyllic if the weather had been kind to us. This gave an opportunity for Jeremy, our electrical

The Helford River

genius, to install an old car radio with an external loudspeaker – *Tanhauser* with broadreaching! Jeremy also fixed the wiring to the battery charging indicator which John Fitzjohn had fitted but not connected.

We sailed the following day with a double reef, but prudence demanded a run into Penzance. Huge Atlantic rollers set us back and it was necessary to motor-sail to get around the Lizard in heavy seas.

A hiccough occurred on entering Penzance where we hung on to a yacht waiting to lock into the inner harbour. When we tried to move when the lock opened, we found we had no power: the engine was racing but we were getting nowhere. Having warped into the inner harbour, with dire thoughts of the propeller falling off, an engine inspection proved that the problem was the gear linkage, which had come uncoupled. So this was fixed very easily and a lock nut added to prevent a reoccurrence.

This time a good start was made on Monday 4th July at 11 a.m. to lock out of the inner harbour and to catch the tide around Land's End. The weather was fine and the Atlantic rollers tamed, but there was very little wind; so by 1415 it was necessary to start the engine for the following three hours.

Whilst a dead reckoning plot was kept going for the whole 1,247 miles of the Rye – Ireland – Rye trip, Navstar was used throughout, which with only one or two lapses performed well. Our last waypoint before setting off into St George's Channel was 5 miles north of the Seven Stones Light Vessel, reached by 1745, after which our next waypoint was the Kinsale East gas platform on bearing 328°(m) 91 miles away.

By 1800 the wind had again died away, and we engined for nearly six hours, speed approximately 4.5 knots. Navstar's first lapse occurred just before midnight when it announced '3 lop differs' and 'posn – lost', but it collected itself rapidly with 'signal found' and a check on position restored confidence.

By 0100 on Tuesday the wind freshened and we were able to put up sails which together with the engine pushed *Emma* along well for the following 14 hours until we reached the Kinsale oil platforms, when the wind improved sufficiently to permit the engine to be switched off for a while. But by 1815 we were back on engine to take us into Crosshaven, the yacht harbour outside Cork where we berthed at 2115. In all, 25 hours 45 minutes on engine out of a passage of 34 hours, much of the time helped by sail. Not an entirely satisfactory passage, but sunshine on Tuesday meant it was not all bad, and after the experience of the Atlantic for the first two days we were pleased to have arrived.

Diana and Rebecca and Florence had arrived by car on the ferry from Pembroke to Rosslare. Staying overnight with Marie's 'Auntie Jo' in Cobh, they arrived at the boat about midday on Wednesday by which time we had taken on board water and 10 gallons of diesel (used since Plymouth). The Maestral was inflated and all ready for the coastal cruise around the coast of Kerry.

The Kinsale oil platform

Cork (Crosshaven) – Baltimore, 6th – 9th July

Diana acted as the shore party, looking after Florence and driving on to Kinsale. Rebecca sailed with the original crew to Kinsale in force 6 winds on the nose, so a rather slow passage along the coast taking nearly four hours with half of this motor-sailing.

Kinsale is said to be the gourmet centre of southern Ireland, and certainly if the number of restaurants is any criteria then it must be so. We decided that this had to be one of the skipper's treats and we all ended up for dinner at a steak house called the Cuckoo's Nest. Looking at the prices at other restaurants this was one of the less expensive, but by French standards, where we are used to a five-course meal for about 80 francs or under £8, a single course here cost £9. Food, like booze, in Ireland is expensive – but excellent.

The following day, Thursday, was a lay day in Kinsale. I tried to visit the harbour-master to get an accurate weather report. A notice in the office suggested opening hours were 9.30 – 12.30, 2.00 – 5.00, but as the office remained firmly locked I asked a likely local where I might find him. 'Ah! but hasn't his brother just died, and isn't he at the funeral?' – the general feeling was that he would not be about for a day or two, and we never did meet him.

It was a beautiful sunny day, and where the sun shines on Ireland it is like a blessing.

The following day, Friday, we left – just the skipper, Jeremy

Emma dressed 'overall' in Kinsale

and Andreas – for Castlehaven, a 40-mile leg in fairly rough weather, half of which was motor-sailing with wind on the nose, tacking into a series of bays: Courtmacsherry, Clonakilty and Glandore. The Navstar signal was again suspect across Glandore Bay, the cross-track error jumping from 0.3 to starboard to 0.4 to port in as many seconds. However we reached our waypoint off Skiddy Isle and so came into Castlehaven where we dropped anchor off Castletownshend at 1830.

The Maestral was duly fitted with our little Yamaha Mariner II outboard and left to pick up Diana, Rebecca and Florence who had arrived by car and were waiting by the jetty.

Castletownshend reminded us of Buckler's Hard, so preserved that it seemed lifeless, not a place we wished to dwell, despite its reputation as a beauty spot; so the following day the same crew left for Baltimore at 1045. More south-westerly force 6 – 7 winds, so with stay furled and main double-reefed we took the route close to Toe Head across Scullane Bay, leaving the wicked-looking 'stags' (rocks) to seaward; then round the outside of Kedge Island. Here we had a triple problem: Navstar was giving 'signal suspect', we were enveloped in sea mist and the wind increased to a force 8. This is a far from friendly coast and there were anxious moments beyond Kedge Island seeking for a break in the mist to identify the entrance into Baltimore Harbour. Finally

Sherkin Island ferry from Baltimore

the lighthouse on the port side and the beacon to starboard became visible and a safe entry was made into the calm waters of Baltimore Harbour, where we unwisely berthed up against the wall of the south quay of the little fishing harbour at 1330.

We weren't sure whether we could touch bottom at the low, so moved *Emma* on to a mooring later, much to Diana and the girls' annoyance. Always a complaint over berthing or anchoring – the skipper prefers the gentle motion on anchor or mooring buoy; Diana prefers the convenience of hopping ashore from the boat's side.

Baltimore is a delightful working harbour, with a constant stream of small ferries taking people to nearby Sherkin Isle, with a larger boat going further on to Clear Island.

Our first gas bottle was exhausted and here we had a supply problem as the only gas bottles in Ireland are the standard Irish yellow bottles, or the French Campingaz type. Our rather larger butane bottle was not available and so a compromise had to be found at vast expense (£46) to purchase one of the small Campingaz bottles with regulator. We would then use this till it ran out, go to our second butane bottle while this was swapped for new, in order

Emma rafted out in the fishermen's harbour

The old lifeboat, Baltimore

Andreas having difficulty with the surfboard

to preserve as far as possible the last large one for the journey home. This problem was solved in Cork, but more of this later on.

We all bought postcards in Baltimore and one particular one titled 'A soft day in Ireland' is now stuck in the boat log. This shows a picture of Baltimore from the inside of a window in town, with everything blurred by rain outside. It seems to sum it all up, and 'a soft day in Ireland' has passed into family folklore.

Baltimore – Sneem, 10th – 16th July

The Sunday saw more gales forecast and discretion, coupled with real pleasure in being in Baltimore decided us on staying. Mr Cotter, the local supermarket, chandler, fishing supplies and diesel merchant was extremely helpful in satisfying all the needs of *Emma* and the family and we also purchased chart 2129 from the local pub! This proved a wise move when on Monday 11th the same three crew negotiated the tricky inland route through the islands to Skull … we certainly couldn't have accomplished this without it. The route takes you out of the north-western corner of the harbour leaving Sherkin Island to port, then on past Sandy Island, leaving Hare Island to starboard, setting a course west-south-west past the dangerous-looking Toorance group of rocks. We passed east of Calf Isle East, although it is possible to go between the middle and East Isle.

The route then became easier by setting a course westwards, leaving all the Calf Islands to port. Mount Gabriel makes a useful landmark and the light at the end of Long Island shows the route into Skull, where *Emma* moored off at 12.30. The girls arrived 2.30. Skull was a great meeting point with Jemima and Graham arriving in the afternoon and Wolfgang and family with their VW Microbus in the evening, having come on the car ferry from Cherbourg to Rosslare overnight. The wind was still heavy and attempts to windsurf were not entirely successful; Jeremy had brought two windsurfers on the top of his car and Andreas tried it across the bay, but whereas Jeremy with his experience could manage it, poor Andreas had a hard time.

Emma having the bottom scrubbed

Even with poor weather Skull is a delightful spot and a decision was made to cut out the more ambitious plans to go as far as Valentia and Dingle Bay, and to settle for the Kenmare River and Sneem. This proved to be the right decision. Rebecca, Jeremy and Florence left for a flat they had arranged in Valentia, but returned the following day, Tuesday, as they found the house had been double booked with another family already asleep and shaken to be woken up at midnight by our lot opening up with their key! They booked into a hotel for the next three days in Skull. Meanwhile Andreas and Derek had got up early to park *Emma* close in to the shore to let her dry out with the legs in position. She was dry by about 10 a.m. and we set about scraping the bottom – in fact this proved an easy task as it was comparatively clean, having last been dried out by John Fitzjohn in February. This also provided an opportunity to check the propeller and stern gear, all A1.

The skipper had to fly to London for a meeting on Thursday,

so on Wednesday we all went for an adventure ashore, taking both cars and climbing Mt Gabriel looking for prehistoric copper mines – found with some difficulty. Wolfgang's family provided a fantastic picnic and we enjoyed the sensational views over the whole of Long Island Bay with the Fastnet looking like an approaching aircraft carrier with the white froth of water on its rocks, which could be mistaken for a bow wave.

In the evening the skipper drove Jeremy's car to Cobh (just outside Cork) where he stayed the night with Auntie Jo, flying the following day to Luton and back the same evening. The problem of our gas bottle was solved by Auntie Jo taking it to the filling plant we had found out about at White Gates, a town close to Cork. I got back to Cork airport at 8 p.m., a 40-mile circuit to Cobh to pick up the bottle and then 75 miles back to Skull arriving at midnight, a little exhausted.

While the skipper was away in London Jeremy skippered a very full *Emma* – Diana, Rebecca, Florence, Graham, Gerti, Ziggi and Wolfgang – taking her across to Carthy Sound. The weather was beautiful and they dropped anchor and spent the day swimming and having a picnic ashore on Carthy Island, seeing baby seals.

The captain of an Irish Navy vessel arrives to pick up the grog

The following day saw the move from Skull towards our furthest destination at Sneem. We decided to spend the Friday evening in Castletown Bearhaven, and after a rare day sailing in light airs we negotiated Mizen Head, crossed Dumanus Bay and sailed across Bantry Bay to Castletown. We had been warned both by Alan Meikle (RIBA Sailing Club) and the Irish Sailing Club's cruising instructions to watch out for salmon nets and we had been on the watch for these – they often extend for 3 – 4 miles with a fishing boat waiting like a spider to leap out to protect them. If the fishing boat sees you approaching it will place itself between you and the net.

In general they are very polite and as long as you play the game they will lead you around the nets; except on one occasion, approaching Crookhaven, we met a rather abusive skipper. We had already seen the nets, started the engine, and were taking evasive action when he arrived with such endearing comments as,

Castletown Bearhaven

'What the fook do you think you're doing, for fook's sake?' and much in the same vein. We left him as he gently backed over his own nets, not watching where he was going! The fishing nets are a nuisance and tales are told of fishermen firing shot guns at the yachts who infringe their waters, but happily we saw none of this.

Castletown is very much a working fishing port; no facilities of any sort, except for a modern supermarket. There seemed little to detain us there and the next day Jeremy and Rebecca left with Florence, taking Graham and Andreas back to the UK, while the skipper, Wolfgang, Diana and Jemima sailed to Sneem in the Kenmare River.

We had purchased chart 2495 from the Sailing School in Skull (we should have had the foresight to buy them in England before leaving as they are so expensive in Ireland: £14.40). The chart proved invaluable to take us through the Dursey Sound into the Kenmare River. Visibility was very poor, and we had to calculate the number of minutes for each course, and fettle our way through the channel with three changes of course to avoid the rocks on either side. The visibility was still poor but we caught glimpses of rocks at Cod's Head and Inishfarnard going north-east up the river towards Sherky Island. The sun finally broke through, enabling a perfect entrance into Sneem Harbour where we anchored off close to the jetty at Oysterbed Pier. The town of Sneem is about 2 miles away and Gerti with Ziggi and Liz had found the road down to the jetty, and after a meal we set off to the local pub with good singing.

Sneem is the most beautiful anchorage, very lonely, only one other boat while we were there. The town on the other hand is on the Ring of Kerry, the tourist route, through which during the day hundreds of visitors spend a few minutes clicking their cameras; but excellent butchers and food stores; no water, diesel, etcetera. Despite this, Sneem had great appeal. We had arranged for Tom Winchester to meet us there the following day.

Irish waters are full of wildlife: we saw seals and porpoises and many different sea birds. I hadn't realised that there would be so many gannets – they abound off the coast and many followed us back on our return trip to England. During the war I had watched gannets diving for fish off the Bass Rock in Scotland, a remarkable sight seen from the air. Other sea birds included the many cormorants, black winged gulls, terns and puffin.

The Skipper

Sneem – Baltimore, 17th – 20th July

The skipper had been given the address of some friends in Castlecove and as the following day, Sunday 17th, was a lay day we decided to sail up to Castlecove after lunch. We tacked up the river against a south-westerly force 5 and it took two and a half hours to get to a position off Castlecove. But even with our new chart the entrance to Castlecove looked altogether too difficult with rocks on all sides; we needed a pilot who knew the way in.

IRELAND 1988

Oysterbed Pier, Sneem

So we decided against it and had a splendid broad reach back past Sherky Isle to Sneem in just over an hour, anchoring at 1730 off Oysterbed Pier, where Tom Winchester found us an hour or so later. Tom had thumbed a lift in a little fishing boat from the pier in the centre of the town at high water.

In the pub in the evening we telephoned our friends, Hugh and Rosie Barton, to say how sad we had been that we had funked the entrance through the rocks into Castlecove. They couldn't have been more charming or hospitable, inviting us over the following day, an invitation we couldn't accept as we had to start the move east towards a return to England. We should have stayed, and regretted not doing so, as Irish hospitality is legendary. So Monday 18th saw the crew, with Diana and Jemima, tacking out of Kenmare River again with a south-westerly on the nose. After tacking for three and a half hours we gave up and turned on the engine to get us up to Dursey Sound, otherwise I think we would be there still. As it was it took until 1300 before we turned into Dursey Sound in much the same visibility as when we first encountered it.

Once through we were able to turn off the engine and had a

good reach all the way past Mizen Head and on down to Crookhaven, arriving 1830, encountering many fishing nets on the way.

The following day, Tuesday, was a lay day and after a shopping expedition in Skull we got back to find Suzanne, a friend of Jemima's, had arrived and was waiting for us. We all set off in the VW van to see Dunlough Castle, said to be the hideaway of one O'Mahony the Migrator. It certainly is remote, on the north corner of the Mizen Head peninsula and almost impregnable from the sea. It has three towers with a romantic lake and is really quite beautiful, and well worth the 2- or 3-mile walk across farmland to find it.

It was Diana and the skipper's turn to host a meal, and the girls cooked roast lamb with all the trimmings for eight people; we certainly tested the extent of *Emma*'s cooking facilities. This was one of the best days of the holiday, weather perfect, and a high for Gerti and family's last day. They left at 9 a.m. the following morning for Rosslare, the ferry to Cherbourg and the long trip back to Austria. Wolfgang stayed for the passage to

Dunlough Castle. O'Mahoney O'Mahoney the Migrator's fastness on Mizen Head

IRELAND 1988

Dunlough Castle

Emma on passage,
Crookhaven to Baltimore

Wolfgang in
characteristic pose

Falmouth and on Wednesday we – the skipper, Diana, Jemima and Suzanne with Wolfgang – left Crookhaven for our last night in Baltimore. No wind at all, so we engined, taking the same route which we had followed on the way to Skull and ending up with the narrow route through the islands into Baltimore Harbour.

We rafted out in the fishermen's harbour, but bearing in mind a dawn start for England on Thursday we left the harbour at night and moored off. Diana, Jemima and Suzanne wisely got a B&B for the night in the town so as not to be disturbed by the salty sailors in the morning.

The return to England: Baltimore – Falmouth, 21st – 22nd July

The log records an early start on the Thursday: engine on at 0450 and anchor up by 0500. The idea was to return to England via the Fastnet Rock and after leaving the harbour we set off south for a mile to clear Sherkin Island, then turned south-west for a waypoint at Fastnet.

There was a heavy swell with little wind, but very poor visibility, and by 0600 off Clear Isle it was realised that we would hit the Fastnet Rock before we saw it. So the decision was made to give up the idea and we turned on to 130° for England, on engine until 1315 but still very limited visibility. After this however we were able to sail well for ten hours till midnight, with an average speed of nearly 5 knots.

In a radio programme George Melly was asked what he thought about sailing. He said he enjoyed sailing, describing it as 'long periods' of tedium followed by 'welcome moments' of panic. This certainly sums it all up: after ten hours of easy sailing the wind suddenly freshened and it was necessary to take in a double reef in the main. In doing so the skipper at the tiller let the boom swing across, knocking Wolfgang flying into the cockpit! No bones broken, but a nasty moment. Soon it was foresails down, main lashed amidships on a dead run with engine until 0300 on the Friday morning when the wind allowed the engine to be switched off. It was good sailing for the next ten hours to a position off Wolf's Rock, at an average speed of 5 knots.

Although the skipper had planned a series of waypoints to take us past Seven Stones, Wolf Rock, round the Lizard and up towards the Manacles and Falmouth, the wind did not permit this and we had to set a course to the north taking us closer to Land's End. Visibility was still very poor, and apart from our escort of gannets we saw hardly another ship for the whole night, and the following day. The navigation was satisfactorily assisted by Navstar (which was behaving itself) and we caught fleeting glimpses of the Lizard as we turned on to 047° towards our goal. It was raining and fairly unpleasant.

But despite this and by using the engine we achieved Falmouth by 2240, mooring off one of the town quays, glad not to have to spend a second night at sea.

We moved to the quay at 10 a.m. on Saturday, flying the yellow, filled in our Customs declaration and were suitably done over by an enthusiastic Customs officer. However he cleared us after a minute inspection of Wolfgang's luggage – clearly this large bearded Austrian without shoes, and wearing an Irish cloth cap was potentially a dangerous fellow! All was well and Wolfgang was given passport clearance. We saw him off on a train for London to catch his ferry at Dover and the Vienna express from Ostende.

Coastal passage to Rye: Falmouth – Plymouth – Portsmouth – Yarmouth IOW – Brighton – Rye, 25th – 29th July

The Saturday was a lay day on which Peter Watson joined *Emma*; we did a proper 'clean ship' job, taking all the duckboarding out and spring cleaning, filling with diesel, water and getting a new gas bottle, all ready for a start on the Sunday.

However the start was like the story of the holiday, a little delayed! South-westerly gales were forecast for Sunday 24th so this gave an opportunity to get Peter used to the ropes. We sailed across to St Mawes and practised a series of tacks in quite rough seas, glad we weren't outside the Fall. We sailed until lunchtime, anchoring off Turnaware Point, the scene of a happy gentle barbecue with the Crabber fleet on a previous occasion. This is still exposed to south-westerly gales so we made the decision to motor up past the King Harry Ferry to more sheltered waters. Wind speed was 30 knots with a gale warning up to force 9 issued by Falmouth Coastguard.

We were seeking an anchorage beyond Trelissick House at Lamouth Creek, passing a white gaffer called *Nefertite*, when we were astonished to hear a voice call out, 'Hello Derek, how's Rye?'

This proved to be Alec Bradley, who keeps his gaff-rigged cutter at Phillips' Yard in Rye and had watched the progress of our family sailing since we first purchased *Midley Belle* in 1980 and made all the dreadful mistakes of the novice. He is a 'real' sailor: he has sailed his 1911 craft down to Biscay or the Scillies, single-handed and without engine, each year since he purchased it in 1954, the year Starkie was born.

After we had anchored we went visiting. Alec invited us over for a drink and then we invited him for a spaghetti dinner. Alec is rich in tales of the sea and it was the greatest pleasure to have him on board.

It was a very quiet night, proving we had made a good decision to stay. A leasurely start was made at 10 a.m. on Monday (25th) to catch the fair tide towards Plymouth between noon and 1830. We tacked out of Carrick Roads towards St Anthony's Head, rounding it by noon and having a fast reach towards Plymouth in fairly heavy seas (south-westerly force 5 – 6) using foresails only.

Another of those 'welcome' moments of panic, when the ring of the Maestral broke and, alerted by the bang, we saw the inflatable going walkabout behind us, engine on, and followed in close pursuit! We tied it on by the side ropes; this however proved unsuccessful and our hero, Tom, proved invaluable in hauling her inboard where we could deflate her, and strap her onto the cabin roof for the remainder of the journey home.

By 1700 we were sailing well for two hours passing the Eddystone Rocks and lighthouse clearly visible. As we approached Plymouth from the west entrance a nuclear submarine left towards the Channel. We moored off Sutton Harbour Marina by 2000, and after a little special pleading – it is after all, my favourite marina – we got alongside and went off to the Indian restaurant for an excellent meal out. Plymouth appeared to be *en fête*, with roundabouts and all the fun of the fair – noisy too!

On Tuesday 26th we got all necessary supplies from a Tesco in town, and diesel at the marina, where we saw a miniature submarine. This submarine apparently is 26 feet long, takes a

Miniature submarine in Sutton Marina

crew of two and can stay submerged for two weeks – but for what purpose, one is forced to ask?!

As we left on the following morning for Dartmouth, Tuesday 26th, we passed a Tall Ship, the *Maria Assumpta*, which had moored overnight. We left from the east entrance, tacking out past the Shagstone Rock and turning on to a course for Dartmouth with all sails up by noon, and sailing well on a broad reach at average of 6 knots; at one point off Salcombe recording 7.2 knots. We arrived at the Dart by 1700 and motored in to the Hotel

Marina, passing *Janna* up against the wall on the way in, but by the time we had got tied up and sorted out she must have gone as we didn't see her again. An excellent dinner on board of roast pork was cooked by Peter.

Wednesday 27th was a memorable day. The skipper had planned to go round Portland Bill on the inshore route for Weymouth at 1530. This meant leaving Dartmouth at 6 a.m. There was a south-westerly force 2 at first and we sailed on a dead run, gull-winging with all sails up, but by 0830 the wind died and we had to motor for about an hour. After this the wind freshened and we sailed well, arriving at the Bill in good time at 1535; but as the weather seemed so favourable the decision was made to take the outside route round, forget about Weymouth and go on to Poole. But by 1615 there still seemed to be plenty of time and a fair wind for the Solent, so again a change of plan, and onwards to the Needles.

We finally reached Yarmouth IOW at 2130, and moored inside the harbour rafted to two or three other boats – no harbour-master at this time of night – and went ashore in the harbour pick-up boat (30p each way) having excellent fish and chips in one of the local hosteleries. We worked out later that we had done 96 miles in 15 hours 30 minutes, or an average berth to berth speed of 6.2 knots, and a lot faster than this for much of the time.

One of the reasons we had decided to continue the previous day had been Peter's advice on the weather: a front was about to come through which might hold us up. This was good advice as the following day, Thursday, the weather was fairly unpleasant, but we decided to continue for Brighton, knowing that there were a number of alternative ports of call if the weather got really bad. In the event, we sailed for nine of the 12 hours it took. One of the 'foredeck gorillas' had trampled on the radio deck plug, and the skipper couldn't understand why, when we effected a temporary repair, this allowed reception while it precluded transmission.

We finally reached Brighton Marina at 1840, and after mooring telephoned Jemima, who said that Diana had taken the car to Rye and was arriving in Brighton by train later. We all met for a drink and Diana joined the crew for the final leg to Rye the following morning.

Tom and Peter on passage to Brighton

The last day of the sail, Friday 29th, was one of trying to sail slowly. High water at Rye was not until 0023 and a call to Dover Coastguard suggested it was OK to get over the bar plus or minus two hours at high springs. This meant we shouldn't cross the bar before 2230. But with only the foresails we were still being swept down the Channel at about 5.5 knots with a strong south-westerly gale.

We made a detour out to Royal Sovereign, and Diana poked her head outside to act the 'salty sailor' bit, to say she had seen it. We still arrived close to Rye buoy about an hour too early and set off on a southerly course for 20 minutes, returning to enter the Rother at 2220, just right to get over the bar and downriver. We tied up at *Emma*'s berth at 2315 having just completed a cruise of 1,247 miles, glad to be home without any mishaps.

Peter, Tom and the skipper put *Emma* to rights, more or less, while Diana cooked a splendid meal of roast lamb which we ate at the house in Market Street at about 0030. It was generally agreed that it had been a great holiday despite, rather than because of, the weather. *Emma* performed well and the crew didn't make too many mistakes.

The skipper's original intention had been to sail to Ireland in *Midley Bell*e, but this had been pre-empted by the purchase in March of *Emma*. On reflection I would not have been happy to have undertaken our Irish passage in a Crabber – this was not just because of the undeniable comfort of the Cutter, but also the greatly increased safety of a larger boat.

A diversion towards Royal Sovereign

'Swept down the Channel by a SW gale ... passing the Seven Sisters on passage to Rye with foresails only'

IRELAND 1988

Dear Derek,

Thank you again for the lovely lift across the Irish sea, as well as the whole trip before. I didn't tell Gnagflow, he for sure would be jaleous (I don't know how to spell that). And if - somewhen - you are in need of a crew, ~~let me~~ I wouldn't mind to be one of them. (If I achieve your standards, of course and I won't drop the gaff, I promise!!!) I also will remember the name of the sails. (Jib-Main-Stay, or is it Jib-Stay-Main?). **THANK YOU VERY MUCH!!!!!**

Wuifi

7

Passage to the Sun: Spain 1989

Coastal passage: Rye – Weymouth, 30th June – 1st July

The original intention had been to sail direct from Rye to Plymouth, from which a week later a new crew would start the 'passage to the sun'. However this was not to be, and although the day started well with all sails up and a light southerly wind, by mid-afternoon

Leaving Rye on 30th June for Plymouth

FAMILY SAILING IN EUROPEAN WATERS

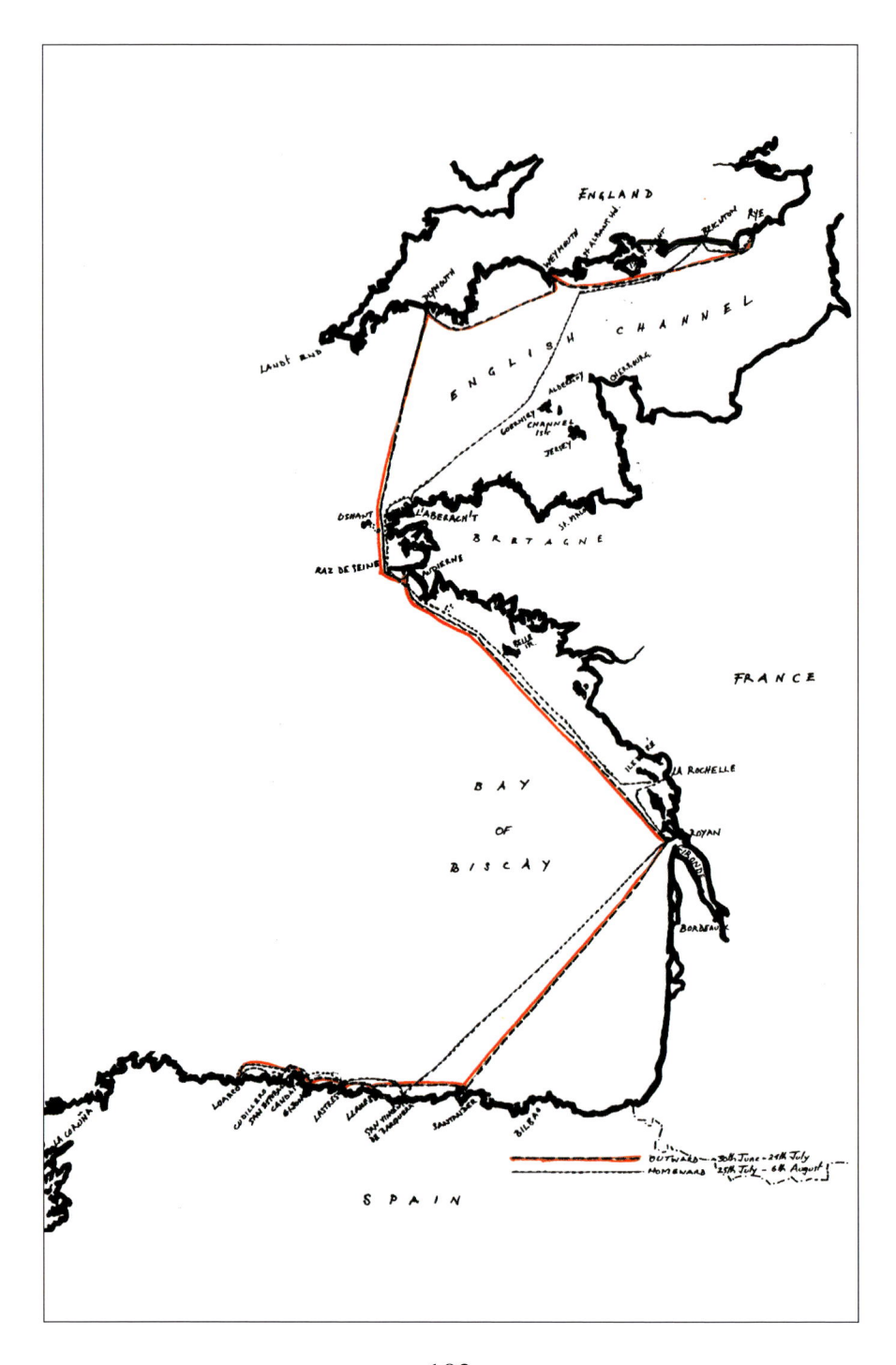

the wind had died and the engine had to be switched on for three-quarters of an hour, after which we sailed until 2030 when it was necessary to motor-sail, beating into a rising south-westerly.

The weather forecast gave a strong wind warning: south-westerly force 6 veering to westerly force 4 – 5 in sea area Portland. Far from this it became very misty and by the middle of the night it was almost impossible to see the St Catherine's light, coupled

Jeremy, Andrew, Steve and Barbara en route to Weymouth

with which the Navstar was playing games with signal lost and eventually gave a single and totally incorrect position, after which we gave up Decca and went over to dead reckoning. The tide was against us off St Catherine's Point and it seemed to take an interminable time to pass it, with visibility still poor. We got a fix on the Needles and Anvil Point at noon by which time the sea state was rough and the main was reefed; with no sign of the wind veering, the skipper made the decision to abandon Plymouth and run into Weymouth when the long line of Portland Bill became clear through the mist at 1400. We reached Weymouth at 1800 and were glad to be there.

Weymouth is always a pleasure and the skipper made all the

Storage of the life raft

necessary arrangements with the harbour-master and the obligatory 'look-see' man to leave *Emma* for the following week. We deserved a meal out, and despite the fact that the excellent Indian restaurant from last year had disappeared we still found a reasonable meal and a beer or so before sleeping on board. Back home for all the crew on the next day, Sunday.

It was not a propitious start for the passage and this experience coupled with a rather unpleasant sail across to Boulogne a few weeks before decided the skipper to abandon the original intention of doing the three-day and night crossing direct from Audierne to Coruna. Notices were sent flying to joining crew that we would take the alternative route down the east coat of Biscay, stopping at Royan near Bordeaux before cutting across to Santander.

Coastal passage: Weymouth – Plymouth, 8th – 9th July

In order to collect our duty free booze it was necessary to arrange for this to be delivered by A.E. Monsen's and sealed by the

Customs officer early on Monday 10th July. This meant arriving at Plymouth's Sutton Harbour Marina on the Sunday ready for as early a start as possible for France the following morning.

The crew arrived at Weymouth on the Saturday morning; or in the case of the skipper and Jonathan on the Friday evening to sleep aboard, enabling them to do the final provisioning for the trip in the morning.

The tide to take us westwards round the Bill at the witching hour of one hour before high water at Dover meant leaving Weymouth at 1300 and rounding the Bill at 1430.

Once again it was very misty and we followed another yacht out of port and towards Portland but in the end lost it in the mist. We used Navstar which had been reinitialised after a telephone discussion with the factory, and this time it worked fine. We passed Portland on the inshore route a 'biscuit's toss' from the shore and set off into a white fog across Lyme Bay, seeing nothing for the next three or four hours.

Alistair tried fishing, having purchased a husky spinning line in Weymouth, and caught a series of mackerel, surely the most stupid fish in the sea.

We had a more successful night sail, passing Start Point about 2 a.m., but the wind had died completely so we were engining from 2100 until berthing at Plymouth, where we arrived at 8 a.m. on Sunday.

Alistair fishing

Alistair and Tony

Tony had contrived to break off the engine key in the lock and it was only due to Alistair's ingenuity that the problem was solved; he had the engine electrics stripped down and the switch removed. A phone call to the local Yamiar agent A.S. Blagdon & Sons, fortunately open on Sunday, and yes! he had the replacement switch. One slight problem: he gave directions as to how we should get there, 'Just a few minutes.' After half an hour's walk it transpired that he thought we were coming by car! All was well however, and £25 poorer we returned to *Emma* and Alistair replaced the switch. I don't know whether *Emma*'s crew are particularly clumsy or whether the engine switch is badly located but it was not more than a few days out that the engine key was bent in half yet again by a clumsy boot; this time we left it bent – it still works fine.

Sunday gave an opportunity for all the other necessary chores to be done: water, diesel, setting in waypoints for the first part of the passage to Spain, relocating the life raft, changing the gas bottle, checking the furling gear, putting all the 23 charts in order for easy reference, and checking the engine oil. And so to sleep, ready for an early start the following morning.

PASSAGE TO THE SUN: SPAIN 1989

To France: Plymouth – Audierne – Royan, 10th – 13th July

Monsen's delivered the duty frees soon after 9 a.m. with Jonathan and the skipper getting final perishable food at the local Tesco at 8.30. The Customs officer sealed the booze locker at 9.30 and at 9.40 *Emma* slipped from her berth and made out of Plymouth bound for the Brittany coast. We were glad to get away early, having a tide to catch down the Chenal du Four towards the Raz de Sein at 10 a.m. the following morning. There was little wind at first and we were on engine till 11.30 when the wind freshened and we sighted Eddystone rock lighthouse soon after midday.

By 1700 the wind increased to a south-westerly force 4 and we were logging a speed of 6.3 knots under sail.

Soon after 1800 three homing pigeons were sighted, looking in need of a home, and two made it on to *Emma*'s stern; the other appeared to have drowned. We fed and watered the pigeons, named Port and Starboard by Tony, which were tucked up below the cockpit seat where they remained all night until encouraged

'Port and Starboard' hitching a lift

to depart the following morning. They flew off towards the French coast and no doubt the French 'ack-ack'. The wind had veered northerly and by 2100 we were broad-reaching until 0300 the following morning when it was again necessary to engine for four hours.

Our aim to reach the Le Four light to catch the fair tide down the Chenal du Four was almost achieved and good progress was made all next day, Tuesday, towards the Raz de Sein. However by 1630 the visibility had deteriorated badly and we went round the Raz using Navstar, seeing little of the cliffs as we went by.

Sailing towards Audierne the sun suddenly shone through in one of those wonderful moments when one minute we could see nothing but mist, and within five minutes the whole French coast was revealed. We anchored off Audierne at 1900.

The town of Audierne is some distance from the moorings, and as we had not yet inflated the Maestral, Tony had to borrow a tender from an accommodating Dutchman, using great ingenuity to pull himself back to *Emma* and yet be able to deliver the tender back to our Dutch friend. All done, it was an early bed with a view to a dawn start on Wednesday.

'A' watch, the skipper and Jonathan, cast off *Emma* at 0530 and engined out of the moorings with a steady barometer at 1024

Royan

and a light north-easterly. By 0530 all sails were set, broad-reaching on a course of 1500 for Belle Isle. However the wind was poor until 1630 when it picked up and we were making such excellent way south that the skipper decided to give Belle Isle a miss and go direct for Royan. A good decision as it turned out, as we then did 160 miles' sailing without recourse to the 'iron topsail' until 2230 on the following evening – 30 hours' sailing at an average of 5.3 knots, all the way to the Gironde, berthing at Royan before midnight on 13 July, the evening before Bastille Day.

Royan was wide awake long after midnight and as the following two days were to be lay days the crew enjoyed the delights of the bars ashore. Whilst not my favourite place it has all the facilities and comforts one can imagine.

Bastille Day saw the ship cleaned and all maintenance work done. The Maestral however proved to be a problem, with the valves having to be restuck in position with Araldite. And more of a problem when the skipper and Jonathan stuck the metal inserts in upside down so the valves wouldn't screw in! These then had to be removed using Alistair's practical abilities, and when restuck they worked OK. So from Royan onwards the Maestral was towed behind *Emma*.

The crew in Royan

The problem of the Maestral

Bastille night, as one might expect for the 200th anniversary, saw great celebrations with I believe the most spectacular firework display the skipper or any of the crew had ever seen, and this certainly included displays seen in Hong Kong or on the Thames. The display just went on and on, with what one felt had to be the finale followed by one even bigger and better, and so on... Breathtaking.

We had flown the yellow in Royan but perhaps because of Bastille Day the Douane was closed and everyone was very relaxed about Customs clearance.

Diana and the shore party were due to arrive on the following day, Saturday, having themselves spent Bastille Day with friends in a village some 60 miles north. Tony and Alistair both had to leave for the UK, after what proved to be some of the best sailing of the trip.

Passage to Spain: 16th – 17th July

If the passage to Royan was good, the journey south to Spain was if anything even better. The crew comprised the skipper and

PASSAGE TO THE SUN: SPAIN 1989

Jonathan, with Jemima and Graham, and left the berth at Royan at 6.40 am on Sunday. We were under sail leaving the Gironde by 0715. The morning wind was light and the engine was needed for short periods until midday when with all sails set *Emma* sailed for 30 hours right down to Santander.

We had known that we would lose the Decca, and using the information from Navstar we calculated losing it in the approximate position 44°50'N by 02°15'W; and this occurred about midnight. We set in a new dead reckoning plot using a speed of 5 knots on a co. of 225°m.

The 'Decca ready' alarm sounded at 0700 on Monday morning and our position seemed to be reasonably accurate with an ETA at Santander of 2300. By 1400 Navstar gave an excellent status of 9.9.9.8 and our position was confirmed. By 1830 we sighted the mountains of Spain, relieved we had made our passage across Biscay successfully: 183 miles in a total of 40 hours.

It was very hot during the day and the only way to keep cool was for the crew to throw buckets of sea water over each other which was a wonderful feeling, the cockpit acting like a shower

The skipper planning the route

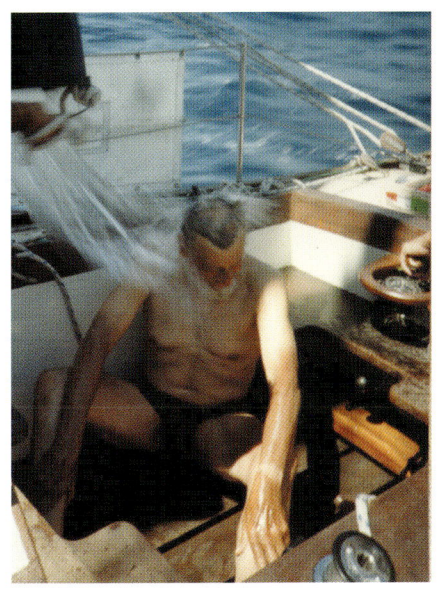

The skipper getting the water treatment

111

cabinet, its self-draining characteristics very useful. We saw a school of porpoises which played around the ship for five minutes or so; nice company. Graham caught a sea bass which made a good lunch for all.

We reached the estuary into Santander at 2200 and berthed alongside in the first marina we found. This was a mistake, first because we couldn't get ashore without difficulty and second, having achieved it and had a beer at a bar, it was equally difficult to get back to *Emma*. This achieved, we decided to move to a position with easier shore access and had just berthed there at about 0130, enjoying a whisky before bed, when another boat arrived whose permanent berth it was and made it clear that we had about 30 seconds to get out! So it was off again to an almost empty marina by the Santander airport about an hour away on engine, and we berthed at 0220, glad to get to bed.

The following day, Tuesday 18th, was a lay day spent in trying to conform to all the Spanish formalities. In the end we gave up as no one seemed to know where the Customs place was, nor did

Sunset in Biscay

it seem to matter. The most important thing was that we paid the marina (£7.30).

Diana and the shore party had arrived during the morning, and had telephoned the harbour-master who told them that yes, *Emma* was in the marina, and that the crew had left by taxi to try to find the Customs. So Diana waited by what proved not to be the Customs, but was at least where we had ended up too. So well met.

The topsail had got badly ripped when trying to get it down one evening crossing Biscay (it was always taken down before nightfall, as this was difficult to do in an emergency in the dark). Santander Marina had useless facilities, but we were able to get some blue mending tape and this, placed on either side of the sail, lasted all the way back to the UK; quite a pretty pattern too.

We didn't much care for Santander, just a very large town, and made the decision not to return on the way home, and to leave from somewhere else. (This turned out to be San Vicente del Barquera.)

Entry to Llanes

The Spanish cruise: 19th – 28th July

The crew now comprised Diana and Derek, Jemima and Graham, Jonathan, Amelia and her friend 'Spacey' Tracy from Hong Kong, and Suzanne; but as two or more people formed the shore party and would take the car on to the next part of call, we were never too crowded on board.

Wednesday 19th July saw the start of the cruise westwards along the Atlantic coast of Spain, the real purpose of our 'passage to the sun', so it was perhaps proper that the first port of call should be Llanes, the little coastal port where we had spent two family holidays in the 1960s. It was quite a long haul, some 50 miles, so an early start was made at 0600 in order to ensure that we could reach this tidal harbour by high water at 1835. The wind starting as a north-easterly force 3 – 4 enabled all sails to be set including the topsail but it was soon necessary to claw back towards the coast as it was impossible to hold a westerly course. We tacked along the coast but a general increase in wind speed necessitated the topsail coming down and two reefs put in the main. By 12.45 we were running before an easterly force 6 with staysail down as well. Tracy didn't like it much!

Llanes has a narrow entrance, and with a force 6, very high

Llanes

PASSAGE TO THE SUN: SPAIN 1989

...up against the wall

Don Paco Hotel, Llanes

The dining room

waves make it look fairly exciting. Clearly the local inhabitants thought so, and we came in between the rocks at 1715, watched by half the town. Llanes dries and so once we had found an empty length of wall to berth against, it was a question of putting down our legs before the water disappeared.

The skipper welcomed this as it provided the opportunity to have a look at the bottom and clear weed off the propeller, and the following morning saw a rather bolshy crew scrubbing the bottom. It was pretty clear, considering it had not been cleaned since the Irish cruise 12 months earlier; one big advantage of a mud berth is that it appears to make antifouling unnecessary – there were no little clinging molluscs to worry about.

Llanes is a dirty and quite charming little Spanish port, almost unknown to tourists, except the Spanish families who come here each year. The following day Diana and the skipper revisited the Don Paco Hotel where we had stayed previously, a converted monastry; nothing had appeared to have changed in 20 years. We ordered 'Chicken in Juices' our favourite dish from the past, with plenty of garlic, and although it wasn't on the menu they made it specially for us. It doesn't always pay to revisit the past, but on this occasion it did.

Lastres

Typical grainstore close to Cudillero

Jonathan left for home from Llanes, but Andreas arrived, having found his way on public transport from Vienna; so you lose one, you win one.

We left the same afternoon at 1700 for Lastres, a short hop of 24 miles westwards along the coast; the wind had backed round to a westerly force 3 and then died completely, making it necessary to motor for five hours all the way, arriving at 2220. We passed the entrance to Ribadesella at 2025 having an idea we might stop there on our return journey, but in the end we didn't.

It was a poor day's sail for Andreas's first day at sea, which was disappointing. However this was made up for by the port of Lastres which is perhaps as typical on any of those along the Atlantic coast. We had averaged 4.5 knots along the coast with 2,500 revs from our GM28 Yanmar, and we calculated that at these revs *Emma* used about 1 gallon in three and a half hours (approximately 15 miles per gallon).

Lastres town rises from the port up a steep hill, and is a real working port filled with fishing trawlers, yet everyone is perfectly happy to see a British sailing boat and there are no berthing fees.

We only paid for berthing at Santander and Gijon, everywhere else along the coast was free.

Having decided to see more of Lastres on our return journey we decided to leave for Gijon the following morning, Friday 21st, with a crew of Derek, Amelia, Graham, Andreas, Suzanne and Tracy. It proved to be a foul day with thunderstorms and lightning.

We left Lastres at 1300 and were immediately sailing, but by 1600 it was necessary to take down the sails and engine. The distance was short, only 18 miles, and we arrived there at 1840.

Gijon has the best facilities of any port that we visited, with splendid showers, diesel and water all easily available. It also has the most rigorous port officials, and the various formalities took the skipper over two hours to get completed. They keep your passport, only retrievable on the day you leave when you have paid your harbour dues (£6.50). Navstar behaved very badly, and I can only think that Decca in this area gives poor signals; it seemed completely up the spout and the entrance to Gijon was clearly visible before we got a position from Navstar telling us it was 8 miles away.

Diana was in the shore party and arrived in time for an evening meal on board for eight cooked by Jemima and Suzanne. We met some charming English people in a Nicholson 32 from the IOW

The port of Gijon

and they invited Diana and the skipper for a whisky aboard before dinner. Their crew comprised their skipper, a Mr Room (I'm not sure of the spelling), his elder brother, both of whom must have been in their seventies, and a female companion – very good company. They told us that they remembered seeing us in *Midley Belle* in Concarneau in 1987.

Their skipper has the problem that as he is retired, he likes to spend a couple of months sailing in the summer but there are few people who can spend so long and he has to arrange a series of fortnightly crew changes. Shades of problems for the future, I imagine.

Saturday 22nd started very blowy and we decided to wait till we saw what the weather would do by lunchtime, as we had a date in San Esteban to meet the Wolfgang clan.

In the event the wind calmed sufficiently to leave Gijon by 1530 and as it was a short leg of 22 miles we felt it would be wise to go for it. We passed Luanco at 1720 but the wind was on the nose and it was all on engine with heavy thunderstorms off Cabo Penas and poor visibility. The crew, skipper and Andreas got absolutely soaked; the passengers, Diana and Jemima remained dry in the cabin. The tide was against us around Cabo Penas and I began to wonder whether we should ever get round. Navstar as usual indicated 'signal lost', so it wasn't much help as there are a lot of off-lying rocks off the Cape.

Finally we got round by 1900 and had a good run on into San Esteban by 2100. There was quite a reception committee, with Wolfgang who had with him Gerti, Daniel, Sigi and also little Eva, and Patrick and Merrill had also arrived.

Having finally tied up along the quay and established that legs would not be necessary we had a really splendid meal with 14 of us at a cheap cafe on the end of the quay. The food was all different sorts of fish, calamares and prawns, including tunny fish, the local industry – which with wine came to about £4 per head.

We decided that in this part of Spain it was as cheap to eat out as it was to purchase the food and cook it on board – food in supermarkets was expensive and the only reasonable food is to be bought in street markets.

With 14 potential crew a selection had to be made for the next day, but the more difficult aspect was trying to find somewhere for everyone to sleep. The Wolfgang lot slept in their VW Microbus, but this still left nine more. Somehow this was coped with, by sleeping bags on the cabin roof or on shore and six in the boat.

Patrick's initiation to the cruise was to be presented by a blocked sea loo, and he used his considerable expertise in these matters to unblock it – despite somewhat dire consequences! He explained that the problem was entirely female.

Our nice English friends had advised us to try the little port of Cudillero only 6 miles along the coast westwards, so as this was

Cudillero, the Maestral being towed back

almost a lay day we did the leg in a couple of hours, arriving 1330 on the Sunday afternoon.

As we had arrived early enough to go swimming all except the skipper, Andreas and Amelia left by car for the beach, and although we didn't know how far this was, we decided to take the Maestral around to find them. It took longer than we had planned, but there was excellent swimming on arrival. On the return journey Diana decided to captain the Maestral, setting off with Jemima,

PASSAGE TO THE SUN: SPAIN 1989

Danny and Andreas. Unfortunately they ran out of petrol and had to be towed into port rather ignominiously by a kindly fisherman. Memo: a full tank only lasts about one hour!

Cudillero proved to be everything expected of it, and we were glad to have made it a port of call, but with no shops open on a Sunday it meant another restaurant.

The skipper, Diana and Amelia drove back to the little cafe in San Esteban for another splendid fish meal, with the rest of the gang eating in Cudillero.

The final westwards leg took us to Luarca; we had originally hoped to get as far as Ribadeo, but time was against us. We left Cudillero at noon, arriving at Luarca in just under eight hours, half of which were on engine, motor-sailing. We came in on a bearing of 1700 as directed in Biscay (South) Pilot. On arrival

Tracy's painting

The thirteen man crew on board at Candas

Patrick dropped an expensive pair of specs into the drink but as even at low water there was about 3 metres of water below us it didn't seem feasible to dive for them. Tracy spent the afternoon painting the central mast pillar in *Emma*'s cabin, and made a good start on it, in her own inimitable style.

So this was as far as we were to get, and the next morning, Tuesday 25th July, we started the journey back eastwards along the coast, the object being to try where possible to run into different ports than on the westward journey.

The first leg was to Candas starting at 0800 for the 40-mile leg. We had hoped that with adverse winds for the most part westwards, we would gain on the way back, but the day started badly with no wind at all! This was the story of the day, with the engine on for seven of the eleven hours it took.

We caught four decent-sized mackerel, and after the skipper had gutted and cleaned them we ate them for lunch. We saw a lot of tunny during the day, and these tend to bask in the sun with one fin flapping above the water.

Our arrival at 1900 was marked by Andreas jumping off the side for a swim having tied up, followed by Diana and the skipper; the water was warm and clean. It was one of the most beautiful sunny days we experienced.

We were warned by a fisherman that where we had berthed alongside the harbour wall would dry, but the Pilot said there would be never less than 2 metres. We thought we should play safe and put down the legs, but in the event the Pilot was right and we never had less than 2 metres below the keel.

As we had spent so little time in Lastres on the westwards run we decided, against the principle of varying the journey back, to spend the following night, Wednesday 26th July, in this charming fishing port. On approaching Lastres from the west we were confused by what appeared to be a lighthouse where none should have been. We saw from the chart that there should be one at Tazones, which we passed, and the next would be at Ribadesella; yet here was what appeared to be a lighthouse high on the cliffs to the west of what had to be Lastres. We were sailing well at this time and it was clear that it was Lastres a mile or so further on when the harbour opened up to us. We berthed alongside the harbour wall at 1800.

Patrick and the skipper had to take the car up to town to collect a new gas bottle and decided to see what the curious tower was, and after a circuitous route we found it. We were really no wiser as it looked just like a lighthouse without a light from close to as well. So the mystery remains unsolved. Perhaps it was an old abandoned light, or perhaps it is in the process of being built – confusing to the simple sailor!

Lastres provided one of the great meals of the trip; 14 of us sat down outside the fishermen's cafe on the quay and enjoyed a fantastic fish meal with all the delights we had learned to order. Jemima's Spanish is very good after her year spent in South America and we all enjoyed the benefit of her making our wishes known. Tracy did a drawing of all 14 of us round the table and this is printed here. Tracy recorded a number of the exploits of the crew, in addition to painting the mast support in *Emma*'s cabin.

Meal at Lastres

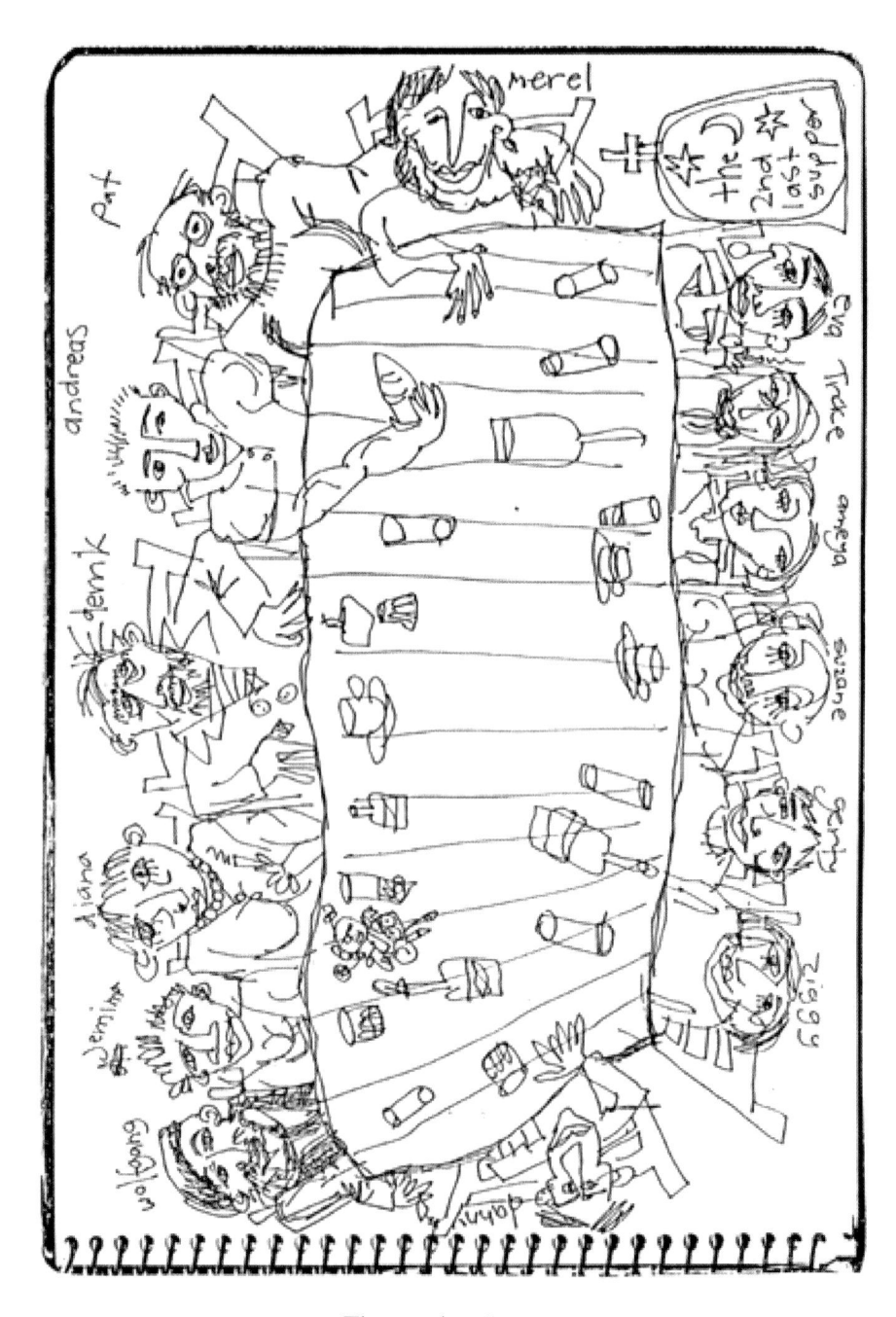

FAMILY SAILING IN EUROPEAN WATERS

The meal at Lastres

The decision was made to stop short of Santander and spend our last day before the northerly leg up Biscay at San Vicente del Barquera.

San Vicente is tidal and the Pilot suggests entry before high water and gives detailed instructions on the approaches, all of which we found invaluable, it not being the easiest of harbours to enter – the ebb runs at 3 knots.

It was around 40 miles from Lastres and calculations suggested a start at 0900 to reach San Vicente to catch the flood in at 2000, and this we did, making slow progress with little wind and the topsail set.

On arrival the ground crew had found a spot for a barbecue, bought all the makings, and burnt chicken was the order of the night.

The following day, Friday 28th, was a lay day, and a 'make

Jemima at the helm

and mend' to get all ready for the trip towards Royan. It was here that Wolfgang's family departed for the 1,000-mile trip back to Austria, leaving Wolfgang on board for the rest of the passage home.

Tom Winchester had arrived also for the trip back and we were to have a crew of six as far as Royan: Diana, the skipper, Wolfgang and Andreas, Patrick and Tom.

It was a beautiful sunny day and we decided on a walk up to the old church above the town. We did final shopping for stores, changed the gas bottle and cleaned the ship ready for next morning's 'off'.

The Return Journey: 29th July – 6th August

We left the estuary at San Vicente on the ebb tide at 0610 to ensure getting out of the river. The route length to Royan was

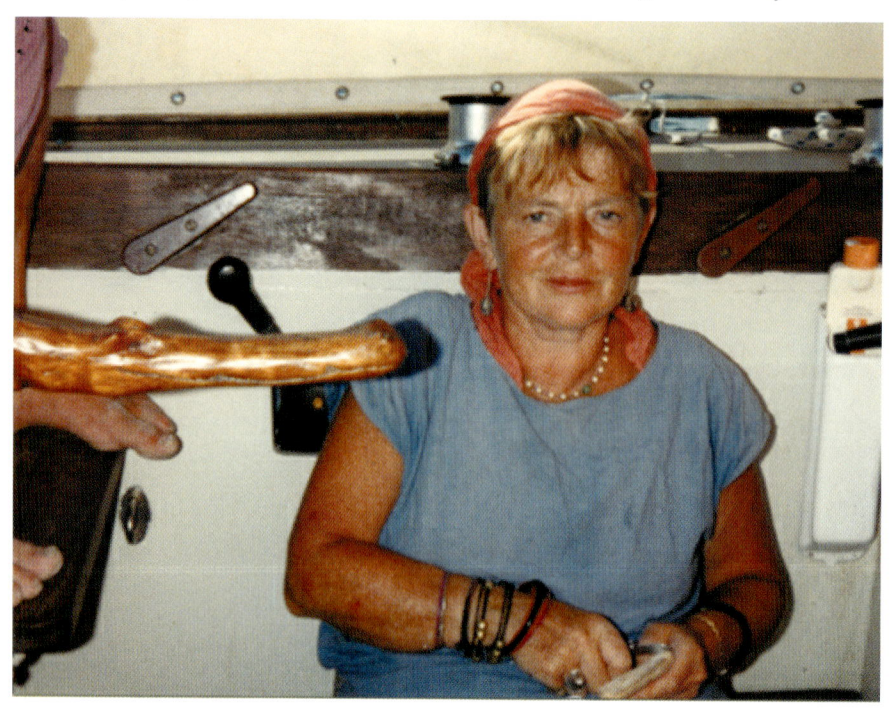

Diana ... on no! Tom

186 miles on a course of 049°. With a north-westerly wind of only force 2 it meant engining despite a beam reach, as we were getting nowhere without it.

We used the engine for 38 hours all told, out of 41 hours 30 minutes, most of it motor-sailing. A night at sea and we arrived at Royan at about 2330 having entered the Gironde from the south, a good suggestion by Patrick.

The Decca ran out in position 44°14'.90N 03°15'.50W, and the change was made to dead reckoning navigation on Saturday evening at 2205; Decca came back at noon the following day at 45°86.70N 02°5.50W (44.3 miles from Royan). The dead reckoning position was about 5 miles out and it appears that Decca can cope with this amount of variation.

The girls arrived soon after we did, having driven from San Vicente across the Picos de Europa on an enjoyable trip. A crew change was made with Diana being replaced by Merrill, and *Emma* left her berth at Royan, having taken on necessary water and diesel before leaving at 1040 on Monday 31st July.

Once again the journey was made on engine and by 1500 the log was streamed as Navstar signals became unreliable. We tried tacking to see if we could maintain at least 4 knots in the desired direction, but this was very uncomfortable with a rising wind now on the nose, force 5 with a strong sea state. By 2200 it was clear we were making little headway against tide and wind and decided to alter course and run into La Rochelle.

The last 32 miles to La Rochelle saw the wind on the port beam and sailing well with a double reef main and jib only. The skipper retired to bed, leaving Patrick and Tom on deck. By 1330 the leading lights of La Rochelle were visible and the skipper was woken up to find the ship heading into wind to lower the sails. This operation completed, the leading lights were lost and our attempt to find the right entrance course into the harbour was frustrated by a series of misleading red lights. Finally we passed to the east of a westerly cardinal buoy, the unforgivable sin. Suddenly with the echo sounder bleeping and ominous crunching from below we turned 180° and left on a reciprocal course, until the skipper spotted another yacht making inwards; we followed

FAMILY SAILING IN EUROPEAN WATERS

The arrival in La Rochelle

Drinks on board France

this, picked up the lost leading lights and entered harbour none the worse (apart from bad temper) for this unfortunate episode. We berthed at La Rochelle Marina at 0420.

Patrick reckoned Merrill had had enough, and when the next day the weather had shown no signs of improvement, arrangements were made for Merrill to return to the UK by train.

The following day, Tuesday, proved to be a bonus: a lay day in the lovely city of La Rochelle. Having tidied the boat, got all necessary stores, diesel, water and gas, we took off by the little ferry to the centre of town.

We found an excellent bar on the *France I*, the first ocean liner of this name and now a museum, and we all sat in the sun

Dolphins

enjoying a beer. After which we found a little restaurant, Le Pilote, in a road just off the popular harbour road, so prices were even more reasonable, with an excellent 90-franc menu with five courses – one of the great meals of the trip.

It was a disappointing day as there was little wind for sailing, but at least we could make good progress in calm seas on engine.

We had no fixed plan of what we could do, as so much would depend on the weather: we knew that to get around the Raz de Sein on the early morning tide on Friday we had to reach the southern point by about 0200, the next opportunity being about 1450 in the afternoon. We could achieve the latter if we arrived too late for the former, by anchoring off Audierne for an hour or two, which would have been comfortable enough.

In the event, whilst the Wednesday winds left us on engine for 16 hours, by Thursday we had a good 12 hours' sailing at 5 knots so that good progress was made in the right direction.

Tom distinguished himself by tying an untieable knot on to a preventer to the main ('I'm good at knots,' says Tom!) so that when we tacked the boom came over and while Tom wrestled with the knot which he had tied to a stanchion instead of the shrouds, the stanchion was bent over by about 15°!

We had again lost Decca off the Ile D'Yeu by midnight on the Wednesday, and gone over to dead reckoning, streamed the log and worked out the tides for the following 24 hours and set these in with estimated course and speeds.

We obtained fixes of lights during the night off Ile D'Yeu and by Thursday morning obtained good fixes off Belle Ile, enabling us to be sure of our course towards Pointe Penmarch, leaving the Iles de Glenans to starboard.

The wind became more favourable and with Wolfgang's excellent helming we used this to round the point and make good headway towards the Raz to catch the 0200 tide the following morning. The Decca had recovered during the afternoon and using the dead reckoning positions based on fixes we checked out that we were in the correct position for rounding the Raz, which like the outward journey was shrouded in mist.

So by 0300 on the Friday we were able to set a course up the Chenal du Four and made the decision to call in at L'Aber Wrac'h for water and diesel, but to stay only long enough for the tide to turn in our favour to get up past the Le Four light and turn starboard towards Guernsey.

We berthed at L'Aber Wrac'h at 11 a.m. and spent a few hours recovering from the two nights at sea and enjoying five hours' relaxation. The shop close to the harbour is expensive and has a poor selection of food, but there was no time to go foraging further.

At 1545 we slipped, and set off out to the Libenter buoy before turning north-east around the coast.

Our return to England from Brittany was depressing, and slightly sinister – there was no wind at all, and the sea was like glass; it was almost like being in the eye of a storm, except there was no storm. At night the stars were perfectly reflected in the sea, like in a painting.

The tide swept us round eastwards towards the Ile de Batz and onwards to Sept Iles at speeds exceeding 7.5 knots, until it ran out of steam by 2200 and started westwards, making the early morning passage with Patrick and Tom on watch depressingly slow.

The skipper was determined to use the tides to cross the Channel and make as far as possible towards Anvil Point, and whilst this all had to be done on engine it worked well and by 0900 on Saturday we were able to check our plot with the tall light-

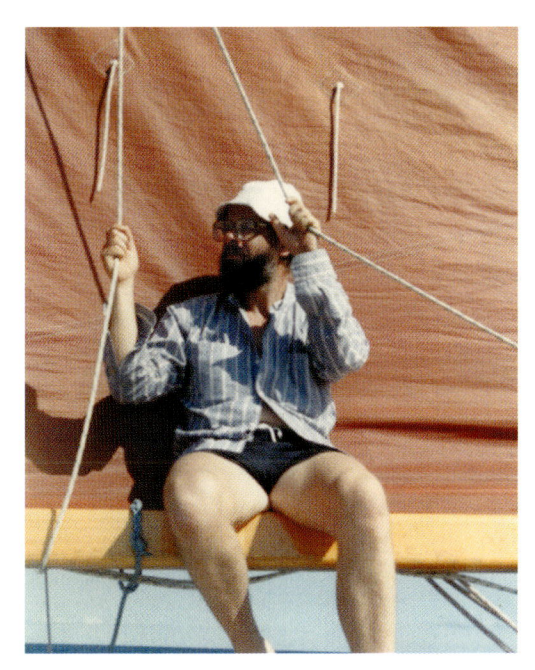

Patrick

Homeward bound!

house on Guernsey and alter course with a fair tide giving us 7 knots towards England. The crew saw a shark during the early morning, but this was not as exciting as being surrounded by porpoises en route to the Raz; they are such wonderful and playful beasts.

At this point we altered clocks back from European time to BST and the skipper badly miscalculated, so that his watch had to do the extra hour ... it will not happen again!

Still a glassy sea, nil wind, and all engine; in fact from L'Aber Wrac'h until we berthed at Brighton Marina on Sunday afternoon we were on engine for 47 hours.

The skipper had radioed ahead to Brighton to request Customs clearance as our first port of call in UK, and two very polite young men met us when we berthed at 1420. We explained we had very little time, as if we were to catch the flood tide down the Rother into Rye we needed to leave by 1600. We achieved this, Customs cleared and diesel purchased, and were exiting the marina by 1550. Still no wind.

We gave Dover Coastguard a TR saying we should reach Rye by about 0200, as we had given an estimate to Jersey Radio of our likely arrival. On this occasion we had requested weather information: variable force 1 – 3 with a north-easterly force 3 – 4 later. What north-easterly? We never saw one! We got a similar report from Portland Radio and we reported to them that from where we were it was nil wind.

The final leg to Rye was a marginal improvement; there was a feeling we had all had enough sailing for a while and a general desire to get home. We obtained a link call by radio to Diana who had arrived back at Bovingdon a couple of days earlier, and she agreed to meet us in Rye about lunchtime on Monday. The wind picked up and we gull-winged down the Channel from 2000, having passed Beachy Head light at 1900. By midnight we realised we would arrive too early for the tide and took down the main, sailing on foresails only. This did the trick and we sailed into the Rother at 0200, berthing in our usual mud berth at 0230. After a quick tidy up, it was home to bed at 10 Market Street.

In all, we had sailed 1 mile less than 1,800 miles. It was interesting to see, when I read Libby Purves's charming book *One Summer's Grace*, that their circumnavigation of England, Wales and Scotland was 1,700 miles, so it is a little bit further to do the Biscay passage.

On Monday, after a good night's rest, we put *Emma* to rights. Merrill arrived by car to collect Patrick and Tom in time for the Great British Breakfast at about 11 a.m., leaving after lunch; Diana and Amelia arrived at 2 p.m. and after lunch with Wolfgang and Andreas we did the final packing and left with Wolfgang and Andreas, arriving at Bovingdon at 1915 – glad to be home, but with some satisfaction at achieving our 'passage to the sun'.

Dear Derek (from Alistair Thornley)

My recollections of sailing on Emma *are more snap shots rather than a coherent narrative.*

On my second trip in 1990, still very much the rookie decked out in a variety of kit, including a set of wets borrowed from the wife of a friend, I was relieved when we turned back to the warmth of Rye and the opportunity to see more of the World Cup. Like many groups of people meeting up for a trip, we discreetly appraised each other: Jonathan, the experienced and trusted number 2 to the skipper, both comfortable with each other; the tall and competitive Tony, bubbling with fun and humour; and Peter Lord, the wild card, a quietly spoken young man who no one had met before but was a friend of friend who said he had sailed a bit in Hong Kong. Once underway, the weather drove us all to don wet weather gear and Peter arrived on deck in an immaculate gleaming white suit in which, even on that grey day, he shone like a beacon. Tony, true to form, came out with a few expletive observations and Peter meekly admitted that the Hong Kong Club had been quite formal and their boats were launched and sails raised by the staff! Peter turned out to know a lot more about sailing than he was letting on, to be good company and a strong team player.

Food was always a high priority, almost as high as the skipper's obsession about fresh water. There must be something in his past that caused the spectre of running out of fresh water to appear as soon as we cast off from land. From my experience we never did come close. The two memorable dishes were roast leg of lamb in a head wind returning from Holland and Diana's signature dish of bread and butter pudding, but wherever we were we ate regally with the appetites of horses.

For thrills, rounding the Raz in poor visibility is the most memorable. Swirling water and large eddies as the currents from the north met the Bay of Biscay. We seemed, like the pre-Columbus sailors, to sail over the edge of the world and drop down to another level, but *Emma* bobbed up and we changed course for Audierne.

On the same cruise, the day after we rounded the Raz we set course across Biscay. A stunning sail with, for most of the time, the sea entirely to ourselves as each watch competed on who could sail the farthest. One afternoon Tony and I were shaken up on our watch when, with nothing in sight, there was an almighty bang and we scanned the horizon to see who was shelling us. The tell-tale vapour trail gave it away and we realised it was the sonic boom of the midday Concorde flight from Paris to New York going over head. The intrusion brought home the price on the environment of technical progress. The hairiest event was entering Royan late at night in 1989, jibbing into a dark harbour which none of us knew to the accompaniment of the fireworks for the 200th anniversary of storming of the Bastille.

Just as arriving in port in a proper and orderly fashion was critical and one of the very few times the skipper got the least agitated (must be that naval training), leaving port in style was equally important, with the relish of sailing out without the motor being the ultimate achievement in the true spirit of the Senior Service.

In 1992, when we were holed up in Dieppe as a gale came through, there was a shouted hello in a broad midland twang. Upon inspection a small gloss white clinker-built dinghy was lurching towards us with an extraordinary collection on board dressed in a variety of garb from oilskins to a motorbike jacket. The boat seemed hardly seaworthy, a pile of wet sails on the open deck and an aged seagull outboard hanging off the back. Once secured, I asked where they had come from, as the name of the craft was the Braunstone Maid. *Braunstone is an area of landlocked Leicestershire as far from the sea as it is possible to get in England. It appeared that they had bought the boat on a canal in Leicester, done it up and then decided to go to the big regatta at Brest '92. This involved motoring on the outboard down the canals and rivers to the Wash, out into the North Sea, down the coast to Dover and a quick skip across the Channel in front of an approaching gale and God knows what other shipping, with only a Michelin map of Europe to navigate by. One had to admire them as they set off next day to harbour-hop round the north coast of France to Brest.

Overall the memory is of fun and good company.

Best wishes

Alistair Thornley

Winging it (from Jemima Pine)

... Drove with skipper's wife (Diana), Amelia, Spacy Tracy and Graham through France, meeting up with Suzanne, the skipper and Jonathan in Royan.

After celebrating the bi-centenary of the storming of the Bastille, and Suzanne's birthday we set sail for Spain, where we were promised we would meet the girls again, who were driving around the coast.

We sailed off as the sun rose ... the wind was perfect ... this was to be my longest sail without touching land. We pulled all the right ropes, the sails filled and for the next 38 hours we goose-winged without engine from the murky grey to the clear blue water ... total heaven!

Once night set in the skipper set the rules for a night sail ... skipper and Graham on one shift and Jonathan and I on the other ... two hours on and two hours off ... when Jonathan and I were on we made it half an hour on and off at the tiller. This would have been fine but both of us dozed off, woken up by the sails slapping.

In my sleep I had gone off course, so got back on course resolving not to nap again.

With no land in sight the curvature of the earth is so clear, very odd and I decided you would have to be a very special person to circumnavigate the earth in a little boat on your own.

On the next day, all suffering from lack of sleep, the sun was warm, and we threw buckets of water over us to cool off. Later that night we arrived in Santander and clambering on to land, *where for the next day I kept reaching for the walls to hold myself up... This is called 'Sea Legs', a feeling I love ... the next morning all the others arrived safely by car...*

Jemima

8

Around the Ferry Ports of France and England 1991

What started off as the rather grand concept of 'Around the Manche in 30 Days' ended up as a visit to the ferry ports.

Everything, of which the weather played no small part, conspired against us; and whilst we set off to go westwards as far as the Scillies, across to L'Aber Wrac'h in Brittany and then east back along the coast of France as far as the Baie de Somme, crossing to Rye for a final leg, it didn't turn out like this at all.

Coastal passage to Weymouth, 22nd – 26th June

After setting off from Rye on 22nd June for the long haul down to Plymouth, the weather seemed reasonable but the wind was on the nose, and after tacking for a couple of hours against a foul tide we resorted to the engine for an hour and a half to get up to Beachy.

By midnight whilst approaching Selsey the wind had increased to force 5 – 6 from the south-west and it was necessary to engine to make any progress. With Alistair and the skipper on deck and Jonathan and Diana below, at about 0335 Jonathan awoke and got up to find he was stepping onto floating duckboards with some 6 – 9 inches of water in the boat.

It was established from the swishing noise each time that *Emma* nosed through a wave that the water was coming in through the keelbolt access panel and that a serious amount of water was gushing in. A temporary stopper was made by wedging the access panel in place with our little dustbin, and the job of getting the water outside the boat started.

This proved the old saying about the best form of bilge pump being a frightened crew with a bucket; it took the skipper and Jonathan half an hour to get most of the water out.

The decision was made to run in to Gosport and after Navstar had gone haywire (its usual mode in any emergency) we finally found the lights to the various Solent forts and arrived at Camper & Nicholson's yard at about 4.30 in the morning.

Diana had slept through most of this, only changing from starboard bunk to port when she found hers to be soaking wet. All the charts, some 25 of them, were sodden, as up till then it had been found that the starboard rear bunk was a good storage place for those not in use. A better place was found later once these had been dried out by Jonathan's parents-in-law who live in Gosport, and the charts now live rolled up at high level, on the port-side bookshelf.

Fortunately the marina has a mega-sized drying machine, and after pounds-worth of coins inserted and about five hours later most things were dry, except the bunk seats which never fully dried out until after the cruise.

The reason for all this dangerous hassle was that the boat builder had stuck in the access panel, and whilst holes for six screws were provided in the flange none had been used so that the pounding of the water up the drop keel chamber had pushed the whole thing off.

The good Alistair put a new panel in, this time tapping and screwing the flange in, and no further problems were experienced. However once the boat was dried out for the winter it would be necessary to epoxy and screw the access panel in, impossible to do with water up to the bottom level of the hole.

The following morning, Monday, we took advantage of the tide running west through the Solent to leave Gosport at about 10 a.m., reaching the Needles by 1300. The weather was very misty but the decision was made to continue towards Plymouth where we hoped to arrive by the Wednesday.

But the best laid plans, etcetera, etcetera... The fan belt broke at about 1700 and Alistair fitted the spare, but in doing so broke off what later proved to be the water temperature monitor, and was concerned that this really should be fixed before going too far. So in a thickening mist we decided to make for Weymouth, where we arrived about 2100, followed by another yacht which appeared to be lost. The first we saw of Weymouth was people fishing on the pier above us!

Whilst I am very fond of Weymouth, I hadn't reckoned on spending any time there on this trip, as we had arranged for A.E. Monsen's to deliver duty frees in Plymouth, but what with weather, boat repairs and crew changes we ended up by staying for four nights, from arrival on Monday 24th to Friday 28th. We did try

The castle at Ope on Portland

to break out for Plymouth one day (Wednesday), to catch the tide around Portland Bill between 1100 and midday but a call to Portland Coastguard suggested a 'strong wind warning' and having seen on a previous occasion what this means off Chiswell Beach we returned in chastened mood.

Emma's sails were needing some repairs, and we took the jib in for maintenance from the local sailmaker, so the days in Weymouth were spent fruitfully with Alistair replacing the engine water thermostat, tightening up the new fan belt and generally making good where needed.

Thursday proved to be a very nice afternoon and we all took a bus up to Portland Bill to see the little castle at Ope; Derek remembered that a friend from London, Jenny Marriot, had moved to Portland a few years back with an address in Ope Road. An

Skipper, Diana, Jonathan and Alistair

enquiry in a local restaurant produced the intelligence that Jenny lived 'next door'. So we met and invited her for drinks on board, having visited a charming little folk museum at Ope after a rather disappointing castle.

Cross-Channel to Cherbourg – Barfleur, 28th June – 2nd July

Due to nearly a week spent so far (we should have been in Plymouth by the Monday) a change of plan was required and the whole of the western half of the passage cancelled: yet another failure to reach the Scillies!

With the change of plan came a change of crew, with Suzanne and Keith Cunningham, who had originally planned to join in Penzance, managing to get to Weymouth after some frantic phone calls.

We had almost despaired of the weather, and certainly of making westwards, but we discovered a window in the weather was predicted for Friday 28th June and by altering the destination to Cherbourg the wind allowed a broad reach for most of the way. We left Weymouth at 4 a.m. with a beautiful sunrise, berthing at Cherbourg at 2000; not the fastest trip – berth to berth was a little over 4 knots – but it was a gentle day and we didn't use the engine, sailing right into the inner harbour.

Jonathan and the skipper

A continuing saga with the Navstar, getting 'antennae fail' although our position seemed credible. On disconnecting the aerial lead it was found to be waterlogged – a result of the pounding en route to Gosport no doubt. Once dried off it seemed to clear, although this was of a temporary nature. However we got a perfect waypoint into Cherbourg harbour.

Saturday was a lay day in Cherbourg; still a lot of drying out to do, duty frees to purchase as we never reached Plymouth – prices very much the same, but the French are more laid back about such things: I arrived at the duty free shop weighed down with ship's papers, passports and the like but all they wanted to know was the ship's name! As the marina is open to the public I imagine there are a lot of fictitious boats collecting their duty frees on a regular basis. We found that there is no longer a duty free shop in St Malo so we were glad to have got a good supply for the journey south, and more on the way back.

We decided a smaller harbour would be more fun and left to

Keith cleaning the bottom in Barfleur

catch the tide around the peninsula to Barfleur on the Saturday, leaving at 1830 and arriving soon after 2200 – a rough passage with races all around the coast where the tides meet.

We moored up against the harbour wall and put our sticks down, allowing Keith and the skipper to scrub the port side of *Emma* at low tide the following day. Barfleur is a charming French fishing port (only 30 francs per night whereas Cherbourg and all marinas vary from 80 to 90 francs).

On Sunday 30th Starkie and Elaine arrived with Hercules; we had found a hotel for them, and we had a huge dinner on board of roast French lamb, excellent quality. Derek had to return to UK for a meeting on Tuesday morning, and caught the midnight ferry to Portsmouth from Cherbourg.

Whilst in harbour in Barfleur two boats were brought in by the local lifeboat; one, a catamaran rejoicing in the name of *Twinnie the Pooh*, had engine trouble; a hiccup not, I understand, brought on by its name.

As Derek was returning to Cherbourg on Wednesday, after catching the night ferry across, it was agreed that the crew with

Towing *Twinnie the Pooh* from Barfleur

Starkie and Elaine would take *Emma* back to Cherbourg. They did their Good Samaritan bit and towed *Twinnie* round from Barfleur, so that Roy the skipper could arrange help from his home port in the UK. But the dawn arrival of the skipper on 3rd July is another story.

Cherbourg – Channel Islands and St Malo, 4th July – 6th July

After a brief but productive visit to the UK for a meeting with Leeds City on Tuesday 2nd July the skipper caught the P&O ferry out of Gosport, arriving about 0600 in Cherbourg. A walk around to the marina found *Emma* moored off at the floating visitors' pontoon. After a bit of shouting Starkie brought the inflatable over and the skipper arrived on board to hear that the outboard was not working and Jemima had lost an oar (replaced in Cherbourg for about £12). This seemed minor compared to the sudden appearance of Jemima on deck covered with the contents of the sea loo which had blown up in her face! The usual problem, the one person we hadn't made aware of this being Elaine!

At this point the skipper was heard to say this was 'the last bloody time' he was ever going to have a woman on board, and threatening to return to England! But as usual calm was restored, the skipper unblocked the sea loo and an agreement was made that Wolfgang should do a large notice to warn the 'frails' (as illustrated here). Tara Pigott arrived off the UK ferry in the late afternoon; she had already been warned!

Wolfgang's notice, now installed in the heads

Emma was moved with the harbour-master's help onto a main pontoon, always difficult to back in; we watched other boats manoeuvering with great skill, but either the skipper isn't very good at it, or it may just be that Pilot Cutters prove a problem in this respect.

The decision was made to sail for Guernsey the following day, Thursday 4th. We left to catch the favourable tide around Cap de la Hague at 1230 and sailed well until 1450 when wind died and the engine was started. But by 1600 there was enough wind available to gull-wing quite nicely, whereas by 1700 a wind increase made it necessary to put two reefs in the main. A strange day, as by the time we reached Sark there was little wind and we engined from 2030 until our arrival into St Peter Port at 2140. We finally got across the cill into the marina three-quarters of an hour later, to find plenty of room inside.

The next day, Friday, was misty at first but with a fair wind,

Keith catching his first mackerel

The skipper gutting the fish

and we decided to make down the coast for St Malo, but as the fair tide south didn't start until 1700 we got out by noon and sailed over to Sark in sunshine, anchoring in a small bay on the north of the island where a few other vessels were parked. The inflatable was taken in to the beach, the skipper remaining on anchor watch. A nice afternoon.

We left for St Malo, catching the tide, but the wind was slight and it was necessary to engine. This really proved the worth of our newly fitted automatic pilot, a Navico Tillerpilot TP1800. With the engine on, and no fear of running down the battery, a very accurate course was steered. About midnight we passed the Minquiers and soon after this were guided by the bright light from Le Frehel. We thought we might have difficulty in getting into St Malo, as on previous occasions we had been confused by the rocks on entering in daylight. At night it proved easier coming in by La Grande Porte channel using the leading lights to come right up to the Port des Sablon and getting to bed by 0600.

After a few hours' sleep we radioed on Channel 9 and were told that the lock would open for the basin Le Vauban soon after midday; we finally got inside about 1300. There was a fair wind blowing and it was quite difficult to get alongside between two rafts of larger boats. It was done with no damage.

We had decided to stay in St Malo for a few days, with crew coming and going, so booked into the marina for three nights.

Keith's family had arrived with two other friends, who were going on for a holiday by car to the South of France; this was therefore the last night that he would be with us. Also it was Jonathan's last evening, so it was the evening for the 'passage dinner' at the restaurant, Port St Pierre of course!

There were 13 of us with the Wolfgang family, all the Phillipses, Keith's family and friends, Jonathan and Tara. The usual fantastic

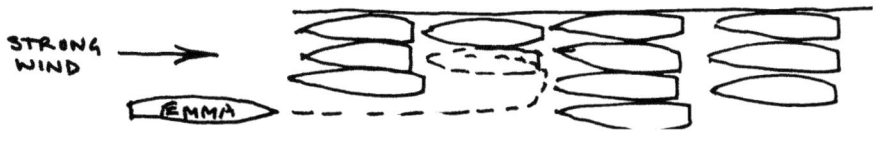

'The parking was difficult!'

FAMILY SAILING IN EUROPEAN WATERS

The trip to St Malo and a picnic

meal was enjoyed, five courses, six bottles of house wine, brandies and coffee all for £17 per head. Why is it that a half-good meal in England costs twice the price? I'm told it's because restaurants in France are family affairs and the buildings are less expensive, but still...! Or is it just that we are all being ripped off in England?

Looking at our original passage plan, down to the Scillies over to L'Aber Wrac'h, and then along the Cote du Nord to St Malo

Keith envying Jonathan's fruits de mer

– we had originally planned to be in St Malo by Friday 5th July, staying until Sunday the 7th – here we were in St Malo at the same time, so we were back on track by omitting the whole of the western section of the cruise.

By telephoning Austria we contacted Andreas and rearranged for him to meet us in St Malo on Tuesday 9th, so we moved out of the Vauban to the *basin du flotte* (Port des Bas Sablons) where we could leave at any time.

An adventure on the Monday was going in Wolfgang's VW Microbus to Concale and on to the Point du Grouin for a walk.

Wolfgang and his family were invited for dinner an board

Dinner on board *Emma*

Emma in the evening. The weather forecast was *mauvais* according to the harbour-master, but the British shipping forecast sounded more hopeful with Jersey at a south-westerly force 5 – 6 changing to a variable force 3 with moderate visibility. A high was expected by Tuesday morning. So we decided to leave on a favourable tide north, provided Andreas and his girlfriend arrived by 1900 the following day.

St Malo – Cherbourg – Ouistreham, 9th – 12th July

The route north using the tides was planned east of the Minquiers, then west to pass south of Jersey, north-east leaving Guernsey and Sark to port, aiming to catch the Alderney Race north at about 0500 to get round Cap de la Hague before the westerly flow started at 1000.

Andreas and Barbara arrived exactly on time at 1900 and we shoved off immediately, starting the 78 miles up to Cherbourg.

The plan worked well, but with little wind in the wrong direction it meant 18.5 hours on the engine greatly assisted by 'George' (the autotiller).

One point worth noting is that the Gros Nez light on the northwest point of Jersey cannot be seen on approaching from the south until you are abeam of the light, which means past the island, so we were confused by not seeing it when we thought we should. A radio call to St Helier established that we should have known this, but I'm still not sure how!

The Alderney Race took us past Cap de la Hague at 7 knots but the 15 miles east to Cherbourg against the now foul tide took a long time and we didn't enter Cherbourg harbour until 1400. A large brunch of eggs and bacon was followed by a visit to the duty free shop, a visit to the diesel point and purchase of Campingaz; then as no one wanted to stay any longer than possible in Cherbourg, we left for Barfleur.

The skipper had had enough, having been up most of the night, and decided to hand the job of getting to Barfleur to the crew, consisting of Wolfgang and Andreas. It was a similar passage to the one on 29th July, with choppy races rounding the Cherbourg peninsula, and while the skipper was having a quiet read below the crew contrived to hit the Basse du Renier cardinal buoy while trying to leave it to port. Fortunately the noise heard from below was worse than the damage – a small scratch on the hull – inspected on tying up against the wall in Barfleur, and putting down the legs.

The following day, Thursday 11th July, we had to wait for the tide to lift us off at noon and then made out for Ouistreham. Very little wind, but as theoretically we had a lot of time we decided to sail gently in the right direction, until we found we were sailing gently backwards, the large lighthouse at Pointe de Barfleur steadfastly moving ahead instead of behind us. Some mistake with the tides! It was such a lovely sunny day and we were sailing, if in the wrong direction, so we decided to have lunch on deck before altering the passage plan.

After lunch a rapid check on the charts showed there was no way we would achieve Ouistreham, and that there was a little

Hitting the Basse du Renier buoy

port called Grandcamp-Maisy where we could get in plus or minus 1.5 hours to high water at 2240, leaving plenty of time for a gentle sail to arrive between 2110 and 0010. It was so lovely not to have the engine and the wind had picked up amazingly in the right direction (north-westerly).

We all waved cheerily at a naval vessel that came to have a look at us and were surprised about a quarter of an hour later when an inflatable, launched rather sneakily from that same naval vessel, approached and wanted to board us. Which of course they did.

A very unsmiling French Customs officer and his mate wanted every bit of ship's paper and all passports, and there was much querying of whether the crew were paying passengers, or friends. After everything was established they asked to go below, but weren't in the slightest bit interested in this and after a desultory look around took themselves off. This is the second time this has happened to *Emma*, the last time being in Dunkirk last summer; again no interest at all in the boat, only in the papers.

We arrived in Grandcamp-Maisy with a number of fishing boats at 2100 and berthed alongside in this fishing port, protected by lock gates so floating. Jemima cooked a splendid chicken meal and then we retired to the pub and played the 'Construction Game' until thrown out about 0100.

The next morning the skipper worked out that the lock gates wouldn't be likely to open before 1000. During breakfast Wolfgang said, 'Surely those fishing boats are leaving?' and they were! So, dropping everything, we got out five minutes later at 0840.

Wind and tide were fair for a run east towards Ouistreham where we had established that the lock gates to the canal up to Caen would be closing at 1450. Initially it was a very fast passage with a fair tide doing over 7 knots, averaging 5.3 knots from berth to lock, arriving at 1445 with five minutes to spare. So through, and on up the canal to Caen. We had to wait for some time at the first bridge and finally berthed in the marina there at 1800.

Honfleur harbour ready for the Bastille Day celebrations

Contrary to popular belief we found Caen rather disappointing, and we left as soon as possible the following morning, getting through the first bridge at 0745.

Wolfgang appeared to have lost his family, due to the enforced change of plan overnight, so he left when we returned to Ouistreham and set off to look for them; later contact was established in Honfleur.

Ouistreham (Caen) – Trouville, 13th – 14th July

We had a good sail eastwards towards Trouville on the Saturday, although resorting to the engine for the last hour, getting into the Trouville yacht basin where the gates were still open at 1400. Originally we had planned to get to Honfleur, but didn't make it by boat. However Wolfgang, having recovered his family, suggested that he drove us as this was the place where Tony was due to arrive at 1800. So we left for Honfleur around 1700 and wished

Gull winging with the topsail set

The Trouville Market on Bastille Day

A last drink for Tara and Jemima before departure

we had got there in *Emma*. Honfleur was preparing for Bastille Day and looked like a great place to be, but it is not an easy place to get into, the tides and wind do have to be right, and we hadn't left enough time from Ouistreham to catch the tide up the Canal de Rouen in the Baie de Seine with the bridge to the Vieux Port opening one hour before and after high water only.

However, amazingly, we did meet Big Tony, and drove back to Trouville where we enjoyed the Bastille preparations there. Dinner at an outside cafe was a 60 franc menu with *moules* and steak, good value, towards the end of which the fireworks started, an excellent display along the seafront. Trouville is a pleasant, alive town and we enjoyed an excellent market on Sunday morning.

Before arriving for the sailing holiday Tara had just qualified as a doctor, and had brought a splendid set of wet gear in celebration. In the evening of Bastille Day, we decided to go to see the celebrations in Deauville on the other side of the river. Deauville is supposedly the upmarket neighbour to Trouville with its fine casino and hotels; this was where wealthy Brits desported themselves between wars. We found several bands forming up, one from the UK, others French, and we found ourselves in the vast throng of people following the bands all the way down to the beach. This is where the fireworks were, and one of the most fantastic displays ever. I remember writing in the 1989 cruise story that the 200th anniversary Bastille night fireworks at Royan were something else. But these certainly came near it.

Tara and Jemima missed the Deauville fireworks as we had seen them on to their bus during the afternoon – they had to go first to Caen and then change for a bus to Ouistreham where the ferry left for Portsmouth.

A drama occurred as they waited to catch the bus. A couple also catching the bus were walking towards it when the woman fell flat on her face. 'Oh it's all right,' said the man, 'she's always doing it.' Something about 'deficiency'. Anyway Tara was able to do her doctoring bit and we were all impressed; she got her onto the bus.

Trouville – Boulogne – Rye, 15th – 20th July

To have kept to our original passage plan, Bastille Day should have seen us in Le Havre, so we felt that we should get there as soon as possible the next day. But we were locked into Trouville and when the gates opened at 1400 and we could leave, we had got just outside when we had a 'hot water' warning, red light and squeals from the engine. Back to berth where Tony (not good at electrics) tightened up a slack water pump drive belt most efficiently and all went normally for the rest of the trip. We reached Le Havre in a south-westerly force 6, a short but exhilarating crossing arriving at 1600, without need for engine except to leave and arrive at berths.

Le Havre must be the largest marina we encountered, you can really get lost in it. Having got to Le Havre we really weren't sure why; the most interesting thing about the town being a huge concrete tower which proved to be the cathedral, which could have been designed by Auguste Perret (perhaps it was). Massive

Le Havre cathedral – the interior

from outside, from inside you look right up, the tower lit by stained glass set between the concrete elements – fairly impressive.

The following day we wanted an early start for Fecamp, so the skipper went foraging for bread at 0600 and we listened to the UK weather forecast at 5.55 (French time 0655). This sounded OK and it proved correct, a south-westerly force 3 taking us gently eastwards, and despite a strong tide across the harbour we waited for the swing bridge to the Basin Berigney to open. It opened soon after our arrival and we moored alongside by 1440.

Fecamp is a particularly nice little town, where the Benedictine monks make that sweet sticky liqueur, and there is cheap food everywhere.

The 17th July, Wednesday, we moved out of the Basin Berigney when the lock opened at 2 a.m. and parked on the diesel pier outside and went to sleep. We finally left for the 30-mile passage to Dieppe at 1000, gull-winging virtually all the way in front of a fresh south-westerly wind; we did the trip in seven hours, berth

Andreas at the helm en route to Dieppe

to berth. We reached Dieppe at 1700, passing a string of nuclear power stations located along the coastline; we passed a beautiful Ocean Youth Club yacht making down the coast. A lazy afternoon, and then a 78-franc four-course meal out at a quayside cafe, four courses – excellent value!

We were assured that the lock gates would open at 0630 the following morning and we left our berth and hung about waiting ... and waiting. Eventually we learned we should have been there at 0600 and that we now could not leave before about 1600. This was really annoying as we even had the harbour-master write down the 0630 time – it meant that we couldn't get into the Baie de Somme at St Valery as planned. Don't ever believe a harbour-master!

It is 54 miles to Boulogne and it seemed the only thing to do; the weather was rough and got rougher till we were moving at 7 knots in front of a south-westerly gale. A very fast journey, averaging 6.1 knots berth to berth, the skipper found it all rather frightening with 30-foot waves following us along. In addition

Diana holding the tiller

Navstar stopped operating at 2100 and gave the same reading until we arrived in Boulogne at 0130 in the morning – but I hear that the Baie de Somme area is notoriously poor for Decca reception. Navstar still read that we were 40 miles west of Boulogne whilst we were lying in the harbour. It was a good thing there are plenty of lights along the coast.

A visit to the supermarket provided our usual diet of coffee, mustard, salami etcetera.

The weather was still rough and we reprogrammed our passage yet again to leave on the Saturday 20th. To get into the Rother we needed to arrive about 1900 on a neap tide, as there was so little water in the river. To make sure of it we left early at 1000 hours, but there was little wind and it was necessary to engine

Amelia greeting us at the end of the journey at Rye

for the first hour and a half, then we had good sailing with the topsail up till well on the way to Dungeness where the wind got up and it was necessary to lower the topsail and double reef the main.

When passing beyond Dungeness we were warned off the coast due to gunnery practice, hailed by a smart pinnace suggesting we listened out on the radio for instructions, when we were told to keep 1.5 miles offshore. Helpful really, as we had arrived rather early and it meant less hanging about off the harbour mouth when we arrived at Rye buoy at 1730 hours.

Finally we entered the river when we considered there was sufficient water, helped by the knowledge of a larger boat going in, in front of us!

We berthed at 1930 and were met by Amelia with the sad news that Keith, who had left *Emma* in St Malo, had been involved in a car accident. [Postscript: he is now back in England at Stoke

Mandeville hospital in the Jimmy Saville wing and is being well looked after – he is very cheerful despite serious injuries.]

After clearing up the boat, Tony was met and disappeared, and Diana and the skipper drove Andreas and Barbara back to stay in Bovingdon, arriving soon after midnight, exhausted.

Analysis of cruise finances – foreign currency converted to sterling

Credits
Cash from UK by skipper £ 725
Additional cash Eurocheque £ 220
Additional cash Barclaycard £ 90
Cash from crew based on
£20.00 per week £ 270

Total £1305
Less: cash spent on trip
for skipper to return to UK £ 60

Total cash spent £1245

Debits
Repairs & parts for *Emma* £ 129.75
Harbour dues
(approx £8 per night) £ 169.00
Diesel £ 34.25
Campingaz for cooking &
water heating £ 51.00
Duty free booze £ 155.00
Food for 4 weeks*
(ave £176 per week) £ 706.00

Total £1245.00

*Note: this includes cost of several meals ashore

Notes on costs

1. Camper & Nicholsons Marina in Gosport was the most expensive night at £20.00.
2. A 'marine call' was surprisingly expensive from Weymouth. Using a new BT £4 card, the card ran out before the end of the marine call. There must be a less expensive way of getting a weather forecast.
3. Average cost for a night in a marina or port in France is £8, small fishing ports such as Barfleur are lower.
4. Prices for meals out in France are much lower than in the UK. A really superb four-course meal with plenty of wine for 13 people in St Malo, cost £220, under £17 per head.
5. Best buys in French supermarkets are coffee and mustard, about one-third the price of the UK equivalent.
6. Duty frees in Cherbourg cost about the same as in the UK, e.g.:
   1 litre Famous Grouse   55 francs   £5.63
   1 litre Gordon's Gin   42 francs   £4.30
   1 litre Blue Smirnoff   41 francs   £4.20
   but can be obtained from the duty free store without any prior ordering and in any nunber. There is no duty free available in St Malo.

9

'A Porto too Far': *Portugal 1994*

FAMILY SAILING IN EUROPEAN WATERS

1: Ian; 2: Jonathan; 3: Skipper; 4: Amelia; 5: Cedric; 6: Jeremy; 7: Rebecca; 8: Tony; 9: Paul, Richard and Fred; 10: Diana; 11: Sian; 12: Jochanen; 13: Wolfgang; 14: Jane; 15 & 16: Adam

'A PORTO TOO FAR': PORTUGAL 1994

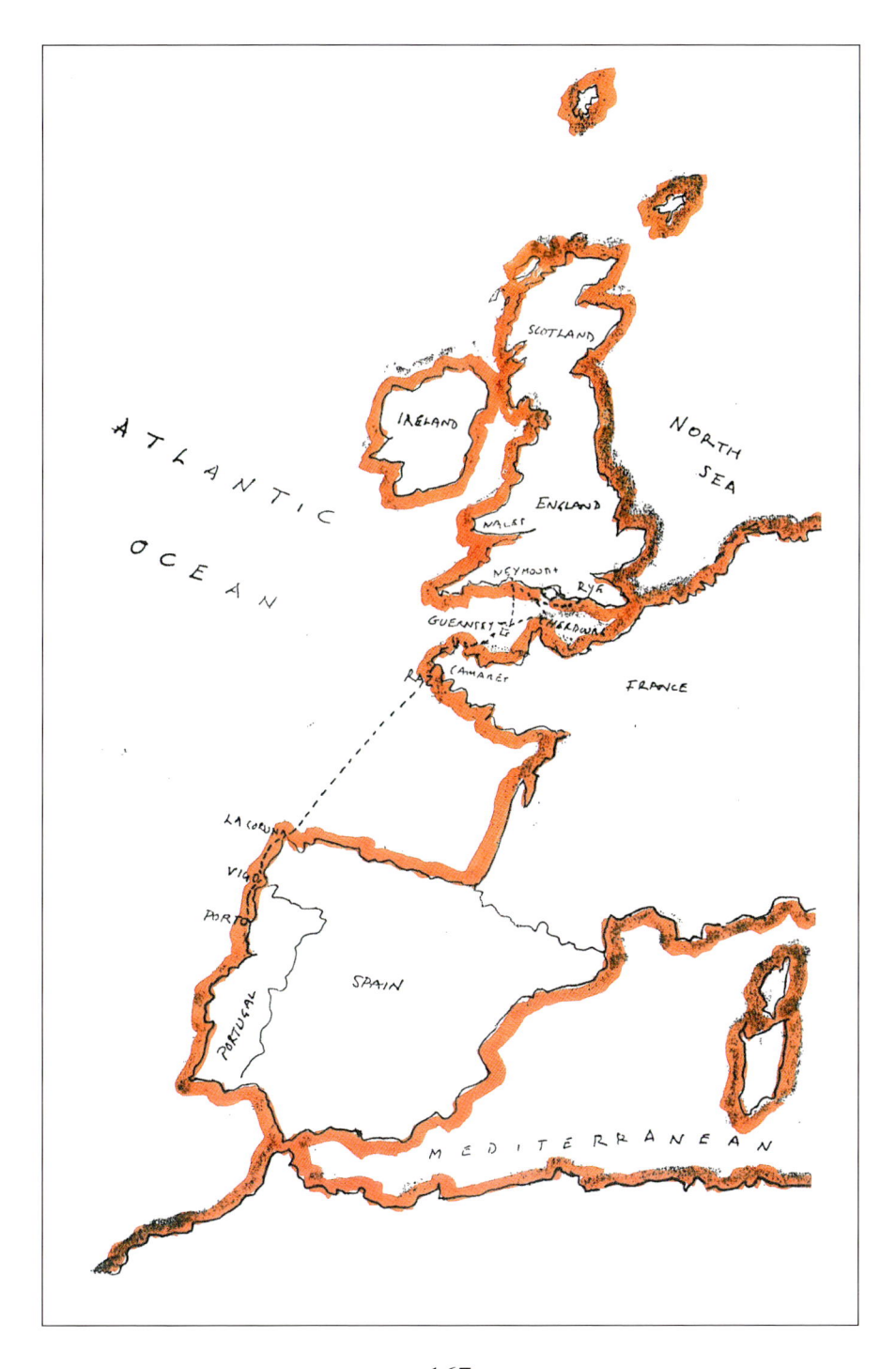

When setting out to plan this year's passage to Portugal, Diana warned the skipper that it might be difficult to find enough crew who could both take the time off their various activities, and afford the travel costs for joining. On reflection she was right.

The passage was to take six weeks with stopovers at some 20 ports. In the end it took seven weeks, we travelled 1,844 miles, reached our destination of Porto, and returned safely home to Rye. But, we did run out of crew, we did have more than our fair share of problems, and decided the next year we might consider Holland!

To Weymouth, 22nd – 24th June

Leaving the River Rother at 1000 on Wednesday with a favourable tide and sunshine, we met a south-westerly force 5 wind which, when the tide went foul by 1500, meant engining towards Brighton. In Bob and Ian the skipper had an untried crew, and in order not to arrive too late in Brighton we ran into Newhaven by 2188 and holed up for the night.

The Newhaven – Dieppe ferry churns up the silt in the estuary to such an extent that it is no longer possible for a boat of *Emma*'s draft (1.1 metres) to leave the marina at low water, and we were unable to leave until 0830 with only three hours of favourable tide left. The sun shone and we sailed for about seven hours rather slowly in light airs, gull-winging at times until the evening when the wind increased and it was prudent to put in a reef before trying to pass outside the Isle of Wight around St Catherine's Point. The tide turned foul at 1800 until midnight and as always the St Catherine's Point light seemed illusively static. However later with the fair tide helping us along we made good time towards St Aldhelm's Head and reached Weymouth by 0700 on the Friday morning.

The Weymouth leg established that the drop keel would not drop, the first of our little problems. Advice was taken and apart from more leeway when beating, there seemed to be no life-threatening consequences, so the problem could be left until *Emma* could be craned out for the winter. The decision was made to carry on without the help of a drop keel.

On arrival in Weymouth the skipper, who had been up for 24 hours departed to bed, so also did Ian. Bob, who was leaving to

Parking in Weymouth. Hooray!

catch a train home, then made his classic remark to Diana (widely quoted by all the crew for the rest of the passage): 'Please thank Derek for all he did, and also Ian ... and if you did anything, thank you!'

To La Coruna, 25th June – 2nd July

Tony and Jonathan arrived at our usual pub in Weymouth, and with an early start at 0500 planned for the Saturday, we all went to bed early.

We collected water from the water point opposite our berth by 0530 and then we were away towards St Peter Port in Guernsey. The following waypoints were set: The Casquets, Platte Fougere, followed by the Roustel light and a check bearing on Tautenay before negotiating the Little Russell with its series of markers, arriving at St Peter Port by 0100 on Sunday.

The skipper had acquired a Garmin 65 GPS at the London boat show, and used this as a backup to Navstar. It may be that experience of GPS is still lacking, but we ran both systems alongside each other, and Navstar is more user friendly. It was wonderful however to know our position exactly at all times from GPS, and of course in Biscay Navstar fails (the main reason for purchasing GPS).

We found it more difficult with GPS to set in waypoints, to change from one to another, and to check cross-track error; but the 'Plot' page on the Garmin, where it is possible to alter the scale, was most useful, enabling one to see the ship's course related to the rhum line to the waypoint. We have a cockpit readout for Navstar which may have a lot to do with it, and a GPS readout is certainly on the shopping list for next year, if such is available. (Later at the Boat Show it was found that one is available from Robertson Stowe at £220.)

Guernsey on a Sunday is controlled by the Methodists, not a shop or a pub open – a good place to leave! And we did, on the tide at 1900 making for the Chenal du Four and L'Aber Wrac'h. However with virtually no wind it was necessary to engine most

The hulk at Camaret

of the way in order to catch the tidal stream down towards the Raz de Sein. The skipper's mate decided that as the shopping facilities in L'Aber Wrac'h are non-existent, we should use the favourable tide to continue as far as Camaret. We arrived there at midnight on Tuesday 27th, completing the 140-mile passage in 28 hours, using the engine for most of the time, averaging 5 knots.

Camaret is a useful stop, you can go alongside a convenient pontoon, there are good showers, and diesel facilities, water, etcetera. The shops are a little far to walk, but the supermarket is happy for you to take a trolley back to the boat – useful with three days and 325 miles' sailing ahead of you.

We filled up with water, diesel (diesel is very expensive, nearly twice the price of Guernsey) and food, leaving at 2000 with a fair tide and a variable force 3 wind forecast for Finistere, not of any great help. The wind strengthened later and two reefs were put in for the night sail. We reached and negotiated the Raz soon after midnight; the lights are excellent, with good visibility and a course was set for La Coruna Co. 214 (m) with a route length of 306 miles. A watch list was posted for the three days, using the naval system of four hours on and four hours off, with two-hour dog watches between 1600 and 2000 to break the sequence.

Emma carries only two 20-gallon water tanks, and to conserve water it was decided that it should be used only for drinking and cooking. All other purposes would use sea water. This worked so well that when we arrived we still had one tank completely full. As a result of this, on the return passage we allowed ourselves water for washing ourselves. Washing up uses by far the most water, and this is adequately dealt with by a bucket of sea water in the cockpit, and plenty of kitchen paper.

We had an excellent cook in Ian, who taught Diana to make bread, so we had fresh bread all the way across Biscay. Ian also made the most tasty pizzas, so we lived rather well.

But not without continued problems: the sea loo got blocked with kitchen paper – we hadn't thought to warn Ian – and having cleared it once it blocked again. This time we took the whole length of pipe off and found its diameter so reduced towards the centre that it was impossible to clear a pathway through it. Jonathan tried pushing a boat hook down without success. A solution was found by cutting out about 3 feet in length, omitting the antisiphon. This worked well for the rest of the passage. The next problem was excessive water in the bilge, so much that it was backing up under the floorboards of the boat. By opening up the engine cover and running the diesel, it was easy to spot that water was spewing out from the flexible water pipes connecting the water cooling system to the engine. Ian showed his many talents and corrected the fault by opening up and reconnecting the pipes and jubilee clips. No further problem. But, as the bilges were now very full, the bilge pump refused to operate (this happens every year). However the good Fitzjohn, *Emma*'s first owner, had amongst his other goodies provided a stirrup pump which, with some difficulty, was persuaded to cope.

One other fault is worth mentioning: this is the effect on the compass of a powerful radio. Tony had brought his radio and placed it in the cockpit close to the compass, and we couldn't understand why, although we were steering the correct course, the course made good was 10 – 15° out. Removing the radio solved

'A PORTO TOO FAR': PORTUGAL 1994

the problem. Not many people know this! Tony must have thought that he was going to fall overboard at night, and had brought an armband with a flashing yellow light on it; happily he never needed to use it.

As predicted, the Navstar Decca failed some 100 miles off the French coast, and was replaced with GPS, coupled with Decca DR across Biscay; we were happy to reinitialise Navstar when it showed 'Decca ready' about 100 miles from Coruna, GPS position being used. It was very comforting to know one's position so precisely.

The voyage across Biscay was not entirely without excitement, on one occasion we saw a whale. We noticed what looked like a large log floating about 30 yards off the side of the boat, gently moving astern; we were wondering what it was when suddenly it spouted water out of a little hole at the top, and we realised this was the 12-foot head of a whale asleep. Later about half a mile astern its tail reared out of the water and crashed down, just like in all the Greenpeace pictures. We were happy that it had been

Dolphins in Biscay

Tower of Hercules, La Coruna

asleep while we were passing by. There was very little shipping, apart from one or two French naval vessels, but dolphins there were in plenty – on occasions we were were surrounded by them.

We arrived in La Coruna early on the morning of Saturday 2nd July, as planned. Winds had been very light, the passage taking three days and four nights to do the 325 miles from Camaret and having to engine for a total of 24 hours out of the 82 hours for the total passage. The first sight of La Coruna is the Tower of Hercules; this was at one time a lighthouse, and can be seen from a long way offshore.

To Vigo, 3rd – 9th July

On arrival in La Coruna we found a message in the yacht club from Amelia and Cedric that they had arrived and were in a B&B near the marina. Tony and Jonathan were leaving for England by plane; we were sad to see them go.

The newly-weds joined us on the 3rd when we set off south towards Portugal; not a nice day! Rainy and windy – sad for their first day at sea.

'Stugeron' sea sickness pills helped, but a force 5 – 6 against meant engining if we were to get to our proposed destination of

Corme. In the end we decided that there would be better shelter from the southerly wind in Lage, across the other side of the Ria, and we went alongside a fishing boat there. We had to move around midnight as the fishing fleet was leaving, and tied up against the now empty wall for a gentle night.

We left early (0730) the following morning, Monday, for Muros, with a complete change in the weather. A gentle sail down the Spanish coastline, past Cape Finistere, the wind having veered to a north-westerly force 3, with a westerly later. We berthed at the fishermen's quay where it was a bit smelly (complaints from Ian) but we stayed there in comfort for the night, but were asked to move the following day. A lay day in Muros meant that we would need the inflatable to enable us to get ashore from a mooring. Ian and Cedric pumped this up while we attended at the diesel quay, enabling us to tow the tender out to the mooring, and get ashore when needed.

Muros is a delightful town, with lovely old streets, and a splendid market building, but not much in the way of boat facilities – we had to pay for water. We renewed the Spanish courtesy flag – it had flown away in Biscay – but were unable to get a new radar reflector which had also fallen off in Biscay; the latter would have to wait until Vigo. The Wolfgang family arrived in Danny's Volkswagen bus late in the evening, bringing Jochanan who was staying with them from Israel.

We left Muros for Porto Nova on Wednesday 6th July at 0830, with a fair wind in the afternoon allowing gull-winging, and a fast run, arriving at 1515, where we moored off. The whole passage south from La Coruna to Vigo is exciting, with a spectacular coastline of rocks on the port side.

Leaving Porto Nova the following morning, Ian agreed to stay on shore, travelling in the bus, allowing Jochanan to join the crew on board for the short passage down to Vigo, arriving just after lunch. Vigo has a fine marina with excellent facilities, but is rather dirty, with the marina full of old plastic bags and rubbish.

Danny is an excellent electrician, and sorted out most of the electrical problems we had experienced crossing Biscay; we bought an electrical tester to help him, enabling him to check over the various

The view of Spain

circuits, so that we now have echo sounder, nav lights and compass light all working again. The skipper was unhappy about the electrics, and whilst nearly everything worked on our return passage decided it would be necessary to have the whole system properly seen to during the winter. Something else to add to the list.

The temporary radar reflector which Bob had provided before we left (after we had discovered that the stainless steel brackets to the 'Fender' type reflector which came with the boat had failed during the winter) had also fallen off in Biscay. A new type of reflector was purchased in the chandlery in Vigo; this is a Swedish invention, very neat, and it can be fixed to one of the shrouds. Wolfgang volunteered to go up the mast to do it – see the cartoon at the beginning of this chapter! This stayed put.

To Porto, 9th – 12th July

Vigo marina has excellent facilities which, for other reasons, we were to get to know well in coming weeks. Jane Priestman arrived by air and had no difficulty in finding the yacht harbour, and we found a rather delightful little restaurant near by (Asturias) run by 'Mama' who looked after us very well. Gerti (Wolfgang's wife) was in her element, as she spends much of her time at home running the restaurant at Gasthof Flackl in Reichenau, owned by her brother. I think we got special treatment!

We left Vigo on Saturday 9th July at 0800 for Viana do Castelo, a halfway house towards Porto. Leaving the Ria de Vigo, we let Bagona pass to port, determined to return there on the way back. On this passage you pass the entrance to the Minho River, the border between Spain and Portugal, at which point we changed our courtesy flag from Spanish to Portuguese. There was little wind and most of the day was spent on engine, arriving at Viana in the late afternoon, a passage of 38 miles. The information in both the 94 Admiralty Harbour chart (3254) and the Atlantic Spain and Portugal Pilot is wrong. The Pilot suggests that you enter the Doca de Flutuacao, and the Admiralty Chart shows a marina beyond the rail bridge. Due to the opening of a new marina before encountering the bridge, all yachts are directed away from the Doca and towards the new marina. (The skipper notified the Hydrographer's Department on his return to the UK who wrote to say that they were informing the Portuguese authorities upon whom they rely for information.)

Viana was the skipper's first encounter with Portuguese bureaucracy; asked to report to the harbour-master's office on arrival and paid the £8 berthing fee, the skipper was directed on to the Customs. This is where every piece of paper to do with the boat, all passports, details of where each person was born, their age and so on, is carefully recorded, taking about three-quarters of an hour. It is clearly shredded the following day, as the whole lot was required again on our return a few days later! (The skipper was apoplectic on this occasion, as all the crew were waiting to catch a restaurant still open at about 2200.)

Despite this, Viana is a delightful little town with a supermarket which is open all Sunday, useful as we had arrived too late to shop on the Saturday.

Later in the day, we left for Leixoes, the port of Porto, arriving at 2000, sailing all the way with a fair wind south. Leixoes is not a very prepossessing place, flanked by oil terminals and industrial buildings it reminded the skipper most of all of Imuijden in Holland, at the mouth of the Nordsee canal leading up to Amsterdam, another sulphurous place to avoid were it possible. But with the difficulties of taking *Emma* up the Douro into the town of Porto, there is little alternative to Porto de Leixoes.

On the evening we arrived it was a fishermen's festival and there was an amazing fireworks display, which seemed to go on for hours.

We had telephoned Sian in the UK and told her we would arrange to meet her at the airport using Wolfgang's van. This we did the following morning and then all drove into Porto ending

'Boats for hire'

'A PORTO TOO FAR': PORTUGAL 1994

The bridge, Porto

Dinner on board

up in the area alongside the River Douro, where all the port lodges are located. Three large yachts were moored alongside, one from South Africa; there was room for no others, and speaking to the skipper it was clear that getting up there unless the tide and wind are exactly right is fraught with difficulty.

We all did the grand tour of the Sandeman Port lodge, and drank rather too much of the free wine. We were glad to have the use of the Wolfgang vehicle, as the next day we drove some 30 miles up the Douro and picnicked and swam there; it made a lovely day.

The Wolfgangs had to leave on Tuesday 12th but we managed to host a dinner party for 14 in *Emma* before they left; a bit of a crush but the chicken and garlic cooked by the frails was wonderful. Ian had decided to jump ship and return with the Wolfgangs, and they all left about midnight for the long journey back to Austria. The skipper wondered whether it had all been worth it for them, such a long car journey for only eight days' sailing.

To Vigo, 13th – 17th July

We left Leixoes on Wednesday at 0900 in thick mist, having filled up with diesel and water. It was necessary to engine at first with a northerly force 2 – 3 against us en route to Varzim, but by noon the wind had increased and backed, making it possible to motor-sail with one reef in the main; but at 1645 the mainsail split along one of the horizontal seams, and was rapidly removed.

We then motored on in rather unpleasant weather to Viana do Castelo with the skipper and Cedric on deck; here we encountered the deadly bureaucracy. However we did manage to catch a restaurant open at 2300, and had an excellent meal consisting of sardines, calamares and chicken piri-piri. Viana turned up trumps the following day, when it was possible to locate a sailmaker who mended the sail in a couple of hours for £12.

As we had to make it a lay day, we cleaned ship and the girls went swimming and shopping. Cedric showed his knowledge of diesels by changing the oil filter, cleaning out the agglomerator and adjusting the fanbelt. After completing this work he found it

'A PORTO TOO FAR': PORTUGAL 1994

necessary to bleed the engine, and this took a rather long time, a bit nailbiting as by then it was approaching darkness.

The decision was made to make an early start at 0400 to make the 33-mile passage to Bayona. We had found from experience that the best time to sail was early in the morning, the afternoons having increasing northerly winds. For a change it was a clear

The sunbathers

The hotel where we enjoyed the Pimentos Padrone in Bayona

morning and we arrived in Bayona at noon, finding a berth alongside. Now back in Spain, there were none of the problems with Customs and immigration, all very simple. Bayona is a magic spot, and somewhere to which we shall return. (It had been recommended to us by Roger Dongray, the designer of *Emma*.)

We had to get Amelia, Cedric and Jane to Vigo to catch their planes back to the UK on the 18th, so were unable to stay longer but had to leave on Sunday 17th.

Bayona is located in a bay at the mouth of the Ria de Vigo, beyond Cape Silleiro, and is surrounded by islands, all of which would make an excellent daysail, with swimming and camping ashore. The Islas Cies are less than 2 miles away, and ferries take holidaymakers there from Bayona. There is a beautifully sited parador above the marina, the site of an old castle. We sat overlooking the bay enjoying the the local wine and Pimentos Padrone. It was only when the bill came and we found we had been charged £11 each for two bottles of the local wine, *vigno verde*, about £1.50 in the supermarket, that we realised just how much we had had to admire the view!

Jane very generously hosted a meal for the crew at a superb little restaurant called El Tunel in the evening, wonderful food followed by spectacular fireworks, a great evening.

On Sunday we left for the short passage of 13 miles, sailing through the islands to Vigo, arriving just after lunch. We all went swimming at a beach nearby, and then to 'Mama's' for a farewell meal in the evening. Cedric and Amelia had to catch a plane early in the morning, and the skipper got up and saw them off in a taxi to the airport at 0630. Jane did not have to leave till the following day, and so we decided to catch a bus and spend the day in Bayona swimming.

Jane having left, the skipper and his mate were left without crew in Vigo for a week. Vigo is an ideal place to be left ashore, with your floating hotel (berthing cost £56.25 for the week). The facilities are excellent, hot showers and all mod cons.

The chandlery at the marina has very limited supplies, but a better one is Vachtsport in the town and after the skipper had removed the bilge pump they effected a repair which lasted till

'A PORTO TOO FAR': PORTUGAL 1994

we returned to Rye. They also supplied the extra length of pipe required to extend the stirrup pump to enable the bilges to be cleared easily, should the pump fail again.

The skipper and mate decided to make the most of the enforced stay in Vigo, and once Diana had recovered from a mild dose of 'too much sun' which laid her low for a day, a number of trips were planned, the most interesting being a train journey to Santiago de Compostela, the main pilgrimage city of Galicia, containing the tomb of St James the Greater. The cathedral is one of the finest in the world, and the day we arrived there was a religious festival with the congregation in traditional dress.

We had decided to leave Vigo on Sunday 24th July when Richard, a new crew member, was due to arrive. In the event he decided to join in Muros but Fred and Paul arrived early; Paul having come from a business meeting in Madrid had a hire car, so for a couple of days we were able to explore the countryside.

We had met Horst, a tax exile from Switzerland, who having sold his business had purchased the most enormous Eurobonker, with three decks, an engine room the size of *Emma* with a completely fitted workshop, a state-of-the-art satellite navigation system, satellite TV, and a motorbike on deck amongst other goodies ... but he was not happy, as he was unable to return to

Horst's 'Eurobonker'!

Combarro – the grain store

Switzerland for more than 14 days in the year, and spent his time wandering the earth! We took pity on him as he was alone and invited him to dinner; I think he must have been starving as he ate like a horse. Thankfully Paul speaks fluent German so conversation was not impossible.

One day we went to the fishing village of Combarro, which is famous for its grain stores set up on stilts, and on our last evening to Bayona where Paul hosted a wonderful meal at a fantastic restaurant, the Los Abertos at Nigran just outside the town, famous for its roast suckling pig and lamb which is cooked on a central barbecue. To bed at 0100 ready for an early start for the journey north.

To La Coruna, 24th – 26th July

We left at 0500 for Muros, starting with a good sail down the Ria before the wind died and much of the rest of the day spent on engine. The passage to Muros (43 miles) is full of excitement, going first through the straights at Isle de Norte, and then skirting Isla Ons, Isla Salvora and Cape Correbedo before entering the Ria de Muros.

We arrived at Muros at 1300, tying up to a buoy, and seeing Richard waiting on the shore. He had only just arrived, having had a fairly tiring journey from the UK delayed by the air traffic controllers' strike. All were exhausted, so we slept till 2000, when we went ashore in the tender to play the 'Oh Shit' card game in a pub, getting back for marinated pork about 2300.

It was another early start to catch the best of the weather at 0600 for the passage past Cape Finistere up to the Ria de Corme y Lage, and the little port at Lage. At 0045 when motor-sailing past Cap de la Nave the gaff spar suddenly collapsed; yet another

The jury rig gaff strop

minor irritation, which had it been in poor weather might have been more serious. The sail was lowered and the engine and foresails used for the rest of the day.

On arrival at Lage, the crew established that the problem was rusting of the stainless steel wire within the suaging of the gaff strop. The whole strop was removed and a jury rig made up of polypropylene rope, which lasted all the way back to England.

Lage is a pleasant place, good for a family holiday, and we all went swimming in the afternoon. Being Sunday we had difficulty in finding anywhere open, but eventually found a small food store where basic provisions could obtained. Richard made an exceptionally good spaghetti bolognese in the evening.

We had an uneventful passage to La Coruna the following day. It was the day the Tall Ships were supposed to arrive, but there was little evidence of them. We had decided to leave the same day, so expeditions for food and chandlery were made on arrival. Diana manfully collected a whole trolley of food on her own. Fred and the skipper found a magnificent chandlery, the best in

Post box in Vigo

Enclosed balconies in La Coruna

Spain – they had everything! We were able to replace all the elements of the gaff strop, so that if we had a failure of the jury rig, we could have replaced it.

We filled up with diesel, the skipper having thoughtfully purchased a further 25-litre can in Vigo, just in case, so this meant that we would cross Biscay with 38 gallons, which seemed to be enough at the time, about 80 hours on engine.

To Guernsey, 26th July – 1st August

Richard had just started a new job, and was concerned that he should return to the UK as close to Sunday 31st July as possible, and had booked a ferry from Cherbourg; so the passage was noted for Richard consulting his watch as we were virtually becalmed in the middle of Biscay, having to use our engine for 76.5 hours overall.

Leaving La Coruna at 1930 on Tuesday 26th we motored all night with no wind, but by 1145 on Wednesday the wind had increased from the north-west and we were able to beat into it with two reefs in the main, but went a long way off course to the east, clawing back the following night, leaving 187 miles to go to the Raz by 0700.

But the wind lessened and from 2100 onwards it was necessary to engine to maintain 4 to 5 knots in the right direction. The skipper had to keep calculating the amount of time to go, related to the diesel available, and was thankful that he had purchased the 25-litre extra tank.

Instead of going through the Raz, it would be quicker to go to the west of the Chaussee de Sein, and a decision was made to alter course for the Chaussee de Sein cardinal buoy, which we finally made early on Saturday 30th July, allowing us to turn east towards Camaret; but by this time we were seriously short of diesel. As we were in a dead calm we even tried towing *Emma* using the tender, but our little Mariner outboard made a poor fist of this.

At one point a French submarine suddenly emerged off our port bow about a quarter of a mile away, and the skipper radioed on

Arrival of a tall ship

Channel 16 asking if they could 'render assistance' (it may seem funny now!). The sub took immediate action: it dived and was not seen again. We wondered perhaps if it should have been there!

A heavenly wind sprung up soon after and we sailed all the way into Camaret at 6 knots with 1.5 gallons of diesel left. Clearly one cannot rely on 30 gallons for the 325-mile crossing; yet on the southerly passage we had used less than 9 gallons.

We filled up with diesel (cost £53.99), went shopping, had showers and got ready for an early-morning start to catch the northerly tide up the Chenal du Four. Late in the evening one of the Tall Ships arrived and anchored in the bay, flood lit at night it looked very impressive.

We left for the 140-mile passage to Guernsey at 0400 the next day, and with that wonderful tidal stream in our favour together with a following wind we had already negotiated the Chenal and

St Peter Port, full up

were approaching the Lizen buoy with the Ile Vierge light massively to starboard by 0900. The rest of the way to Guernsey went well, catching the easterly tide to arrive at St Peter Port at 1000 the following morning, delivering Richard in the tender to the ferry port for his homeward journey, still looking at his watch!

When the water was high enough we entered the innner harbour, and then went off to the pub and to find fish and chips, very good in Guernsey.

To Rye, 2nd – 8th August

Once again we had crew problems, Paul would have to leave ship on arrival back in the UK leaving only the skipper, the mate and Fred to get *Emma* back to Rye, so phone calls were made, arms twisted and the result was that Adam together with Jeremy and family would join us in Weymouth. Adam's son Ben, now 14, who lives in Austria, was at present staying with his father. The original idea was that Ben would spend two weeks with Adam on his Folkboat, but one week of this would now be spent helping the skipper to get *Emma* back to Rye.

We left on a misty and unpleasant day for Cherbourg, negotiating the little Russell without difficulty, and setting course for Alderney, to get the maximum benefit of the tide, before turning east for Cherbourg. A number of other boats left at the same time, once there was water over the cill in the inner harbour. There was little

Emma parked in the marina

opportunity to sail north, and after a while all boats were engining. We did not arrive in Cherbourg until 2300, too late for the splendid duty free shop, but not too late to walk up into the main shopping street which was alive and well at 0100. Time for a drink, then back to *Emma* for a short sleep before leaving for Weymouth at 0400.

A sail across the Channel with a fair south-easterly was a joy after so much engining, and we managed the 65-mile crossing in 17 hours, not a fast crossing but a pleasant one. We had to engine for the last two hours to meet Paul's deadline as Judy was picking him up by car. The skipper hosted a dinner in a rather nice Chinese restaurant, before Paul and Judy departed for home.

The following morning the good Fred got up early, and by the time the skipper was up he had had a new gaff strop suaged at a local engineering works, using all the parts purchased in La Coruna, and was busily fixing it in position. Friday being a lay day, the skipper and Diana went swimming on the beach with a million other people, a gentle lazy day. Jeremy and family arrived, also Adam and Ben, so we were able to set off for the Solent.

We left at 0600 and made good progress eastwards, seeing the Isle of Wight by noon, even getting the topsail up, but by the time we were at the Needles Fairway buoy, the wind had died and we needed both tide and engine to make progress towards Gosport, where on advice from an old salt in Weymouth we discovered the Haslar Marina, an excellent alternative to the expensive Camper & Nicholsons next door. (Haslar cost £10.74. per night whilst four years ago C&N had cost £20, never to be repeated.) The skipper had marinaded some pork for dinner and we were joined by Diana, Rebecca, Florence and Jamie on arrival.

Rebecca decided to join the crew the next day, while Diana looked after the kids and drove the car to Brighton, where *Emma* was due to arrive in the evening. As it was it was a most unpleasant day – back in England with a vengeance, a north-easterly force 5 – 6 on the nose all the way – Rebecca loved it! We arrived at Brighton Marina at 2230 where the car was taken into town, and an Indian fish and chipper, which was about to close was persuaded to produce the answer, which was excellent.

There was a good deal of debate the following day as to whether we should continue to Rye or leave *Emma* in Brighton, but as the wind had eased a bit we decided to go for it, leaving at 1100 to fill up at the diesel quay, then on towards Beachy. It was impossible to maintain anything like the right direction with sail alone, so the rest of the day was spent motor-sailing.

High water at Rye was at 0043, so we planned to arrive about 2200 to get down the river on the flood. This was a mistake as it was a strong spring tide; we should not have attempted it until closer to midnight, and in the event we had difficulty in getting into our berth due to the flood which carried us past the berth on our first try, and made life difficult on the second, breaking off a stanchion on an adjacent boat with our bowsprit as we angled our way in.

Amelia was at the house and Diana had arrived by car, so that once we had tidied up they cooked a huge bacon and egg meal for all of us.

The general feeling about the cruise was that although it had been fun, it had been a port too far, causing problems with finding sufficient crew, having always to meet deadlines so that although we were away for seven weeks, it had been too much of a rush. It was thought likely that the plan for next year would be both closer to home, and with longer stops between each leg.

The skipper had proved (to his own satisfaction if to no one else's) that he can be macho; in future it was time to sail for pleasure and this would be to everyone's benefit.

Cruise finances 1994

All members of the crew were asked to contribute £55 per week, the same as for last year's passage to Ireland. This was sufficient to pay for all expenses on board. (One week in Vigo there were only two crew, although the berthing for the week cost £56.25.)

Credit from all crew, 30 man weeks	£1650.00

Expenses	
Expenses for boat	£ 656.00
Expenses for food and drink	£ 994.00
Total	£1650.00

Breakdown of boat expenses	
Berthing	£ 218.99
Diesel	£ 201.92
Gaz	£ 38.86
Boat bits	£ 204.23
	£ 656.88

Analysis: cost per week	
Food and drink	£ 142.00
Boat	£ 94.00
	£ 236.00 per week

Notes:

All foreign currencies converted to sterling

Additional cost of £311 for hire of life raft, donated by Jonathan, Tony and skipper.

10

The Halcyon Cruise: The Netherlands 1995

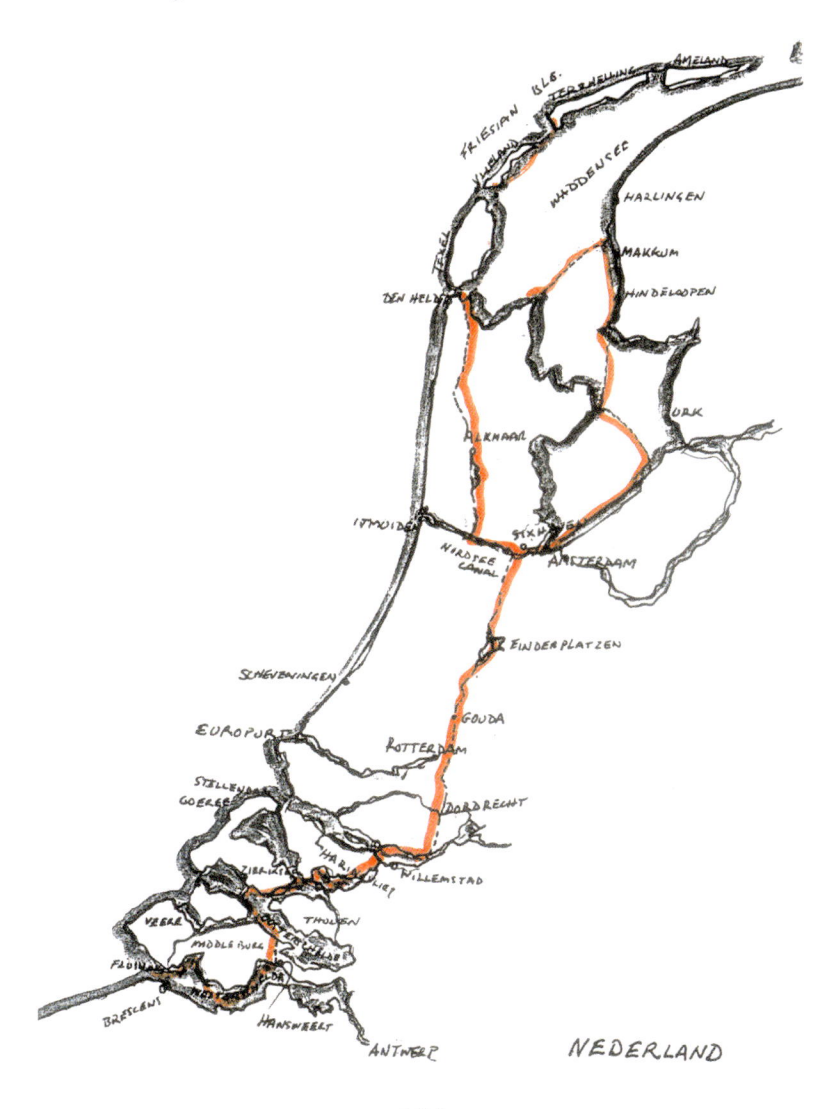

Holland seemed like a good idea after the problems with the boat on the passage to Portugal in 1994, and so it proved to be. We had no problems with the boat, the weather for the most part was perfect, the crew turned up on time, and we lived like millionaires.

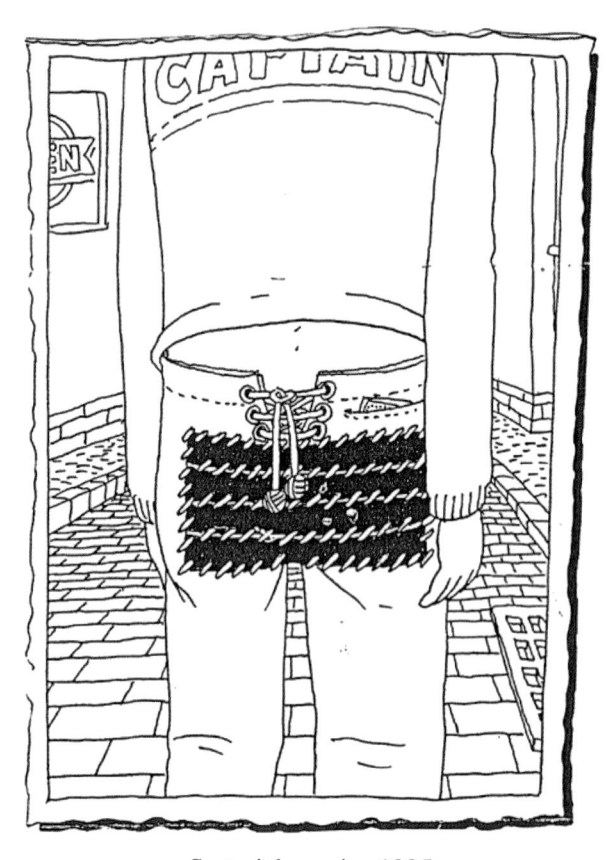

Sartorial repairs 1995

The crew gathered at 10 Market Street on Friday evening, 14th July, with a dinner at the Ypres Tower, and all ready for the off to catch the midday tide down the Rother the following day. Barney and little Paul had arrived late, with a new-look Barney, short hair!

There was some preparatory work to do, getting the inflatable from the house and into the port lazaret, and generally preparing for sea. The sea was quite rough (south-westerly force 5 – 6) but

THE HALCYON CRUISE: THE NETHERLANDS 1995

1: Skipper; 2: Young Paul; 3: Jonathan; 4: Sian; 5: Diana; 6: Wolfgang; 7: Jane; 8: Paul; 9: Tin Tin; 10: Jeremy; 11: Rebecca; 12: Fred; 13: Jo; 14: Andreas; 15: Ian; 16: Cedric, Amelia and Poppy; 17: Chris; 18: Barney

we decided to try it, and in the event we left our berth at 1300 and sailed all the way to Boulogne, arriving just before 2000, our usual seven-hour passage. The wind had decreased by Dungeness, and it was a pleasant crossing. In a way this was to set a pattern for the holiday, as we spent very little on diesel this year, and this mostly in negotiating the Dutch canal system – it was a sailing holiday.

The next day being Sunday, and the Boulogne supermarket closed, it seemed sensible to carry on north towards Calais, so we took the tide around at 1130, arriving at 1530. A minor problem on arrival, with ferries milling around in every direction, was that the staysail furl refused to work, and Big Paul had to wrap the sail around in order to reduce the wind; this was later solved by renewing the string with a narrower one.

At Calais, you have to wait for the bridge to open and close which it does twice a day, so we decided to leave the following morning, following a string of boats out at 0400. The weather looked fine, and instead of stopping at Dunkirk, our original plan, we sailed fast all the way to Ostend, arriving at 1430 in time to see something of the town. Belgium is very expensive due to its hard currency, the berth costing £14 for the night. Big Paul cooked two small chickens which cost about double the price in the UK. (He committed the cardinal sin of throwing away the parson's noses, the skipper's prerogative.) The harbour-master was complaining that the hard currency had hit their tourist industry badly.

The weather worsened and the following day one distressed yacht was brought in by tug, and the inshore life boat had a busy day. Ostend is an attractive town, so we decided to have our lay day in the Mercator marina there. We took the opportunity to belay the lazy jacks (these had been omitted when the boat was put in the water after the winter), and new longer ropes were fitted with young Paul up the mast to secure them. They can now be altered from the deck.

The Yacht Club has a bonded stores facility, and provided booze is ordered in the evening, it is delivered to your boat at 9 a.m. the following day. The shipment is followed by a Customs officer who seals it into some appropriate cupboard – in our case the gas locker!

The prices were as follows:

Fletcher Whisky	£4.50
Silver Top Gin	£3.83
Bolskaya Vodka	£3.50
Wine cartons	£1.80

The wine was the only disappointment, a very undistinguished rosé, the same quality a French supermarket sells at 80p. Otherwise the prices were similar to bonded stores in the UK, when years ago we used to pick them up in Plymouth.

The following day, 19th July, we decided to take a look at the sea outside (the forecast had been for a south-westerly force 3), and found that it had calmed down sufficiently to continue north towards Holland. Leaving at 0900 with a foul tide, it took nine hours to reach Flushing (Vlissingen) and a further two to negotiate the lock, bridges and canal up to our berth at Middleburg, a total

Emma in harbour

of only 32 miles. It had taken five days from Rye to Holland, in keeping with our desire for a gentle cruise this year.

Big Paul had arranged for his company plane to pick him up from the little airstrip outside Middleburg, and as young Paul and Barney were also leaving, he was able to give them a lift home to Luton Airport.

Winter work

Emma had been lifted out during the winter with the mast lifted off by crane. As a result of this we had none of the hassles of last year, and it might be useful to list the various repairs we had carried out over the winter, as a result of all the problems the previous year:

> Fit a new bilge pump.
> Renew the 6-foot antisyphon pipe to the sea loo.
> Get the plate to drop – it had stuck in the 'up' position.
> Renew the bush to the cutlas bearing to the stern gear.
> Renew the bearings to the rudder.
> Navico tiller pilot serviced.
> New fanbelt fitted.
> All sails valetted, and the main double sewn.
> Kicking strap block replaced.
> Normal engine maintenance.
> Electrical circuits checked.

This year the engine started on the button every time, the 19-year-old sails all performed well, the tiller pilot worked, as did all the electrics, and navigational aids. It was a trouble-free cruise, and well worth the time and cost spent during the winter on getting things right.

Middleburg – Amsterdam, 22nd – 28th July

Middleburg is a delightful town, and as we were picking up crew we booked for three nights. The second day we agreed with the harbour-master that we could spend the day in Veere, and return in the evening. Veere is a delight, and no one should miss it. We went for a slow (little wind) sail in the Veerse Meer, before taking the Walcheren Canal back to Middleburg, where the following day Sian, Andreas and Jonathan joined us. April had originally been coming too, but alas decided to have a baby! On Sunday 23rd July we left at the first bridge opening at 0830 for Amsterdam, stopping briefly in Veere to see if anyone had found Diana's purse which she had dropped while shopping the day before, but no luck.

We had a good day's sailing, through the Veerse Meer, and through the Zandkreeksluis into the Oosterschelde, and then north to the Zeelandbrug which gives access to Zierikzee. The skipper always likes to have 13.5 metres clearance for *Emma*, and we called up the bridge control on Channel 18 to establish that there was sufficient height, and were told there was 15 metres, but it is always slightly heart-stopping as you get close; but all was well, and our burgee appeared to have a good 2 metres above, as we went below.

Willemstad

Dutch barge

It had been a very hot day, and it was nice to go ashore at Zierikzee, where we berthed at 1600. It is a lovely old city, with interesting shops and streets, but we decided to carry on the next day, leaving at 0850 for Willemstad. A call to the bridge established there was sufficient height, and we passed under with rather more confidence, negotiating the Oosterschelde, and on through the Krammersluis into the Volkerak by 1300. We stopped for lunch alongside the *sluis* (lock), and as it was sunny and warm, all plunged in for a swim, not leaving for Willemstad until after 1500. This was all a part of the new-look gentle passage.

There is little need for navigation in the inland waters, as the buoys are plentiful, and unless the weather clamps down, or you are really stupid, it is difficult to see how you can come to much harm, provided you equip yourself with the excellent Dutch *Hydrografische Kaarts* for the different waters (Oosterschelde is 1805). It is as well to update these as the Dutch do have a habit of altering the buoy numbering.

We had excellent sailing with the topsail up, reaching the *sluis*

THE HALCYON CRUISE: THE NETHERLANDS 1995

at Volkerak by 1800, then round the corner to Willemstad, where we berthed in the old harbour soon after 1900. I think that the harbour-master must recognise *Emma* by now, as we give him a wave, and he doesn't insist that we go into the modern marina. This year we chose all our favourite ports, and Willemstad is another at the top of the list.

There is an excellent chandler there and as we needed to replace a block to the port backstay, he modified one to fit, while we watched. We also purchased a Dutch 'curvy' jackstaff, as we found this allows our red duster to fly properly. After a lazy morning we left, sailing under the Haringulietbrug then making excellent time broad-reaching towards Hellevoetsluis, where we moored off for a swim before entering the marina. Hellevoetsluis is a useful stopping-off point for Stellendam, the opening to the North Sea, and a 0730 start was made the following day to cross the few miles to the dam; through by 1900, and set Navstar for

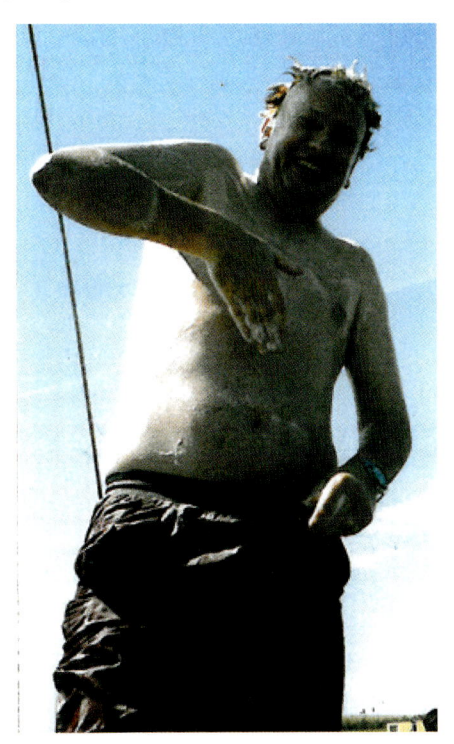

Andreas   Jonathan

a waypoint at the Hinder buoy, before making the turn easterly past Europort. From Stellendam to Hinder is a buoyed route, and it is vital to follow this, and not make direct for Hinder, as the area around the Goree estuary is fraught with shallows.

Unlike Andreas, he had a problem putting up the topsail, got it in a muddle, had to go up the mast while under way and whilst getting it down tore it!

Weatherwise

A note here about the weather, so that it will be unnecessary to keep mentioning it. We thought that our barometer was broken, it never varied day after day until we got back to the Belgian coast towards the end of August – long, gorgeous, sunfilled days; we felt it was too good to last, but it did. We understand that it was just as good at home, which of course was slightly irritating! But such a long period of high pressure must be pretty exceptional.

Diana had made a cockpit cover against the sun, thinking there might be a time to use it. In fact we used it whenever we stopped,

The Belage Museum

THE HALCYON CRUISE: THE NETHERLANDS 1995

Schreveningen – full up!

Willemstad

providing necessary shade. It stretched over the boom, being attached by elastic string and nylon clips to the stanchion rails. We also made good use of a hammock as the weather was so good; Andreas slept in it on deck each night.

We had passed Europort without difficulty by midday, but soon after this, the wind freshened out of the north, and it was necessary to motor-sail for two hours to make way towards Schreveningen, where we arrived at 1600. The latter is very expensive, and overcrowded (£27 for two nights, twice the price of Middleburg). A wonderful supermarket close to the marina, and Diana and Sian went marketing.

The skipper had, before leaving the UK, talked to Martin Richardson, an architect working in Holland, who gave us some advice about things to see in the town, and together with Diana visited the Haag's Gemeentemuseum designed by Berlage, a most interesting building with much of Frank Lloyd Wright about it. The building was in course of renovation, so some galleries were not in use, but there are works by Monet, Mondrian and Picasso, with sculpture by Rodin, Hepworth and Marini.

Before leaving we had a major spring clean, floorboards up, bilges cleaned through, sea loo washed out and deck scrubbed, so a new-look *Emma* finally made it out of the melee of boats by lunchtime en route for Ijmuiden, on Friday 28th.

Wind was non-existent, so as we were engining, we tried out the autopilot (repaired from last year) and it worked fine. To Ijmuiden by 1730, where we helped tow a small yacht through the lock, as its engine had failed, and after two hours sailing up the Nordsee we berthed at Sixhaven Marina in the centre of Amsterdam.

Sixhaven is a delight; it is located opposite the main railway station, from which free ferries take visitors to and from the centre leaving about every ten minutes day or night, so getting into the centre of Amsterdam is no trouble. The harbour, the cheapest we encountered at £5 per night, is surrounded by trees and is pleasant and quiet, usually pretty full, but the harbourmaster is helpful in always finding you somewhere for the night. Andreas, as he is the youngest member of the crew, was christened 'the Boy' and was led astray in Amsterdam by Diana, Sian and Jonathan, taken to the red-light district and purchased naughty substances!

Sadly Sian and Jonathan had to leave, but not before vying with each other to produce the most wonderful food. Sian bought and cooked some huge prawns, out of this world!

Amsterdam – Harlingham, 29th July – 4th August

Both Tin Tin and Wolfgang arrived on the Saturday. Wolfgang had had an uncomfortable journey by train from Vienna; he arrived looking like a zombie, having to stand all night with backpacks blocking the corridor, so it was virtually impossible to move. Hey ho for the comfort of *Emma*! We decided to leave after lunch on Sunday, giving Andreas an opportunity to visit the Van Gogh museum in the morning.

On leaving our berth we crossed the river to see if we could visit the *Batavia*, which we had seen being built at Lelystad in 1999. Apparently it has been having some problems, and was in an internal dock so we couldn't get close, and it had gone by the time we returned to Amsterdam on 16th August. So the nearest we got was to see her masts and spars from across the river.

Into the Ijsselmeer, and a good sail up to Hoorn arriving just before 2100 in the evening; by the time we had eaten we didn't have time to visit the town, as it is quite a walk from the marina, but we had done the town before, the town of Tasman and the famous Hoorn Tower, and we needed to leave early in the morning to get across the Ijsselmeer to Urk.

We left Hoorn early for the lock at Enkhuisen, which takes you from the south to the north Ijsselmeer, but the wind was very light, and even with the topsail up we made poor progress, having eventually to engine for one and a half hours north-eastwards to the lock, if we were to make our destination at Urk before nightfall.

We were through the lock with some beautiful Dutch barges by midday, and stopped at the third marina for diesel, giving Diana and Wolfgang a chance to do the marketing. We sailed well to the east with a freshening wind, berthing at Urk by 1745, where we all cooled off with a swim. Tin Tin, our Vietnamese cook, and Diana made a splendid stir fry to complete the day. We were beseiged by butterflies on the way across, they came over in droves, flopped into the water, and were gobbled up by the fish.

The lock at Enkhuisen

Model of a Dutch barge purchased in Urk

THE HALCYON CRUISE: THE NETHERLANDS 1995

Gerrit Pasterkamp's wooden boat

We looked up Gerrit Pasterkamp but found that he had left for the UK the day before in his Pilot Cutter 12, *Jacoba Maria*. The skipper had invited him and his wife to dinner by letter before leaving the UK and it was sad that he was not available. We spoke to the harbour-master who pointed out to us a brand new Cornish Crabber, all wood, that Gerrit had made (presumably from plans obtained from Crabbers). It was nice to see a brand new all-wood version, it reminded me of *Midley Belle* in her heyday! In the evening we met his daughter and husband, but it was not clear whether Gerrit intended to keep both boats.

Urk is another of our favourite Dutch towns. It was once an island, and the population still regard themselves very much as an isolated entity. The skipper went looking for a model of a Dutch barge to adorn his chart room at home to keep the French *Sloup Entirement Ponte* company. They must mass produce these in Holland, as they are available in other towns, but at Urk it was the cheapest we found at £41; the French one had been £100 in 1991. We stayed a couple of days in Urk enjoying the swimming, marred only by Diana repeating her lost purse trick, this time over the side, and despite efforts with magnets it was not recovered. After this we attached a large float to the purse and had no further mishaps.

We broke our passage to Makkum at the north of the Ijsselmeer, by a stop at Hindeloopen, a tiny town with a huge marina. The marina had everything, including a swimming pool, restaurants, children's creche and a price to match, and we were not sorry to leave for little Makkum the following day, 3rd August.

We had slow sailing with a force 2 – 3 wind from the north; many sailing boats were out on this hot and sunny day.

An amazing change has taken place in Makkum since we were last there. It is entered down a long channel, and the south side of the channel is now lined with marinas. But remembering happy days inside the town, we passed all these by, and sure enough the lock into the centre still operates, and we passed through, berthing alongside right in the centre of the old town, which has hardly changed.

There is an excellent chandler in Makkum, and the skipper was able to pick up the *Tidal Stream Atlas* for the Waddensee (*Stroomatlas Waddensee West HP17*) an invaluable document when approaching the *Riddle of the Sands* country.

In the evening the skipper hosted a meal of mussels at an excellent restaurant called De Waag (the weighbridge); they charge a fixed price for the dish with chips and salad and you can eat as much as you fancy – this appealed to Wolfgang and Andreas. It was interesting to see in a shop window in the town a picture of the large motor yacht we had seen in the boat building in 1985: it was called the *Montkai*, and was clearly something of a sensation for the town; in the picture it is being pulled up the channel by two tugs. When we saw it, it was being given a final polish, and looked as though one of James Bond's 'very bads' was about to take it over, and would certainly have had a submarine parked in its bowels. (Could this have been the *Lady Ghislane* of Robert Maxwell?)

We left Makkum lock early when the lock opened, and set course for the Kornwerderzand lock giving access to the Waddensee; once clear we turned east for Harlingen, our next pickup point. This is approached by a buoyed channel avoiding the shoal water, showing 1.8 metres in the channel in places, with 0.3 metres just outside. We didn't see anyone aground, but were glad to arrive.

Jeremy, Rebecca and the children had just arrived by train and we met up on the quay. They had a fairly tortuous journey from Bristol, leaving at 1500 on Thursday via train to Harwich, night ferry to the Hook, and several train changes later to Harlingen on Friday to meet *Emma*.

It was Tin Tin and Andreas's last night; we had a wonderful fish meal cooked by Tin Tin, and they left in the morning.

Financial

The last time we had been in Holland, berthing had been about £4 per night, so it was a bit of a shock to find that this now averaged about £9, also with food and everything else higher. Diesel is twice the cost of the UK, 11 gallons costing £28.

I suppose it is still a shock to realise that Britain is now a 'third world country'. It is impossible to purchase Calor gas bottles in Europe, and we had brought three of the 4.5 kg bottles with us, each lasting 9 – 10 days, we had also brought three of the Campingaz bottles (2.72 kg); each lasted five days, but when had we had to replace them they cost more than the larger Calor gas. I've never fathomed this one out, but it does seem that there must be a favourable market for Calor in Europe, since it costs less than half the price of the monopoly Campingaz.

Vlieland

Harlingen – Friesian Islands, 5th – 11th August

The harbour-master provided the tide tables for Harlingen, and we worked out that we would have a fair tide out to Vlieland by leaving in the early afternoon, so after a general tidy and check-up we left, in company with a number of other boats; but not before Diana and Rebecca had visited the supermarket, as prices were likely to be higher in the islands.

We had done this trip before in *Midley Belle*, and had found ourselves being passed by other boats all the time; it was a pleasure that in *Emma* we more than held our own, it taking only four hours to arrive and tie up in Vlieland's crowded harbour.

The position we found meant that it was necessary to retract the bowsprit, never necessary before. This was accomplished with comparative ease, and it no longer bothered us when we found it necessary on a couple of other occasions, where 'bow on' to the pontoon, the bowsprit would have obstructed access.

The skipper remembered John Fitzjohn, the first owner of *Emma*, telling us that on one occasion he had been asked by a marina to pay the extra 3 metres for the bowsprit, and had retracted it instead. A useful tip for the future, if any greedy marina attempts the same.

In Vlieland we had the only boat problem we encountered during the passage: we noticed that the bilges seemed to be filling excessively for no good reason, even when we had not moved. The problem was investigated by Jeremy who discovered that it was not salt, but fresh water. The problem was solved when he found that the outlet cap on the port water tank had become cross-threaded so that the drinking water had been seeping out. All was corrected, and we had no further trouble.

The story of Vlieland is not so much about sailing, more about family holidays, with swimming and catching crabs, bicycling and enjoying the spectacular weather. There are no cars, and everyone bicycles all over the island. We hired bicycles and went to beaches on the far side. Jamie spent his time catching crabs, and Florence and Jamie played about in the inflatable, our good little Marina outboard starting first pull, after not having been

THE HALCYON CRUISE: THE NETHERLANDS 1995

Bowsprit retracted

Terschelling – buoy park

used for nine months. The town is about a 20-minute walk from the harbour, but an excellent travelling shop arrives at the marina each day, and this provides all the necessities, including moderately decent wine.

We stayed three days in Vlieland, then sailed for Terschelling, where the harbour was less crowded and the town more interesting. There are cars here, but the swimming is still good, and the place relaxing, so we stayed three days, before returning to Vlieland.

Emma in the Friesians was like living in a first-class seaside hotel, without the bill at the end. Fantastic food on board, and every day an adventure.

Jeremy, Rebecca and the children left on the ferry for Harlingen on Saturday 12th August to start the long trek by public transport back to Bristol via the Hook and Harwich. Jane and Chris arrived in the evening, all set for the next leg as far as Amsterdam.

Foodstuff

Food on any holiday plays an important part, and when as in the case of *Emma* meals out can be afforded only on rare occasions, it is important that the food on board is varied and exciting. I don't know whether it is that excellent cooks are attracted by *Emma*, or whether the skipper's Machiavellian crew selection results in what could be called the 'gourmet cruise'.

Tin Tin and Ian both cook for a living; Tin Tin, who is Vietnamese, cooks the most wonderful fish meals, Ian makes delicious pastas and pizzas, but these are the professionals. Jonathan and Sian are both superb, and this year we had Big Paul cooking. I should also of course mention the skipper's mate, Amelia, Jane and Jo; it appears that all members try to vie with each other when it is their turn to cook. I mention this now to avoid continual food talk, but the skipper does make a passable spag bol.

THE HALCYON CRUISE: THE NETHERLANDS 1995

Vlieland – Amsterdam, 12th – 17th August

Sunday 13th saw *Emma* leave the harbour in Vlieland and set off against a foul tide westwards towards the open sea, in order to catch the fair tide south-west down the coast of Vlieland towards Texel, and ultimately round the corner to Den Nelder. Once round, the wind out of the north west and tide were perfect and *Emma* flew, doing the 34 miles at a speed reaching 7 knots; with a berth-to-berth speed of 5 knots, despite the slow start.

This was particularly nice for Wolfgang as it was to be his last day and it was to be all canals until leaving Holland on reaching the Westerschelde at Hansweert, in ten days' time.

This year's passage down the canals was all a part of the plan for a gentle cruise, taking us from the north of Holland through Amsterdam, and onwards to the south.

Den Helder is an excellent spot, despite it being a naval base; we parked easily alongside, and made for the friendly club house. Matthew, the son of our next-door neighbour, is a pilot, and very kindly borrowed his father's plane to fly Amelia, Cedric and Poppy to Holland. When he filed his flight plan to the airstrip at Den Helder he was told that this was a military airstrip, and he consequently had to fly into Schiphol! Thankfully not on the same

Tin Tin

runway as the 747s: there is a separate runway for private planes. The three arrived about 1900, having had an expensive taxi ride across to the other side of the airport and a train north.

Emma now had to adapt to having a two-month-old baby on board, and this she did with remarkable ease, Poppy's bunk being at the aft end of one of the cosy doubles, shared by Amelia and Cedric.

The following morning Wolfgang left for the long trek back to Vienna, stopping in Amsterdam, where he had the advantage of seeing the Tall Ships and the *Batavia* being towed out on her way back across the Ejsselmeer to Lelystad.

We had a little difficulty in locating the correct bridge leading to the Noordhollands Canal south through a large *sluis*, where we just tucked in behind a tanker. The route to Alkmaar, our destination for the night, takes one through 11 bridges, and a stately journey was made on engine. Our *Nauticring Vaarkaart* (picked up at the London boat show), identifies all the 'fixed mast routes' in the canal system, and is helpful, but insufficiently detailed, and a good deal of imagination is needed too.

Alkmaar is a quite delightful spot, where we stopped for the night, with a lazy lay day following. We entered one of the little canals where access was gained through a wee opening bridge, with only four other boats inside. It was beautifully quiet, and we were therefore quite surprised during our walk around the town to find that Amsterdam is not the only Dutch city to have its red-light district, they are alive and well in Alkmaar and no doubt elsewhere!

The bridge opened at 1000 to let us out, and we engined the whole way to the Nordsee canal. You have to cross the Alkmaardermeer, assisted by well-placed buoys, stopping at the picturesque town of Wormerveer for lunch, reaching the Nordsee, a port turn, sails up, and we sailed all the way into the centre of Amsterdam, berthing alongside a large German sloop in the Sixhaven Marina by 1700.

Chris left the following morning – a lay day in the city – and Jane in the afternoon to spend some time with friends in town. Fred and Jo arrived having also spent a few days' holidaying, so we were complete for the next leg, which would take us south to the Westerschelde, then back home. With six of us on board and Poppy we were not just complete, we were full up.

Chris   The canal at Alkmaar

Amsterdam – Brescens, 18th – 22nd August

As we did not have to leave until midnight, to catch the railway bridge out of Amsterdam, we had the Thursday to ouselves, and visited the ship musem. This is an interesting museum, the best part of which for the skipper was a visit to the *Amsterdam*. Whilst being a replica, since the original was sunk on its maiden voyage to Asia in 1749, the ship gives an authentic experience, even to the 'crew', a bunch of scurvy-looking ruffians who give their services free to show visitors around the ship, cook meals on the stove, and allow children to swab the decks! It all adds to the 'original' atmosphere. They are also very well informed and happy to tell.

To reach the canal system south, it is necessary to cross from Sixhaven to the Oude Houthaven, go through a bridge which

The 'too high' barge or the 'too low' bridge

opens, and wait. You wait for the mainline railway bridge into the city to open; it opens once a day and there is no set time for this; depending upon an eccentric timetable, but generally between two and three in the morning. We all went to sleep, and woke to the sound of other vessels leaving – the bridge was about to open. It was 0230, and panic stations as the engine key was lost. It could not be found immediately and at Amelia's suggestion we got a tow through the bridge from the boat on our inside. A 24-hour delay avoided!

By the time we got towards the second bridge, the mate (who we suspected had hidden it all the time) found the key and we were able to proceed independently through the next eight bridges with the little flotilla of other ships. It is all beautifully worked out, with the bridges opening in sequence as the first of the boats approaches and closing immediately after the last one, and this is all before light.

The Schiphol bridge opened at 0500, and having negotiated this we parked alongside the canal opposite a garage, and went to bed by 0540 not entirely certain where we were.

The garage was very helpful in the morning, supplying milk and certainty. We had not yet reached the Aalsmeer, so stopped there the following morning for provisions.

Amelia had friends who have a house on the side of the West Einderplatzen, the largest lake along the canal, and they had arranged for us to use their mooring, flying a red flag for indentification. This was a joy in all respects; once entering the lake we were able to put up sails, and tack across to their house for a lazy day of swimming in the lake and a meal sitting in the shade in the garden with cold beer, real cutlery and china, then sailing off the mooring towards the other side, and back into the canal system and Gouda.

What was amusing live theatre for us, as we waited for one of the bridges to open, must have been very much less amusing for the barge which attempted to go below the bridge (their usual procedure, they don't have to wait, as do we of the fixed mast). There was a splintering sound as the roof of the cabin was torn off, with shattered glass, made worse by the attempt to reverse and try again. We never knew the reason, but assumed that due to a lighter load than usual, the barge was higher in the water; the owners would not have been best pleased.

We reached Gouda just in time to miss the last bridge opening at 2140, so had to spend the night moored outside the town, getting through the following day and finding an excellent mooring in the centre of town. Gouda is a lovely town and it was market day. As an example of how kind the Dutch are: while we were mooring in the centre an old lady came up and asked if she could photograph the boat; we said of course. As Amelia and Cedric left for the market she ran after them with a teddy bear for Poppy. After we had done our shopping, and sat in the square over a beer, we got back to find that she had had the film express processed and wanted us to have the results. Could this happen in England? Perhaps!

We left after lunch for Dordrecht, a very large town, but we were too late to get into any of several marinas, and parked outside one for the night. Happily this was by an excellent pub, where we played cards. The pub was unique for having a hi-tech loo where on pulling the flush a hand comes out and grabs the seat, turning it through 360 degrees, presumably with disinfectant added, before stopping and withdrawing.

As it was Sunday the following day, we left early to catch the bridge out of town when it opened: this occurred at 0900, and

FAMILY SAILING IN EUROPEAN WATERS

The *Amsterdam*

Lunch in the sun

we were on our way for the short hop to Willemstad. This was the one occasion we ran foul of the Dutch river police. We were boarded just after we had made a port-hand turn into the Dordtsche Kil leaving the Oude Maas. We had apparently made two mistakes: first we had cut across the corner, instead of going at right angles from the far side of the Maas, and we had not been listening out on Channel 4. However they were extremely polite and after checking our certification, radio licence, up to date flares etc, he said he would record a 'warning'. At this point the skipper breathed a sigh of relief as he had not requested sight of the dreaded *Binnenvaart Politie Reglement* (BPR) published as Vol 1. of the *Almanak voor Watertourisme* which all yachts are required to carry in Dutch waters; but as this is not available in English, the skipper has never thought it worthwhile. It is expensive and useless to a non-Dutch speaker and thankfully the skipper has never yet been asked to produce it.

Once out into the Hollandsh Diep it was sails up and a good wind from the east took us to Willemstad, which always seems like our home port. We anchored off for an hour or so for swimming and lunch, and then into the old town harbour for the night.

Monday 21st was magic sailing with a north-easterly force 3 taking us through the Volkeraksluizen and the Krammersluizen, then south west around St Philipsland and Tholen to Wemeldinge, the start point for the Zuid Beveland canal. Cedric got very competitive and we spent the afternoon racing two sloops down the Oosterschelde, at 7 knots – our performance not being improved when the skipper and Fred attempted to raise the topsail. The infernal thing got stuck, and Fred manfully went up the mast to release it. After one and a half hours it was decided to put 'that sodding thing' away.

In February 1995 the *Practical Boat Owner* had published an article saying the old route from the Oosterschelde to the Westerschelde via the Walcheren canal, Middleburg and Veere would soon be overtaken by the route we were about to try, from Wemeldinge to Hansweert, and then starboard towards Brescens. Wrong! Not our experience.

Fred up the mast

Wemeldinge is a 'nothing' town, the Zuid Beveland canal is totally without interest, and one gets held up for long waits at bridges; having finally left Hansveert, one is embroiled in a frightening stream of commercial shipping in and out of Antwerp. Never to be repeated!

The saving grace was that having extricated ourselves from all the shipping, we caught the fast-flowing tide west coupled with an increasing north-easterly for a fast sail down the Westerschelde. We finally made Brescens (very well organised but expensive) where Ian was waiting for us on the pontoon, having taken the morning ferry from Harwich. Ian arrived with a book of the photographs he had taken on our trip to Portugal last year, he is a very good photographer (as well as a good cook).

THE HALCYON CRUISE: THE NETHERLANDS 1995

Brescens – Rye, 23rd – 31st August

Thick mist in the morning of Wednesday 23rd, and as the fair tide towards Ostend was after lunch, we decided to leave at about 1300, when the mist might have cleared; but thunderstorms were forecast for the Belgian Coast. However the skipper got his tides muddled up and as a result found we had to buck a westerly tide, so eventually ran into Zeebrugge, leaving early the following morning and catching the correct tide towards Ostend, arriving by breakfast time, averaging 5 knots berth to berth.

Friday 25th marked a change in the weather: from the warm sunshine of July and August, it became very unpleasant, and when we left early the following morning to keep to our original schedule for Calais and home, discretion demanded that we returned to Ostend. We were glad we did, as the weather got progressively worse and we were unable to leave until the following day. The skipper found a chandler who was able to supply more detailed charts of the Belgian and French coasts, which we lacked. It also gave an opportunity for Ian to remove the alternator and replace a worn nut, which was making it difficult to adjust the fanbelt.

Amelia, Cedric and Poppy left on the ferry for home – more room! The plan for the 26th was influenced by the forecast which suggested that the wind would reduce to a force 3 – 4 out of the north by the afternoon, so we left to catch the tide and hoped for wind at 1600. In the event the wind did not veer as suggested and remained in the north-west, so we had a lumpy passage motor-sailing to Dunkirk – Jo was not happy! Coupled with this, in negotiating the Passe de Zuydcoote we briefly touched bottom, when too close to the E6 buoy, but we soon moved to deeper water.

We reached Dunkirk before dark, and were delighted to see another Pilot Cutter on the visitors' pontoon; we parked alongside for the night, which was very bumpy, so in the morning we arranged with the harbour-master to take a berth on the inside, and found that the other Pilot Cutter was *Grace O'Malley*, the boat Libby Purves had written up in *One Summer's Grace* when

223

she and Paul Heiney had spent a year circumnavigating the British Isles.

The weather, far from improving got worse (force 8 outside) and after a very quiet night within the protection of the harbour, we were surprised to find that the other Pilot Cutter was still bucketing about on the visitors' pontoon. On enquiry we found the the new skipper had strained his back, and was unable to move the boat, so we suggested we did it for him. This done, we invited him to dinner that evening.

There was a Tour de Dunkirk going on during the day, with a million bicycles racing round and round the town. The French take bicycling very seriously: it is a sport for them as opposed to the Dutch, for whom it is a functional transport system, and the whole town was taken over for the race.

Dinner with Lothar

Over dinner that night the new owner of *Grace O'Malley*, a charming German artist called Lothar Pannitschka, told us his story. He had purchased the boat through an agent, picking her up in Cornwall three weeks before, from which time he had had

THE HALCYON CRUISE: THE NETHERLANDS 1995

all sorts of problems. He was sailing single-handed, and the main difficulty had been with the engine, which had failed on three occasions. He had run into Salcombe where he was held up for a week, while the diesel tank was removed and modified. On another occasion when the engine failed he had to sail in the wrong direction in the middle of the night, and had been hallucinating. Now he had reached Dunkirk having injured his back and was telephoning his wife to try to get a crew to sail the boat back for him to his home port of Cuxhaven. And we thought we had problems last year!

Because of the weather we were unable to leave for Calais until Tuesday 29th when it was still lumpy, and Jo decided that she would rather take the ferry across to Dover instead of coming with us the next day.

The entry into Calais had been difficult with five ferries milling about going in and out of the harbour. You have to lock in and out of the yacht harbour in Calais and whilst we got in at about 1400, this meant that we could not get out until a similar time the next day (as 0200 did not appeal to us).

The *Master Builder*

As we left Calais, we were followed out by the *Master Builder*, one of the Ocean Youth Club boats. She looked wonderful under full sail, but we were surprised when she turned to starboard and appeared to go straight across the Ridens de la Rade, which we had been so careful to avoid the previous day. With a draught of at least 2 metres we felt he was chancing it a bit, but no harm was done, and we put this down to his considerable experience, and high water!

We arrived in Dover at 2030, with all that port's legendary courtesy, now improved even more by the new all-tides marina, so no more locking into the Wellington Dock. Jo was awaiting us on the quay, having spotted us from her ferry as we sailed across.

To get into Rye at high water the next day we had to dump Fred and Jo on the quay at 0700 where they departed for Preston, and Ian and the skipper sailed *Emma* back to her home port, arriving on top of the tide; as we had sailed rather faster than anticipated we had to hang about before entering the Rother. But we were all tied up and shipshape by 1500.

Whilst we could have done without the hassle of the past five days, arriving four days later than planned, overall it had been one of the most wonderful and trouble-free holidays we have enjoyed.

Cruise finances

As in previous years each member was asked to contribute £55 per week, but it was found that this year, due mainly to the devaluation of the pound, this was insufficient. Berthing was a major expense totalling £380 (last year was £218 on our passage to Portugal for the same time scale). Food on the Continent had also increased in price. It was necessary for the skipper to subsidise the cruise.

Total credit from all crew, 31 man weeks	£1705.00
Additional contribution from skipper	£ 316.00
	£2021.00

THE HALCYON CRUISE: THE NETHERLANDS 1995

Total expenses for cruise

Expenses for the boat	£ 753.90
Expenses for food/drink	£1267.10
	£2021.00

Breakdown of boat expenses

Berthing	£380.00
Diesel	£ 55.80
Boat bits	£318.10
	£ 753.90

Analysis

Cost per week (7 weeks)   Total £288.00

Food and drink	£180.38
Boat	£107.70
	£288.00

Note: All foreign currencies converted to sterling. Exchange rates experienced were as follows:

UK/French franc	7.46
Belgian franc	44.00
Dutch guilder	2.41

Charts for Holland 1995

Planning charts

Beachy – South Foreland	*2451*	1:150,000
Dover – Scheveningen	*1406*	1:250,000
Dunkirk – Flushing	*1872*	1:100,000
Zeegat Van Texel	*1408*	1:300,000
Vlieland – Den Helder	*2593*	1:150,000

Dutch charts

Detailed:

Westerschelde	*1803*	1:250,000
Oosterscheide	*1805*	1:250,000
Volkerak/Hollandsch	*1807*	1:250,000
Ijsselmeer	*1810*	1:250,000
Waddenzee Westblad	*1811*	1:250,000
Waddenzee Oostblad	*1812*	1:200,000

Rye – Boulogne:

Beachy – Dungeness	*536*	1:75,000
Dover Straight West	*1892*	1:75,000
Dover Straight East	*323*	1:75,000

Boulogne – Flushing:

Oostende – Flushing	*325*	1:50,000
Oostende – Dunkerque	*102*	1:60,000

Flushing – Texel (Amsterdam):

Goree – Texel	*2322*	150,000
Europort Approach	*122*	1:50,000
Noordzee Canal	*124*	1:20,000
Westkapelle – Goree	*100*	1:75,000

Canal Map Nederland   *1:400,000*

THE HALCYON CRUISE: THE NETHERLANDS 1995

Vlissengen – Dunkirk	*1872*	1:100,000
Dunkirk – Calais	*1406*	1:250,000
South Foreland – Beachy	*2451*	1:150,000

Dutch Tidal Stream   *Waddenzee West HP 17*
Atlas   *Westerschelde – Oosterschelde HP 15*

11

Cruise to the Sun: Brittany 1996, July – August

FAMILY SAILING IN EUROPEAN WATERS

1: Paul; 2: Diana; 3: Jonathan; 4: Wolfgang; 5: Skipper; 6: Jane; 7: Florence and Barbara; 8: Sian; 9: Deke; 10: Jeremy and Jamie; 11: Rebecca; 12: Cedric; 13: Amelia and Poppy; 14: Andreas; 15: Julian; 16: Becky; 17: Jay and Verena

232

Introduction

It was realised that the successful cruise to the Netherlands in 1995 would be a difficult act to follow, and in choosing the islands off the southern coast of Brittany it would all be very different, and thus incomparable. It proved to be so.

We had been as far as the Morbihan in 1992, and remembered long sunny days, a factor in our choice of a 'cruise to the sun'. In the event, the exceptional summer of 1995 proved unbeatable, and rereading the log for 1992 it hadn't been all that sunny anyway, so much for memory!

The *Riddle of the Sands* cruising area and the Friesians has the great advantage of proximity for a boat starting from Rye; so to overcome this, we arranged that we would sail *Emma* down to Plymouth a week or so in advance of our start date. This enabled us to cross direct to L'Aber Wrac'h on a night sail, to be at the heart of Brittany the following day.

With the exception of a couple of not entirely minor hiccups, *Emma* survived the cruise, arriving back within a day of our original plan, berthing without incident at Rye Yacht Basin after a magic night sail from Dieppe.

Skipper and Mate swimming

Plymouth – Concarneau, 7th – 12th July

The crew, comprising the skipper and his mate, Paul and Jonathan, assembled in Plymouth by lunchtime on Sunday 7th July, and after filling up with diesel and belaying the bowsprit (which had had to be retracted for the two weeks at Sutton Harbour Marina) *Emma* set sail on her passage to the sun at 1315.

As we left Plymouth the royal yacht *Britannia* was steaming into port looking quite marvellous, with large ensigns flying from the three masts. One hopes that talk of scrapping her comes to nothing – they don't build them like this any more! Past Eddystone light at 1600 averaging 6 knots, but the weather, which had started fine and sunny, became rather heavy. With the wind from the north-west it gave us a fast passage across the Channel, where we arrived at L'Aber Wrac'h five hours before our planned ETA, doing the 115 miles in just under the 24 hours (an average speed of 5 knots) double-reefed. The engine was used to leave and enter port only.

Diana had cooked a chicken for the passage, but due to the sea state none of us had felt like eating it; in fact the skipper had not even felt like going below, so this was consumed with relish on arrival.

There was a pre-Brest Festival in the town the following day, and so we stayed over, dressing *Emma* overall in every flag we could find. It was an exciting evening in L'Aber Wrac'h, as a large number of the Tall Ships en route to Brest arrived and anchored in the harbour. We took the inflatable out and motored around them taking photographs, a wonderful sight. After an excellent meal out at L'Escale restaurant, we adjourned to the Welcome pub where we were playing 'Oh Shit' when all the lights in the town went out. It seemed no one had thought of providing candles, so it was back to *Emma* to finish the game.

Wednesday: with sea mist rolling in, we couldn't see across the harbour, but we hoped that this might clear before we planned to catch the tide down the Chenal du Four at 1400. It didn't, but relying on Navstar we left for Libenter buoy anyway, and using the Decca buoy hopped down to Le Conquet. It was quite eerie, particularly as we didn't see the entrance to Le Conquet until we were about 200 metres from it. But all went well and we tied up to what we thought was a mooring buoy, until being told by a fisherman that it was a lobster pot marker. We found another more suitable one for the night.

Thursday dawned bright and clear; this was the Biscay we had come for, and better still we had a grandstand view of the Tall Ships as they passed Le Conquet on their way to Brest, a wonderful sight. The skipper believed that *Emma* had picked up some unnecessary cargo around the prop whilst engining the previous day; after suggesting that 'someone' should go down and have a look. Jonathan offered his goggles! So it seemed that it was up to the skipper, who nobly stripped off and used a sharp knife to cut away the polyprop rope that had wrapped itself around. He felt a hero, particularly as it was very cold.

We left at 1345 to ensure our passage through the Raz de Sein with the tide about 1800. A wonderful north-westerly wind ensured that we didn't have to use the engine until reaching Audierne where we again moored off for the night. I think this was also on a lobster keep but we left early the following day to continue

Concarneau

FAMILY SAILING IN EUROPEAN WATERS

A peaceful anchorage, Audierne

The Skipper and 'that rope'

our passage to Concarneau. The wind had died, and sadly this was an engine day, all seven and a half hours, except for a little wind towards the end to allow us to enter Concarneau under sail. (We have some pride.)

Concarneau saw Paul and Jonathan leave for the UK, catching the TGV train to Paris, and then the Eurostar to London. We spent two days in Concarneau, one of our favourite haunts, the skipper buying a replacement for his Breton trousers, and his mate a matching tan shirt. (Not before time, as anyone who saw last year's ten-year-old pants will agree.) Andreas Stefferl arrived from Munich during the afternoon and Amelia and Cedric brought Diana's car by way of the Roscoff ferry, joining the boat with Poppy for the following week: the new crew had arrived.

Concarneau – Quiberon – Concarneau, 14 – 21st July

As we were unsure of how Poppy would react to sailing, the decision was made for Diana, Amelia and Poppy to drive along the coast to Port Louis, whilst Cedric and the remaining crew sailed the 30 miles there; the aim being to sail the short distance to Ile de Groix the next day.

The plan worked well, good sailing down to Port Louis leaving Concarneau at 1400, arriving Port Louis soon after 2100, using the engine for leaving and entering port only. A short passage across to Port Tudy on Ile de Groix the following morning, Monday, establishing that we could leave the car at Port Louis, and that Poppy would remain with *Emma* for the rest of the week.

There was good swimming at Port Tudy, and afterwards Cedric and Andreas lit a barbecue on the beach and we stayed there until it got dark.

The following day was spent in Port Tudy, exiting through the gate at 1600 en route for La Palais on Belle Ile, with a fair east-north-east wind taking us fast down to Belle Ile, with the topsail up. Once there, we found we had missed the lock into the inner harbour, and had to moor outside with a large number of other boats. After a very lumpy night Amelia established that we could lock into the inner harbour at 0630. This we did. Many boats left. Belle Ile is a lovely island, good for a family holiday; so it was decided to have a lay day to do some shopping, go swimming and the Bank. Diana bought two live crabs which the skipper cooked and cracked open for a great lunch of dressed crab.

We left when the lock opened the following morning, Thursday, at 0730, and moored off in deep water while Amelia and Cedric went for bread, croissants and a supermarket. After breakfast we left for Quiberon, and planned a course to take us through the passage de Teighouse and round the corner to Port Haliguen. Arriving off Port Haliguen around 1500 we anchored off the coast, taking the inflatable ashore, and spent the afternoon on the beach before motoring into the marina.

Port Haliguen is a comparatively new marina, and I don't think existed when we had come this way before in 1987 and 1992, when we had cruised in the Morbihan; it is well organised, cost 110 francs per night (£14, about par for the course this year) but there is nothing much there, and if we had had the time it would be better to go that little bit further on to La Trinite.

Cedric and Amelia had to catch the Roscoff ferry back to the UK on the Sunday, so it was necessary to return to Port Louis on Friday. With a force 2 wind we made slow progress, but without the diesel, berthing in Port Louis by 1900, in time to take the family for a farewell dinner at the Hotel du Commerce (our intelligence being that this would be both good and reasonable).

Port Louis proved to be a charming town and not, as the skipper remembered previously, 'just moorings in front of a wall'. There was a wonderful market on the Saturday, and it is certainly a place to revisit. Amelia and Cedric packed up Diana's car and left in the morning, and we left later for the Iles de Glenans.

Andreas is a strong swimmer, and is happy to dive off the boat and swim round it when we are sailing at 4 knots, climbing in by means of the bobstay up to the bowsprit. This however was not one of those occasions, as there was so little wind that we were forced to engine, using the autohelm; it was slow progress, arriving 2030.

We found a suitable anchorage off the Ile de St Nicholas by

2100, and settled down for the night. It was a rare, warm and beautiful evening, and we watched the sun setting to the west of the islands. The Glenans are a beautiful series of islands, and are home to the largest sailing school in Europe. They produce the Glenans *Manual of Sailing*, which is the definitive wisdom on the subject.

Belle Ile

We departed the Glenans at midday leaving Les Grands Porceaux rocks and the Rochers Leuriou to port; in time to get to the supermarket in Concarneau by 1600, only to find that it closed on a Sunday at 1200 – so no food!

Wolfgang and family had seen us come in when on the beach at 1500, and after drinks on board, we had to go out to a restaurant in the evening. It was Andreas's birthday (it usually is!) and so it became a celebratory dinner.

Concarneau – Roscoff, 22nd – 28th July

Monday saw the arrival of the new crew, Jeremy, Rebecca and family, and after replenishing our food stores at an excellent supermarket close to the fishing harbour, Andreas left to catch his bus, then the TGV to Paris and on to Munich.

Rather than spend yet another day in Concarneau, it was decided to sail out to the Glenans again, so that the children could spend time swimming and crabbing on the series of beaches there. We anchored off St Nicholas and used the inflatable to get ashore the following day. Wolfgang had decided to spend a day with his family, so a rendevous was made at Benodet for the next evening. Jeremy and Rebecca got up early in the morning and went skinny-dipping in the beautiful clear water, followed by Florence and Jamie.

A minor hiccup occurred when the skipper was attempting to board the inflatable from the beach and fell backwards into the water, only discovering later that his much-loved Olympus XA Camera was in his back pocket! Cameras and seawater are not great mixers, and despite efforts to revive it, the XA never recovered; the skipper finally managed to find a replacement in October. These cameras are 'collectible' now.

We sailed off our anchorage at 1500, this time leaving the Ile aux Moutons to starboard to take us further westwards towards Benodet.

We found that Chart 2352, the *Anse de Benodet – Presqu'ile de Quiberon* (updated to 1995) is essential to navigate in what can be difficult waters. The buoys are excellent, and the Rouge de Glenan west cardinal allows a straight course towards Benodet, which we reached at 1800, sailing on a port tack all the way.

Wolfgang and family met us as arranged, and a nice pub was found for the evening on the west side of the river, before the bridge.

It was an early morning start on Wednesday for which, as it was to be a long day, the children joined the shore party and Wolfgang sailed with *Emma*. Leaving at 1045 with a north to north-westerly wind freshening to a force 4 during the day, but

CRUISE TO THE SUN: BRITTANY 1996, JULY – AUGUST

Iles de Glenans

lessening by 1700 to a force 3, we sailed well past Pointe de Penmarche and on to Audierne, where we anchored at 2100.

We had never before entered down the river to the centre of the town at Audierne, and resolved to do this the following day after getting advice. We moved *Emma* at 0900, berthing easily at the centre of the small town. The harbour-master was most helpful, and provided a map he had made of the route down the river. We

Cedric, Amelia and Poppy

FAMILY SAILING IN EUROPEAN WATERS

Skipper, Diana and Wolfgang

Rebecca

Jeremy

CRUISE TO THE SUN: BRITTANY 1996, JULY – AUGUST

Florence

Jamie

also worked out that it would be impossible to get around the Raz the following day if we left when the tide allowed in the morning; it would be necessary to move in the evening and anchor outside so that an early start could be made by 7.30 a.m.

Audierne is a delightful town, and we realised that we should have been into the centre before, but in the past we have generally been in a hurry to move either north or south, and have never thought it worthwhile. We spent a lazy day doing a little make-and-mend, and visiting the shops. We left down river about 2000 using the harbour-master's excellent 'chart' which was all that was needed we were grateful for it, anchoring off by 2100. It was a somewhat uncomfortable night at anchor, the skipper getting up at two-hourly intervals to check our relationship with other boats, but all was well.

The children were taken off in the inflatable at 0700 to spend the day with the shore party, and we left at 7.30 for our trip along the coast, around the Raz and up to Camaret. Wolfgang had had to drive to Brest to pick up Danny from the airport, and so was not on board, the crew consisting of Jeremy and Rebecca.

It was a fast sail westwards with a north-easterly force 3 – 4 along the coast at 6 knots, meeting heavy swell when rounding the Raz, despite the tide being in our favour.

The rest of the morning saw a gentle sail north, rounding the corner into Camaret by 1600. An interesting ship was parked on the mud at the end of the harbour, called the *Antarctic Endeavour*; it looked as though it had been designed to ride up over the ice, there being no keel. It was very large, with the tallest mast I have seen (including *Velsheda*). The deck housings were faired into the ship like a space structure. It made a strange contrast with the Camaret hulks, that seem to multiply every time we go there.

From Camaret we left the next day in mist at 0900, but in order to sail we had to tack right across to the Goulet de Brest, and to catch the tide up the Chenal du Four we had to engine for an hour up to Pointe St Mathieu, before turning north for L'Aber Wrac'h. Even so, the tide had turned against us by 1600, and with little progress being made, we engined towards Libenter, and into the harbour at L'Aber Wrac'h by 1735. The shore party had

CRUISE TO THE SUN: BRITTANY 1996, JULY – AUGUST

The *Antarctic Endeavour*

Parked at Roscoff

arrived, and it was agreed that we should have a meal ashore at the L'Escale restaurant – this was generously hosted by Gerti.

As the passage to Roscoff was to be Rebecca and family's last day it was decided that Florence and Jamie should come with us; so with Wolfgang we were a full crew of six. It proved to be a long day for the 32 miles, but was enlivened by The Battle for Roscoff which took place just as we arrived, with a splendid re-enactment of some past naval bombardment. There was lots of gunfire from the attacking ship, and this was returned from the shore batteries. It had obviously been well advertised, as there was a large crowd gathered on the quay.

Leaving the Ile de Batz to port we finally entered the *vieux port* laying alongside the wall, as in the past, and putting down our sticks. We had calculated that we should arrive close to high water, and that when the harbour emptied, the skipper would have an opportunity to clean up the hull and check the propellor.

This was all done, but in addition it was found that the bolt retaining the rudder had come off, and the screw had worked loose, slightly damaging the hull. It was a good thing that this was discovered, as we were ill prepared for losing the rudder! Jeremy decided he would be the cook for the evening, and we fed all the shore party on board, 13 in all.

Monday 29th was a lay day, with a general clean-up, and make-and-mend. The Jeremy party left to catch the Roscoff ferry during the morning, and we awaited the arrival of our next crew.

Roscoff – St Malo, 30th July – 2nd August

Jane Priestman arrived on the Monday evening, having spent the weekend with friends in Paris, and missed a train connection from the TGV, having to wait for one and a half hours at Morlaix.

After dinner on board we went to bed early for a 6 a.m. start to catch the tide out of the drying harbour the next day, when we planned to go the 44 miles to Treguier.

The wind was a north-westerly force 4, with heavy swells, and it took some time navigating north of Les Sept Isles to catch the benefit of the wind, but it then meant a long haul to the SE with the wind almost dead behind – uncomfortable. On reaching the entrance to Treguier at the Basse Trublent light it was clear that we would require the engine, but once we turned starboard into the estuary we had the engine alarm and red lights, so had to turn the engine off (more of this anon). Wolfgang was steering with the skipper navigating, and without the help of the engine was unable to avoid going to port of a red buoy, thus hitting a rock. This was quite dramatic, with the ship turning almost on its side.

Action was taken as follows: the anchor was lowered sufficiently to hold our temporary position, the drop keel was raised to ensure this did not become encumbered in a crevice in the rock, the sails were lowered, and Treguier radio informed of our position and situation. The tide was rising and the ship soon righted itself, and an attempt to restart the engine was successful, so that it was possible to back away from the rock into deep water.

After radioing to Treguier that we no longer required assistance (though we were uncertain whether it would ever have been forthcoming), *Emma* had an uneventful passage down the 2 miles of river to moorings in the town. We had a wonderful meal at a traditional pizza place we had remembered from some years back and it was just as good.

Skipper, Jane and Wolfgang

Treguier is a lovely cathedral town and we were able to get all necessary stores the following day. The skipper also located the best ship chandlers of the trip, the wonderful sort which goes on and on into deeper recesses, with ropes and other goodies hanging from the old timber ceiling and, best of all, less than average prices: 15 metres of strong mooring rope for 180 francs.

(A note on the engine: the failure in Treguier proved to be intermittent, it occurred also the following day at Lezardrieux, and it was found that stopping for a short while, then it started again. The fault was finally diagnosed to be the water pump thermostat which was sticking, and this was replaced later in St Malo.)

We caught the tide downriver from Treguier at midday, leaving by the north-east passage to Les Jument des Heaux, where we turned east before taking the 160° passage towards La Vieille du Treou starboard-hand buoy, leading down channel to Lezardrieux.

The engine problem occurred again but this time was less dramatic as we managed to hail a passing yacht for a tow; but as the engine started again this was not required, and we reached Lezardrieux about 1800 for a meal on board followed by the pub.

It was now Wednesday and we had to be in St Malo for Wolfgang to catch the train for Vienna on Saturday, so it was decided to get as far as St Quay Portrieux the following day. This proved to be an excellent sail down the coast for 24 miles, leaving at 0845, arriving 1700. We hardly needed the engine, but it still played up, and it was necessary to switch off and then on again, so it was essential that it got properly serviced in St Malo.

During the afternoon five sloops from the Glenans Sailing School arrived and berthed close by. We were sitting having a drink on deck about midnight, when we noticed that the first of these boats left her berth followed by the remaining four. No engines were used, and they departed northwards in complete silence, an impressive experience. We imagined that perhaps this was the final passing-out examination for their crews.

On Friday we left St Quay Portrieux with Wolfgang and the skipper getting up for a 0600 start northwards to avoid the rocks to starboard. We had liked Portrieux and hoped to return another time.

It is 34 miles to St Malo, and as what wind there was, was on the nose, it meant nearly eight hours on engine, passing Cap Frehel at about 1000.

The engine performed, so it seemed that once it got going it stayed going, but the skipper was taking no chances, and once berthed in the outer harbour at St Malo we arranged for an engineer to look at the water pump and do any necessary servicing (Chantier Naval de La Plaisance). The fault was indeed the thermostat and this had to be replaced together with the impeller and belt (the latter provided from ship spares). Total cost was 778.05 francs (£101) which we thought was quite expensive, until we found he had renewed all the jubilee clips with stainless steel.

We moved into the Vauban town harbour, when the lock opened at 2000, with considerable relief. The Vauban is right in the centre of the old town, whereas the outer harbour is a very long walk into town.

It was here that Wolfgang had to leave to catch his train on Saturday, and Jane had to leave on the Sunday for Paris. Due to unforeseen circumstances we did not leave San Malo until Thursday

St Malo

FAMILY SAILING IN EUROPEAN WATERS

St Malo

8th August! This gave ample time for swimming on the excellent beaches and to have our usual spectacular five-course meal at the Porte St Pierre Restaurant (110-franc menu – it would cost more than double this in the UK). When the skipper booked in the morning, he asked for reassurance that the management had not changed. He was told very firmly that it has been run by the same family for over 60 years!

San Malo – Cherbourg, 6th – 9th August

The swimming in San Malo is excellent, either on the main beach or in the tidal swimming pool opposite the old town. The skipper and his mate then did all the household chores, as we waited for the arrival of the next crew, Sian, her sister Grania and Deke. They arrived on Monday 5th August having been led initially to the outside harbour. Unfortunately Grania did not feel well on arrival, and decided to take the ferry back to the UK the next day.

This was perhaps a good thing as she would have felt a lot worse the next day when we left the Vauban through the lock at 1100 with the 55-mile passage to Guernsey ahead. This was not a good day! We had the wind on the nose, and a heavy swell, starting as a force 4 – 5, and increasing to a force 6. After we had only progressed 9 miles on engine in three and a half hours with a further 46 to go, a decision was made to return to San Malo, having a fast trip back with only the foresails up, reaching San Malo outer harbour by 1745. The lock to the Vauban did not open until 2240, by which time the cill into the outer harbour was clear, so we moved, to find that our favourite position close to the main gate to the old city was still free. (We felt they must have known we would be back – we were not the only ship to wimp out! Another British ship returned after having got as as far as the Minquiers.)

So yet another lovely day in San Malo, staying until an early morning start on the Thursday, getting through the lock at 0400, with a complete change in the weather – a lack of wind. We left

Deke

Sian

St Malo

the Minquiers to starboard, but only had sufficient wind to sail for four of the 14 hours it took to reach St Peter Port. We arrived in time to get into the inner harbour by 1800 and to enjoy our usual Guernsey fish and chips.

In Guernsey we met Chris and Monica from Rye, who rather shamingly had heard our radio message when hitting the rock in Treguier!

CRUISE TO THE SUN: BRITTANY 1996, JULY – AUGUST

Sian and Deke, who had both been taking sailing classes in the Port of London, and who had had a really bad first day, began to get the benefit when we left on Friday for Cherbourg, after getting diesel.

To reach Cherbourg it is essential to catch the Alderney Race north; so we left via the Little Russell from St Peter Port the next day at 1415 when the inner harbour cill was clear. We had an excellent sail, and Deke was persuaded that sailing was really great fun – he was reluctant to leave the tiller!

The tide turns soon after the time one reaches the top of Alderney, and on previous occasions it has been a long old haul past the Cap de Hague and on to Cherbourg; but this time the wind was just right and we made a fast passage even when the tide turned foul about 2100, arriving in Cherbourg and berthing by 2200 ... very dark and the marina not the easiest place to find.

We decided that Cherbourg was 'out to lunch': everything seemed to be closed, the bonded stores shop, the restaurant, and even the engineers were reluctant to help. It was interesting that a neighbour of ours, who owns a little aeroplane, tells us that he landed at the Cherbourg airport en route to a destination in Europe to find no one there to accept his flight details, no one in the tower, and it was lucky that he didn't require fuel, as there was no one there to serve it. The strange thing is that the ferries are arriving all the time, so should be generating a good income. Our view of Cherbourg was further clouded by the worst meal we have ever had in France, this because the waiter assumed that because we were English we would accept garbage. By the time we had refused the wine and each dish as it was presented, the waiter changed his views!

Sadly Sian and Deke had to catch the ferry home on 10th August, and we felt that they had drawn the short straw, only two decent days of sailing during their week; we were sorry to see them go.

Cherbourg was where our next little hiccup started – water in the boat! (This is against Bob Read's principle of 'people in the boat, water outside'.) By the time our next crew arrived – Jay, Verena and their two children, Julian and Becky – we were finding it necessary to bail out the bilge every four hours, and when the bilge pump broke down we had the unenviable task of using the heavy foot pump. The Jay family did not have a good start! But after taking the bilge pump to pieces we found the usual problem, a piece of wood stuck in the inlet value. Whilst this didn't solve the water problem, it made it easier to handle.

Jay

St Vaaste La Hougue

CRUISE TO THE SUN: BRITTANY 1996, JULY – AUGUST

The transport to the Ile de Tatihou

St Vaaste La Hougue – the entrance

Cherbourg – Rye, 12th – 19th August

We had originally planned to go south as far as Grandcamp-Maisy, a drying harbour which would get us closer to Ouistreham, and ultimately into the Seine and Honfleur. But this would have meant a 40-mile leg and it was thought better to go only as far as Barfleur.

Getting around the corner from Cherbourg to Barfleur means negotiating a series of races and choppy seas, but it was only 16 miles and meant we could catch the tide around by leaving at 1630, tying up against the wall soon after 2000.

The skipper was anxious to examine the hull to see if the water intake had anything to do with 'l'Affair Rock'. Happily after a 0400 inspection it revealed only two fairly minor scars on the port side of the hull, so the mystery of the water intake remained. The skipper was not a happy bunny, muttering about 'holidays in caravans next year'!

As *Emma* leans forward when on sticks, all the water collected inside (before the sea had drained out of the harbour) went forward, so that the duckboards were floating in 6 inches of water, which could not be pumped out until we were afloat again.

After establishing that there were no engineers available in Barfleur, the advice was to go the following morning to St Vaast La Hougue, only 11 miles further south. This was very good advice, we left when there was sufficient water by 1000 and reached St Vaast by 1300 when the lock was still open, so we were able to berth inside.

The happiest possible memory of St Vaast is that they had an engineer (from Contentin Nautic), who came and solved the water problem in less than half an hour – to the shame of the skipper who had not thought of checking the intake pipe to the water pump!

It appeared that when the new jubilee clips had been installed after the repair to the thermostat in San Malo, one must have cut into the pipe, thus causing the leak. Oh happy smiles; no longer talk of caravans!

There is an amusing amphibious vehicle which takes visitors

from St Vaast to the offshore island of Ile de Tatihou; it lumbers off down a slipway to sea which seems its more natural habitat.

Leaving St Vaast at 0900 we sailed quite well for most of the day with a north-easterly force 3. Julian tried his hand at fishing and caught ten mackerel and Jay, who is an accomplished folk singer, sang sea shanties. He knows all the words, and we poor crew could do no more than join in the choruses. Jay even knew all the words to one of my favourites, 'The Leaving of Liverpool'.

We had to rely on the engine when the wind died for the last four hours, arriving at Ouistreham by 2040, but having to wait until 2200 before being allowed through the lock and into the marina. The place is the pits, basically a ferry port and the way up to Caen. Our radio call made it quite clear that we were not allowed to wait on the outside pontoon during the night, which we would have prefered, allowing an earlier start in the morning, and saving us a 123-franc marina fee. We could also have negotiated the Seine, and got to Honfleur, but the place continues to elude us; as it was we had a very pleasant day in Trouville and Deauville. The latter has a very nice market. Verena went shopping and bought some chickens – the last of the long-distance runners!

Time was now beginning to run out, as we had to get the Jay family back to Rye at the weekend, and it was now Thursday, so the original idea of going up the coast as far as Boulogne was ruled out, and a decision was made to make our Channel crossing overnight from Dieppe.

On Friday we sailed for Fecamp, leaving at 1030, and by 1325 were moving nowhere, nil wind and slack tide. So it was swimming for all. The sun was shining, the sea was warm and the French coast was about a mile away. Our long five-rung ladder contributes an essential safety factor on such occasions. The skipper cleaned all the dirt and oil off the waterline – we had to look a bit smart to come home. We berthed in the avant port at Fecamp by 2015; they also would not sell us diesel.

Leaving Fecamp at 0900 we had a south-easterly force 3 to take us north-eastwards towards Dieppe but by 1100 the wind died and it was necessary to engine. By noon a little wind arrived, and we were able to sail again, it was the first time the skipper has used the autohelm when sailing, keeping battery 2 in reserve for starting. Jay mastered getting the topsail up which added a knot to our speed.

We were followed by a Cornish Trader (*Romain*), owned and sailed single-handed by a Frenchman, and we sailed in company for an hour or so, when he departed seawards. He did not arrive in Dieppe until late evening and told us he had 'gone fishing'.

Romain

The Duquesne harbour is being redeveloped, and all ships have to moor in the outer harbour. We were now getting short of diesel, as the last time we had got any was in Guernsey, and there was also none available in Dieppe ... but we were lucky enough to meet a delightful English clergyman called Peter Rose living in Dieppe, who had come down to have a look at *Emma*. He offered to take us in his car to his garage on the outskirts of town, and we picked up 30 litres there; more than enough to see us back to the UK if the wind was of no help. Is it our imagination, or is it getting more difficult to obtain diesel in France? It had been unobtainable in St Vaast, Ouistreham and Trouville.

As Sunday was to be our last day in France we decided to eat ashore in the evening, and ignoring the upmarket restaurants, we found a delightful little bistro with an 88-franc (£11.50) menu for a five-course meal. It was good too. We had a certain déjà vu about the place as we were fairly sure it was where we had been before some years ago.

Skipper's 'Mate'

Sunday was a lay day until we were to leave for the night sail across to Rye, and we found a supermarket open until 1500 where we bought some essential items for the passage across; unfortunately the money had run out so we couldn't stock up with all our usual goodies.

The passage home to Rye was magic, and made up for the hiccups we had experienced over the past six weeks. We left harbour under sail at 2030, with one reef put in (our usual practice when night sailing). The wind was light at first and we motor-sailed for the first three hours, after which we sailed all night, using the North Star as our guiding beacon. The skipper was even allowed a few hours' sleep, but was wakened up by the mate who was worried about a bright white light which seemed to be approaching us from the north-east. It certainly presented a problem

– was it an aeroplane or another yacht quite close? It was when it started to rise well above the horizon that it dawned on us that it was Venus, the brightest planet in the heavens!

We shook out the reef at sunrise, and sailed well to Rye arriving early at 1330, with a strong flood tide, enabling us to get over the cill into Rother river, but too strong to allow us to make it safely down river to our mooring. We hung onto a fishing boat by the Harbour Office while we had lunch. High water was at 1439, so we left to go downriver at 1400, arriving at our berth dead on the high; we didn't wish to repeat the experience of two years ago.

It was a longish passage, over six weeks and 1,307 miles, and when Adam kindly brought the car down to drive us home to Bovingdon it was a great joy to be home safely, and tucked into a real bed again.

Safely home in Rye

Cruise finances

This year there were fewer crew over the six-week period from 7th July to 19th August. All crew were asked to contribute £60 per week.

Berthing was still a major expense, this year £435. In Holland it had been £380 in 1995 and in 1994 £218 in Spain and Portugal, each for a six-week cruise.

Food in France was not dissimilar to UK supermarket prices, but in restaurants a 109-franc (£13) menu will provide a superb four-course meal (wine extra). Restaurant meals in France are excellent value and quality.

Credit from skipper and all crew,

26 man weeks @ £60	£1560.00
Additional cash to meet high berthing costs	£ 100.00
Total	£1660.00

Expenses

Expenses for food and drink	£ 954.00
Boat expenses	£ 706.00
Total	£1660.00

Breakdown of boat expenses

Berthing	£460.00
Diesel	£ 55.00
Boat bits	£ 64.00
Repairs	£127.00
Total	£706.00

Analysis of costs per week

Food and drink	£159.00
Boat stuff	£118.00
Total	£277.00

Exchange rate used: £1 to 7.7 francs.

Additional note on preliminary costs:

In order to have a faster passage to France, *Emma* was delivered to Plymouth two weeks ahead of the start on 7th July.

Rye – Plymouth, 17th June – 22nd June

New charts for Biscay	£ 76.45
Berthing en route	£ 65.90
Food	£ 60.00
Diesel	£50.22
Sutton Harbour Marina (2 weeks)	£150.09
Total	£401.67, say £400

This extra £400 was considered well worth it, since it allowed *Emma* to reach Concarneau in the first week of the passage, in time for the Bastille night celebrations.

12

*Not so Much a Cruise – More a Doddle:
Holland 1997*

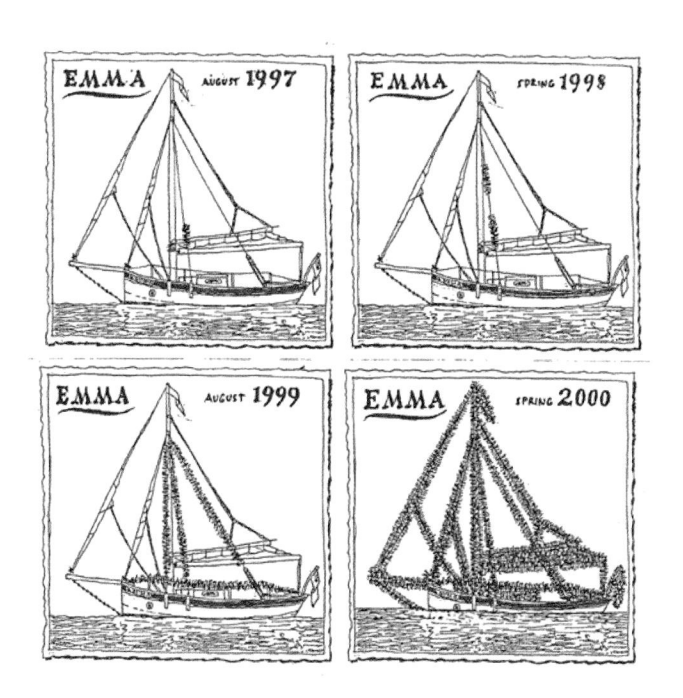

FAMILY SAILING IN EUROPEAN WATERS

1: Jonathan and Skipper; 2: Diana; 3: Jonathon Pine; 4: Jane; 5: Tin Tin; 6: Fred; 7: Chris; 8: Barney; 9: Sue; 10: Wolfgang; 11: Elan; 12: Mandy; 13: Paul; 14: Ian; 15:Andreas; 16: Bill

264

Introduction

This year we made a return to Holland for a reduced cruise: five weeks – we felt that the six weeks last year had been a port too far.

Holland is one of our favourite cruising grounds, and this year we had decided to spend more time in the various towns along the way, starting at Antwerp in Belgium and taking in a number of places we had not visited before, such as Bruges, The Hague and Dordrecht, as well as all the old favourites.

Another reason to choose the Netherlands is the ease of travel for crew and this was proved by the speed of take-up, the crew list being complete soon after we had worked out the passage plan – some coming from as far away as Israel, as well as our faithful Austrian contingent.

We did not suffer from bad weather, and the sunshine we normally associate with Holland did not fail us. There were a few minor problems mainly associated with the water pump, but nothing life-threatening. All the crew turned up in the right places and by planning a looser passage plan we enjoyed new places along the way.

The crew in Gouda

Rye – Antwerp, 13th – 19th July

A quick shakedown cruise took place on the Saturday before starting, as the weather had been so unpleasant that this was the first time we had taken *Emma* out since putting her in the water; it was useful for Jonathan to check out the rigging and sails. We were back to berth by 5 p.m.

Josephine, Fred's wife who was not able to come this year, very kindly hosted a meal in her absence for the crew at the Flushing Inn in the town. A wonderful meal, after which we all slept on the boat, setting the alarm for 4.30 a.m.

On Sunday our intention had been to go only as far as Dover, but to catch the tide down the Rother meant that it was necessary to leave at 0445, and with nil wind, it was motoring for four and a half hours to Dover where we had a hearty breakfast. Rye no longer has facilities for the supply of diesel, so we purchased 15 gallons and made the decision to carry on to Calais; still no wind. We waited for an hour for the lock to open into the Basin de L'Ouest, berthing by 1930 (ET).

Another British boat crew who had been several times to Calais told us of a wine shop in the main square, where they have casks of wine from which you can taste Bordeau, Côtes du Rhône and Chardonnay. They sell it in 10-litre boxes for about 100 francs (Chardonnay a little more expensive) so we bought one of each to try. It was very good, and we promised to pick up more on our return to take home, we did!

The cooking on this leg was provided by Tin Tin and Jonathan, vying with each other to be the best, to the benefit of all. Tin Tin produced some excellent Vietnamese meals using a fish sauce he had brought, which he used for everything. This smelt disgusting! But whether it was fish or chicken the meal tasted wonderful: Diana learnt something of Vietnamese cooking. Jonathan cooked an excellent spicy pork dish with lentils. As it was Bastille Day we went down to the beach to watch the fireworks.

On Tuesday we left for Blankenburg, a 52-mile leg. Leaving at 0715, a following wind allowing us to gull-wing past Dunkirk, arriving in Blankenburg at 1830, with an average speed berth to berth of 4 knots.

Blankenburg is close to Bruges (the *raison d'être*) and we took the little train from the centre of town to Bruges the following day. Fred and Tin stayed and explored Blankenburg. Bruges is a delightful city, but heaving with tourists. There is a constant stream of horse-drawn carriages, with special leather 'catchers' below the horses tails, to ensure that the town does not get lost in a flood of manure.

We found a quiet little restaurant beside one of the small canals for tea to escape the other tourists.

Deciding to give Brescens a miss, we did the extra mile or so as far as Terneuzen: we had arrived in Holland. The map shows the fact that the Dutch retained control of the east side of the Schelde. We had not realised this, and had thought we were in Belgium!

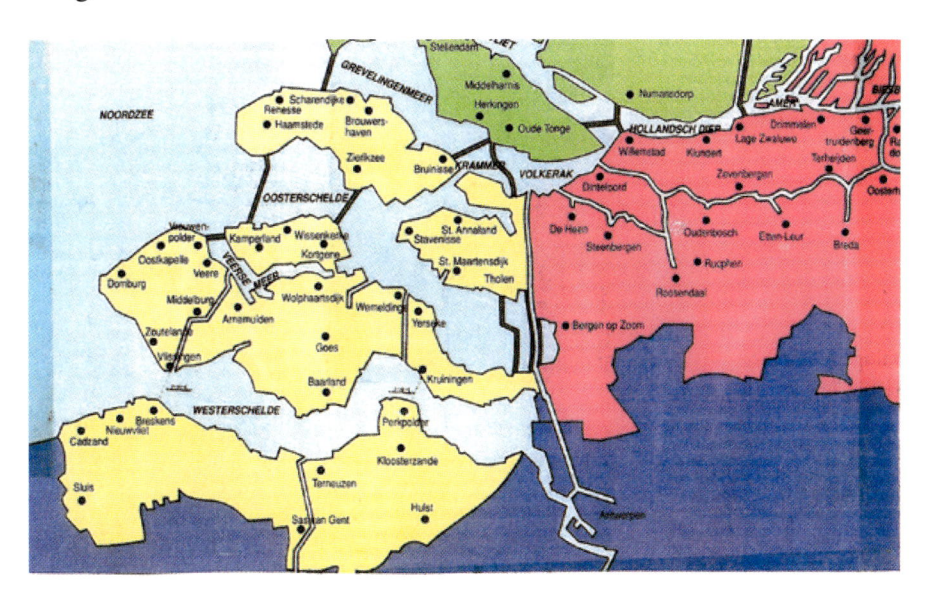

Terneuzen was a strange place, all dressed up and nowhere to go. The main street was full of restaurants and pubs and if the sun had been shining it could have been delightful ... but there were no people! The harbour-master said the town suffered from a drug problem: Belgians came across the border to buy, as hash is not illegal in Holland. The lack of people we were told was because it was too early in the season! The next day, Friday, was windy and raining hard and as we had never attempted the route up the Schelde to Anwerp even in fine weather, we decided to give it a miss.

Hellevoetsluis

Saturday dawned fine and clear, glad to have waited, and we left for Antwerp at 0845. Quite a complicated passage, with all that commercial traffic, but we arrived in good time to catch the lock into the Imalso Marina by 1515.

Antwerp is on the opposite side of the Schelde to the marina, and to get to the town, you have either to catch the metro, or walk through a pedestrian tunnel, either way it is a long walk! Antwerp, once you are there, is a fine city and well worth a visit, but I don't think I would repeat the visit by boat! We spent the

Sunday visiting the cathedral, the maritime museum, and also went to see the main station, now under reconstruction. A model in the station shows the whole development which is extensive, but it is difficult to judge it at present.

It was pouring with rain, and that with the thousands of tourists coloured our view of the place. Antwerp was our first crew change, and saw the arrival of Chris Oakley and Jonathon Pine; with Tin Tin and the other Jonathan leaving to catch planes back to the UK – we missed them. Fred stayed.

Antwerp – Amsterdam, 20th – 26th July

We were unsure of whether we could make it through the dock system into the Oosterschelde, without long delays at locks, so having got out into the Schelde, we decided to go south as far as Hansweert and north through the South Beveland Canal. We had noticed that there had been a water leak from the engine water pump which had got worse and we had been using the bilge pump (63 pumps a day) rather a lot, so we called in at Wemeldinge, where we found a Yanmar agent.

The engineer put on a reconditioned water pump (£126) and we hoped that all would be well in the future, more of which anon. Wemeldinge had changed little since our last visit in 95 and was still as uninteresting, the Dutch Milton Keynes, but as it had now got quite late we stayed over for the night.

Water still remained the problem, this time from the sink unit, leaking into the food cupboard below, tackled by Fred. The waste to the large sink had corroded so it was removed, and we couldn't use that sink for the remainder of the passage.

En route through the well-buoyed channel past the end of Tholen, the weather was quite rough, and after putting up the main we had to reef it down briefly to get round in safety to the Keeten, and on past the *sluizen* at Krammer and Volkerak to round the point into Willemstad, like old times. It was a good day's sail and Willemstad really is a delightful spot, and we chose our favourite restaurant for a crew meal out of mussels and chips

(£15 each inclusive of wine). A lazy morning next day, seeing the sights knowing that it was only a short daysail (20 miles) up the Haringuliet to Hellevoetsluis, which we made by 6 p.m.. A lovely couple in a bar insisted on buying us drinks, and attempting to teach us how to pronounce *sluis* – it sounds like 'sloish'.

Hellevoetsluis is a good kicking-off point for the lock at Stellendam which gives access to the North Sea, but as provisions were running low we needed to find shops; this was magnificently provided by a supermarket with its own mooring, accessed by lock into the town. A great place to stop.

We left for Stellendam, sailing well, entering the lock at noon and out into the North Sea by one o'clock. Followed a course to avoid the shallow ground off Goeree taking us out to the Hinder buoy, from which we set course north past Europort.

From past experience we had expected the usual panic stations, weaving between the commercial shipping entering Rotterdam; but on this occasion we were lucky, and hardly had to change our course at all towards Scheveningen, where we arrived at 7 p.m.. Very crowded and expensive as usual, Scheveningen would not

Hellevoetsluis – the shopping centre

have been our choice but for the fact that it is an easy train journey to The Hague, where we went the next day (all a part of the plan for a new-look cruise).

The Nieuw Centrum by the American architect Richard Meier is a major part of the redevelopment of the centre of the town, and is mind-blowing. With the skipper's increased interest in daylighting, this building alone made the visit worth while. First of all its size – it is immense, containing commercial and government offices, shops, the public library and restaurants. And a central daylit atrium so large that the offices on all sides appear to be naturally lit at all 12 levels, reminiscent of an Escher.

Back at the boat we were accosted by Gerhard Moller, a German who had met *Emma* both in Falmouth and at San Vicente del Barquera in Spain in 1989. He sails his 70-year-old steel gaff-rigged cutter *Niobe* down to Spain from Germany single-handed each year. A consummate sailer, he taught Diana how to make 'baggywrinkles'! The skipper went aboard *Niobe* which was a joy, fitted out for single-handed sailing, a place for everything and everything in its place. A diesel-operated heater also acted as a cooker! Gerhard gave the skipper a photograph of *Niobe*, showing the self-steering gear.

Niobe

Jonathon distinguished himself first by blocking the loo (sorted out as usual by the skipper) and then sitting on and breaking the compass binnacle. 'Jono the Blocko', as he became known, magnificently rehabilitated himself by mending the binnacle with fibreglass, in such a way that it was now far stronger than before.

We left Scheveningen for Amsterdam on Saturday to enter the Nordsee Canal at Ijmuiden, but troubles never come singly, and having sailed well towards the lock we started the motor for the final approach, and after a few minutes got red warning lights and alarms, so switched off. Fortunately a passing yacht gave us a tow into the new marina, situated before you reach the lock. More engineers looked at the water pump, and finally the problem was solved, allowing us to leave through the lock and up to Sixhaven using only the foresails. Sixhaven was full up as usual, but the amazing harbour-master always fits you in somewhere, and he did, although we had to retract the bowsprit.

Sunday was a crew change, with the arrival of Jane Priestman, Wolfgang and Barney Noblet (he was with us in Ireland in 1993) and his partner Mandy. Jonathon, Fred and Chris left. We walked into Amsterdam, and guided by Jane found the American Hotel, where we had tea and cakes at the art nouveau coffee house, and then watched street buskers. We love Amsterdam!

Amsterdam – Terschelling, 27th July – 2nd August

Monday was a beautiful day, and we left Sixhaven at 10 a.m., going out through the locks into the Ejsselmeer, where with light airs we made slow progress past Pampus.

By the afternoon the wind had picked up and we had a nice two hour sail on a port tack at 5.5 knots towards Hoorn, another of our favourite towns, arriving by 5 p.m., mooring in the old harbour or Vluchtaven (shallow mooring 2 – 2.1 metres depth). I should mention here that Diana and Barney got the topsail up! The skipper has given up on this. Hoorn has all the charms, with some lovely old houses and we wandered around the next morning taking it all in.

NOT SO MUCH A CRUISE – MORE A DODDLE: HOLLAND 1997

We left soon after midday going through the lock at Enkhuisen by 4 p.m.. We had intended to go north to Medemblik (described in *Seafile* as 'an idyllic town'). On the way the weather was so lovely that we went close to shore and put our anchor down for swimming. After having tea we all decided it would he nicer to spend the night there, and setting up anchor bearings, we relaxed, had dinner and watched the sun go down.

Going to Makkum is like going home, and we met the same nice Dutch people, met two years ago, who have a daughter called Emma, who we invited on board for coffee and cake. A busy morning was spent visiting the chandlers, where we replaced the ropey navigator's lamp for a new and neater one, and also got the Friesian courtesy flag. Barney sorted out the cockpit table, stripping it and making it like new; Jane polished the brass on the Taylors heater and the anchor lamp – all very industrious!

Barney restoring the table

We left soon after lunch, going out through the Kornwerderzand lock into the Waddensee, then starboard to follow the bouyed channel up to Harlingen, berthing before 6 p.m. We had wonderful views along the way of sky, mud flats and sea. Dutch barges using the tide park temporarily on the mud flats and spend a few hours having picnics and games. We had a wonderful meal in the evening with Diana and Jane preparing pork using one of Tin Tin's recipes. Mandy made a splendid starter with cauliflower, beans and cheese.

All was set for the next day's passage out to the Friesian Islands. As Jane would have to return from Terschelling, she decided to jump ship in Harlingen.

As the marina was very crowded, and the gate opened only so often, we had to wait for a while to leave. This was good, as while waiting we talked to a Dutch skipper on an adjacent boat, who told as that due to silting the passage we had planned, and which was shown on the chart for Terschelling, was impassable; it would be necessary to use the Slenk channel. This was very useful information and we followed his advice. Down the Slenk we were boarded by the Dutch Customs, who wanted to see our papers. They were very polite, quite different to the French we had experienced in the past.

Arriving in Terschelling, three rafted out, amongst all the old barges and gaffers. Sunday was a lay day, with a crew change: Barney and Mandy left by ferry for the mainland, while Sue and Elan arrived from Israel, and Andreas from Munich. Cornish Crabbers were well represented here: we had met a Yawl on the way in, several Shrimpers and a Crabber (number 526).

Terschelling – Dordrecht, 3rd – 9th August

After a very pleasant day in Terschelling (less crowded and nicer than Vlieland, our old port of call) we left at 9.30 a.m. on Monday for Den Helder. It was now high tide, and seeing another boat leaving the 'old way' we decided to follow; this saved a good hour from having to depart via the Slenk. We had a wonderful sail using the tide from passing Vlieland as far as the entrance to the Molengat channel into Den Helder, where the tide turned, so a slow few miles at the end; but it had been 6 knots all the way till then.

We arrived at Den Helder by 5 p.m., where there is a very pleasant little bar, and the harbour-master's wife does good food.

Andreas had taken the engine control apart and, properly greased, it now performed well; also the loo handle had broken, and this was riveted up by the harbour-master in his excellent little workshop. Andreas tried his hand at fishing and caught three mackerel; Elan also tried, without success!

Leaving the following day and buying diesel, we clipped another boat on the way out; no damage, but the German skipper made a great fuss, demanding an exchange of insurance papers. Happily we did not hear from him again!

Now we came into the Nordholland Canal, with a gentle passage south to Alkmaar, able to sail using foresails only, very sedately arriving at 5.30 p.m. Alkmaar is a beautiful little town (surprisingly

City sculpture

with its own red-light district) where we were able to get into the same little canal as in 1995 for the night. The harbour-master bicycles around opening up the bridges, and tells you when you can leave. The town is noted for its cheese fair, but this was not on.

Jochanen, whom we had last seen in Portugal, was travelling by car around Holland, and met up with us for a couple of nights; as we were continuing for Amsterdam the next day he was waiting by the canal. We decided to stop for lunch and a swim, and as there were no mooring points he drove over the mooring lines. A first for *Emma* to be moored by a BMW! There are a large number of bridges to negotiate, and although the majority are opened when you approach, it can still be a slow process.

As we did not reach the final bridge into the Nordsee Canal until nearly 8 p.m., we decided not to go up to Sixhaven, but to moor alongside the railway bridge, at Houthaven, to wait until the bridge opened between 2 and 3 a.m. It only opens once a day, so you have to be there! Sue made a delicious vegetarian pasta for dinner.

On the past occasion when we left Amsterdam by night into the canal system, it had been magic, in a flotilla of some 30 boats; as the first boat approached the next bridge, it would open and stay until the last boat was through, then on to the next bridge, no delay at all. This year it was chaotic: each bridge waited until all the boats were milling about waiting, and nearly backing into each other, before opening. The whole process of going through some 11 bridges took nearly three hours. The skipper eventually went to bed, leaving Wolfgang and Andreas to take *Emma* on to a mooring near Aalsmeer by 7 a.m. No one woke up until nearly 11 a.m.

In future a better solution will be to go into the canal system at Haarlem, where you do not have to start by negotiating a bridge in the middle of the night, and can rejoin the canal at Aalsmeer and go on down to Gouda from there.

On to Gouda the following day: ten more bridges! The last bridge had closed for the night by the time we arrived so we had to wait outside in a dreary part of town. Gouda is a most exciting place once inside with a great market, unfortunately not open on Fridays.

NOT SO MUCH A CRUISE – MORE A DODDLE: HOLLAND 1997

Emma

Skipper

Diana

Wolfgang

Elan's pictures

Andreas

We had a very lazy day sunbathing on a lawn by the boat, and in the evening Elan and Sue hosted a meal in an Indonesian restaurant, which was excellent. Sadly Diana had had too much sun, and stayed on board, feeling sick.

Elan, as well as being a well-known psychiatrist, is a considerable artist, and did portraits of the skipper, Wolfgang, Diana and Andreas, all recognisable!

Saturday saw us sailing some of the way, but mostly motoring down the wide canal to Dordrecht, arriving by 5 p.m., where we met David and Marion Proctor, whom we had met in 1995 in Wemeldinge, and who keep their beautiful Dutch barge at Paal on the Schelde halfway up to Antwerp.

Our new crew, Paul Heimburger, with a whole contingent of family arrived on Sunday and we had a party in the local bar alongside the marina, joined by Tony Cotter who owned a Dutch barge – except that it wasn't! It was a fibreglass clone, made in Norwich. Ian, who had had some difficulty in finding the Nieuehaven, arrived later, as did Bill Crawforth, a new member of the team.

Gouda

NOT SO MUCH A CRUISE – MORE A DODDLE: HOLLAND 1997

...in the bar!

The happy couple!

During the day we investigated the town. Our marina was close to the Great Church or Grote Kirk, a beautifully daylit church; this seems to be a feature of the Dutch churches, and the skipper nearly killed himself climbing to the top of the tower for a fantastic view of the rivers and countryside. Dordrecht is a town of great interest. Wolfgang left to catch a plane back to Austria. Elan and Sue with Andreas also left, but not before, with Diana's help, they had made two baggywrinkles, which Andreas fixed to the shrouds (see picture on page 281).

Dordrecht – Rye, 10th – 18th August

The bridge out of the Nieuehaven opens every half hour, and to catch the railway bridge out of Dordrecht we tried to leave at 9.30 am, but we had problems with the batteries, and had to get the marina to provide a starter. This delayed us for a couple of hours and we finally got through the railway bridge by noon on a very hot day.

We sailed using the foresails only down the Dordtsche Kil to the Hollandsch Diep and on past Willemstad towards the Volkerak and Krammersluizen (the opposite way round to our inward passage) and sailed well at 5 knots into the Ossterschelde, and below the bridge up to Zieriksee. Even though the water mark tells you there is 14 metres clear below the bridge, it is always heart-stopping as you see the mast appearing to touch it, although there is actually a good 1.5 – 2 metres clearance. Its good to be through! It was getting dark as it was nearly 10 p.m. before we berthed rafted out five boats alongside at Zieriksee. One of the boats on our inside said that he had been in the chaos with us through the bridges in Amsterdam and had also decided that he would choose the Haarlem route another time.

It was too hot to cook, so we ended up with smoked salmon and salad. The new exchange rate allowed us to shop more exotically this year – no problem affording smoked salmon.

On Tuesday we made a change to the passage plan: instead of leaving for Middleburg, we had heard on many occasions the

NOT SO MUCH A CRUISE – MORE A DODDLE: HOLLAND 1997

Andreas and baggywrinkles

beauty of Goes (pronounced Huus!) so crossed the Oosterschelde on a very hot and steamy day, entering the canal down to Goes, first making a navigational error and entering the wrong canal. Goes is as beautiful as we had been told.

Arriving in Goes by 3 p.m. we found the old marina, which was enchanting, had a late lunch and swimming in the warm water. The following day when we wanted to leave to catch the bridge out of Goes, there was a battery problem again. Ian solved this by diagnosing that the charge switch fitted this year was smoking, and that the problem was again one of the batteries. A long walk into town located a new battery, and we got a taxi back, fitted it and we were away by 1050 to catch the 11 a.m. bridge.

Into the Veerse Meer en route for Veere, time was against us and as we needed to be into Middleburg for an early start the following morning we had to give Veere a miss (we have been there many times before, so no hardship). We had a night on the town in Middleburg, after berthing with ease by 5 p.m.

Thursday was an unpleasant day: first we got held up by the bridge not opening outside Middleburg for about an hour, and by the time we had negotiated the obstacles and were out into the ocean at Vlissingen it was already 1 p.m.. The wind was on the nose all the way down the coast so we had to motor-sail, and instead of reaching our planned destination of Nieueport we ran into Ostend, mooring at 7.30 p.m.

The following day was a complete change, calm and beautiful, and we decided to go for Calais (45 miles). The tide would be against us for the first few hours, but OK for the most part. You have to navigate carefully towards Dunkirk, to negotiate the Passe de Zuydcoote. This completed we were only a short way off Dunkirk on course for Calais when it was necessary to switch on the engine.

We are getting quite used to red lights and screeching, so it was engine off and we tried to sail into port, but finally had to hail a passing French boat for a tow into the harbour. The second time this year.

Dunkirk is a pleasant harbour, with a yacht club that serves excellent food (unusual), so the skipper hosted a dinner, which cheered everyone up. The good Ian diagnosed the problem of the engine might have been a plastic bag over the water intake; anyway he tightened both fanbelts, started the engine, water coming out, seems all OK and it was all the way home.

We made a start at 5 a.m. on Saturday, to catch the fair tide towards Calais, and buoy-hopped down the coast, arriving by 10.30 am to pick up a buoy to wait for the gate into the inner harbour to open (10 – 12 a.m.). The gate opened at 11.30 and we moored opposite the yacht club.

We revisited the wine shop discovered on the outward trip, and bought ten boxes (10 litres each at £10) so we should have enough to last till Christmas. We bought Côtes du Rhône, Bordeaux and smaller boxes of Chardonnay, all excellent value.

Bill and Paul had discovered that it was the skipper and his mate's wedding anniversary (16th August 1952) and bought champagne, and then hosted a dinner at the San Diego restaurant opposite the harbour. This was wonderful; the name must have been chosen by Paul, our American! Whilst it would have been possible to have gone straight for Rye, we decided to take an extra day, sail to Boulogne, then do a night sail to Rye arriving midday on Monday, a day late. Shades of 1996, with a successful night sail to bring us home. The five-week cruise this year had been the right length, and had it not been for the water pump and battery problems, it would have been perfect. As it was, we all enjoyed it and were looking forward to next year, which might be Ireland!

Cruise finances

This year each member was asked to contribute £65.00 per week, which due to the exchange rates for sterling in the different countries was sufficient. This made it unnecessary for the skipper to subsidise the cruise. The cruise was only five weeks long, of which for three weeks there were five, and for which for two weeks there were six crew.

Total credit from crew (27 man weeks)	£1755
Expenses for cruise	
Expenses for boat	£ 630
Expenses for food and drink	£1125
	£1755

Breakdown of boat expenses

Berthing	£166
Diesel	£115
Boat bits and repairs	£349
	£630

Analysis: cost per week (5 weeks)

Food and drink	£225
Boat	£126
	£351

Note: all foreign currencies converted to sterling.

French franc	9.80	Comparison in 1995	(7.46)
Belgian franc	59.00		(44.00)
Dutch guilder	3.20		(2.41)

Note: the 'boat bits' were inflated by the need to purchase a new battery for £100 in Holland, together with some repair work to the water pump. The exchange rate helped us to break even.

13

Passage to the Mediterranean I: Rye – St Jean de Losne 1999

Introduction

After last year's exploration of the French canal system around Calais and the Baie de Somme, we read Raymond Andrews's excellent log of his 'retirement cruise', entering the canal system at Le Havre, and thence via Paris to the Mediterranean. This inspired us to try a similar route via the Seine, the Marne, the Soane and finally the Rhone, although we never got that far.

Sailing from Rye as far as Honfleur on the Seine, the mast was removed and from then on we were under engine as far as St Jean de Losne near Dijon, where *Emma* was looked after for the winter by the H20 marina.

Our plans were then unclear, but the likelihood was an early spring passage down the Rhone to Port St Louis near Marseilles; returning to the UK, then making the decision whether to carry on to Malta, the original 'gleam in the eye', or perhaps stopping off on the way to explore the delights of Spain. Ah! the joys of retirement.

Preparation

Over lunch at Simpsons, Raymond was kind enough to give me the benefit of his expertise in negotiating the canal system – invaluable advice, the first of which (since I had been in the Navy during the war) was to join the Royal Naval Sailing Association (RNSA).

Essential navigational information

Navicartes: *Carte-Guide De Navigation Fluviale* (Published by Editions Grafocarte, 125 rue Jean Jacques Rousseau-BP40-F – 921 32, Issy-les Moulineaux Cedex.)

For our passage the following five were needed:

    1. La Seine, aval du Havre a Paris
    3. La Marne, de Paris a Vitry Le Francois
    8. Champagne Ardenne, Vitry Le Francois-St Jean de Losne
    10. La Soane La Seille, de Corre a Lyon
    16. Le Rhone, de Lyon a la Mediterranee.

The Navicartes provide all the essential information of the route, the locks, the stops, water and diesel points, the distances in kilometres, together with pictures and travel information along the route. I had made the mistake of buying an expensive book on the inland waterways of France, which had proved quite useless;

the Navicartes are all that is required when planning routes, times and distances.

The only slight caveat being that piped diesel is shown in some locations, where in fact you are pointed to a local garage! *Emma* is economic with diesel, and we experienced little difficulty. Our main tank holds 20 gallons and we carry 10 extra gallons in carrying tanks; on two or three occasions we had to fill these up at local garages.

Permissions

It is necessary to obtain a *vignette* from the Canal Authority. This may be obtained from any of the Voies Navigables de France (UNF) Offices. (Typical is: Le Havre: UNF La Citadelle Avenue Lucien Corbeaux 76600.)

We were unable to obtain one either in Honfleur or Rouen, and eventually got ours at Conflans before entering Paris. Although dire warnings are issued to boats entering the canal system without the *vignette*, everyone seemed very laid-back about this.

The cost for *Emma* worked out by some abstruse equation between length of boat and beam, to be 853 francs for a month (£88). You are required to fill in a form showing which days you were travelling, lay days not being counted.

Protection

The old system of hanging car tyres down the sides is not welcomed; the tyres fall off and foul up the locks. The method favoured, and the one we used, is to hang a series of fenders on each side of the boat, in our case six per side, and to protect these by hanging wooden boards outside. We picked up 12 new fenders from a 'boat jumble' near Southampton, and the boards were cut from a single piece of 8 by 4 shuttering plywoood, being 12 inches by 8 feet each, two per side end to end. A strong central cleat is an essential when negotiating the locks, and these were fitted before leaving Rye. In addition we had four metal spikes made from angle iron, for mooring to the bank.

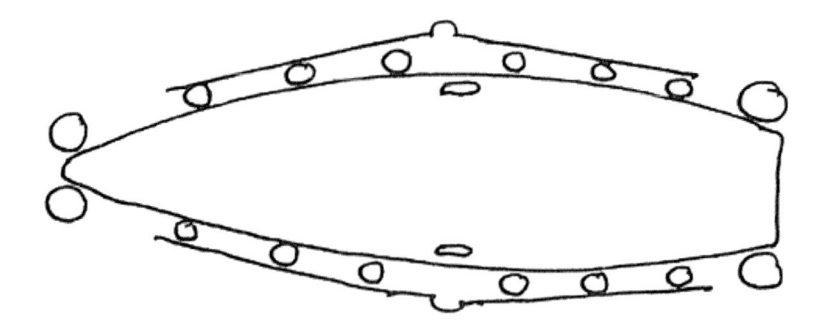

Dismasting

To assist with dismasting we needed to carry the main weight of the mast forward, using the tabernacle as a position for a forward crutch; the top of the mast being supported by the rear steel crutch normally supporting the boom. This we made from a half sheet of shuttering ply, proving entirely satisfactory.

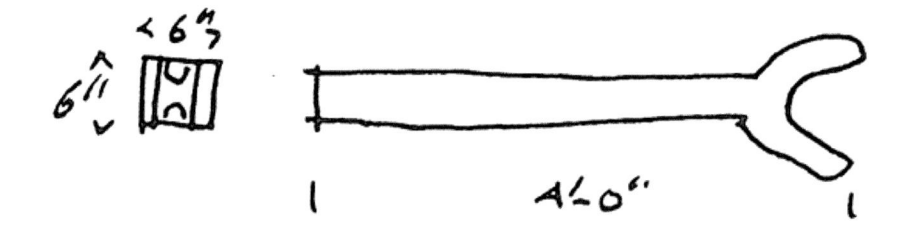

Communication

It was foreseen that there would be difficulties with communication for crew joining, and a decision was made to invest in a mobile telephone; the one chosen being a Vodaphone with facilities for use in France. A car cigarette lighter plug was installed in *Emma* to keep the phone charged. This proved satisfactory, the downside being the bill for calls received on our return to the UK – £78 for July and £221 for August. We hadn't realised that we would be charged £1 per minute for calls made to us! With the mast down the radio aerial is disconnected, so it is necessary to provide a temporary aerial, for radio connection to some of the locks. This was inexpensive.

The new crutch

Dismasting in Honfleur

Mooring spikes

Emma rigged for the canals

PASSAGE TO THE MEDITERRANEAN I: RYE – ST JEAN DE LOSNE 1999

THE CREW 1999

TIN TIN & RACHEL

IAN

REBECCA

MICHAEL

JAMIE

JEREMY

FLORENCE

CEDRIC & AMELIA

BILL

POPPY

JEAN

NOAH

291

Rye – Honfleur – Paris, 24th July – 3rd August

Leaving Rye at 0830 with a fair wind for France, we did not expect to reach Dieppe till dawn the following day, but in fact arrived soon after midnight. The wind had died by 1600, and with the engine on making 5 knots we had a fast and uneventful crossing. Ian had just passed his Yachtmaster's and kept us all according to the book, particularly when approaching Dieppe; we were sad that he had to leave there. We came into the Duquesne harbour in the morning and spent a lay day in Dieppe on Sunday, with an excellent meal out in the evening.

Setting off at 1030 the following morning when the Duquesne opened, we left for Fecamp in a force 4 from the north-east, ideal weather; but the wind freshened to a 7 – 8 by mid-afternoon, and we were glad we had put in a reef in Dieppe. Michael proved to be an excellent helmsman, coping with a lot of weatherhelm; it was quite a difficult entrance into Fecamp, turning into the wind and taking down both the main and the jib, whilst starting the engine. But all went well and we were parked in the avantporte by 1545 after a fast but rather unpleasant passage, only five hours for the 30 miles (6 knots average speed).

Fecamp is the home of Benedictine, and we were glad to have an enforced lay day due to the blustery wind (force 7 to 8), in the Channel the following day. There was an interesting summer exhibition of modern art in the monastery, with pictures by Le Corbusier amongst others, followed by a wonderful meal of seabass cooked by Tin Tin on board in the evening. But we had lost a day in the scheme of things.

Leaving on Wednesday for Honfleur at 1190 to catch the westerly flowing tide, the wind was still out of the north-east but decreased to force 5 – 6 which by the time we were off Le Havre had decreased to a 3 – 4. The skipper always finds it a little hairy crossing the mouth of the Seine and kept a close eye on the depth-sounder until picking up the marker buoys for the channel. However we completed the 37-mile passage to Honfleur in good time, getting into the lock which now opens at low tide to take you in, berthing in the Dieux Bassin by 2930.

Honfleur is a joy, and particularly parking in the centre of town. The facilities are excellent with all sorts of charming bars and restaurants right by the side of the harbour. In addition the local *chantier* has a useful little chandlery, where I was able to complete my selection of Navicartes (No. 1 not being available before leaving the UK). The following day, Thursday, I thought I had arranged by letter with the harbour-master to have the mast lifted off, but my French being what it is, I found this not to be the case! We moved through three bridges to the inner harbour and negotiated with the *chantier* to have the mast lifted the following day, so on the Friday we spent the morning in getting all ready for the lift: sails, spars and running rigging off, standing rigging loosened to ensure no hold-up on arrival of the crane, so that when it arrived at 1400 the lift went smoothly with the mast laid gently onto the new forward crutch, and the rear boom crutch, then tied down.

We were all ready for the off up the Seine, but with a second day lost. Up early on Saturday, to catch the 0700 lock opening despite the low water, we made it out into the main channel and set off for Rouen at 0710. We had planned that although the tide was foul for the first hour and a half it would be better to make some headway, however slow. We reached the magnificent Pont de Normandie by 0800, and by 0930 our speed had improved to some 15 km/hour as the flood tide took effect. We calculated that with 90 km to go, we should arrive soon after 1700. We actually berthed at the Halte Plaisance de Rouen at 1730.

The Seine is huge, and as our first experience of the French canals, somewhat daunting. There were fewer vessels than we might have thought, although some of them were immense, particularly the two-storey car carriers, two barges end to end; we calculated that together they carried some 140 cars, and we imagined that they would be transfered at Le Havre to ocean-going vessels.

The skipper was up early to get the croissants and baguettes, taking in a short visit to listen to a mass in the cathedral. Tin Tin and Rachel jumped ship in order to spend a little time in Paris, knowing that because of the two-day delay we would not now arrive until Tuesday 3rd August. We left Rouen at noon, getting piped diesel before setting off for les Andeleys, where, using the mobile, we had arranged for Jeremy and Rebecca to meet, they having flown to Charles de Gaulle airport at lunchtime. They finally arrived after dinner, excited but exhausted, having successfully negotiated the French railway system.

The 'automatique' control

The stop at Les Andeleys, where Richard Coeur de Lion had built a castle, was delightful, in a little cul de sac off the main river. A new pontoon had recently been completed, so the cost for the night with virtually no facilities was rather expensive (113 francs) As the harbour-master told us, they had to try to reimburse themselves for the new pontoon! This compares with excellent facilities elsewhere at 35 francs per night. Jeremy and the children climbed up to the castle before breakfast.

We had encountered our first lock at Ampreville, and the next day there were two before Meulan where we stayed the night, and two more before Paris. We had still not managed to purchase the *vignette*, but at Rouen had been told that this could be done at the UNF Office at Conflans, where piped diesel was also available (shown on the Navicarte). Stopping first at the diesel quay on the starboard bank, we went to the port side and the skipper walked up to the UNF Office, and purchased the *vignette* (853 francs or £88.30) so we were now legal. By now the Navicartes had became invaluable, marking each kilometre with all necessary information along the route, so that by the time we were approaching Paris on 3rd August we felt like old hands. Although later we found out that this was a gentle initiation for the days when we had 16 or more locks to deal with. The approach to Paris is quite spectacular, with views dominated by the Eiffel Tower, finally approaching the Isle de Cite and Notre Dame, then turning to port and through the lock into Arsenal, the Port de Plaisance de Paris, close to the Place de la Bastille and the new Paris Opera.

To catch up with our passage plan, meant that the planned three days in Paris had to be reduced to one lay day, but this proved not to be a hardship, as it coincided with Paris being suffocatingly hot; so much so that apart from an excursion to the Pompidou Centre (covered in scaffolding) we did little other than try to find food shops, mostly closed because Paris is on holiday during August. Rebecca and family explored the shops, but didn't get up the Eiffel Tower!

Paris – Epernay – Chalons en Champagne, 5th – 9th August

So far, the worst experience was nasty black smoke appearing from the engine compartment, which proved to be caused by a loose alternator fan belt; also a smell of diesel caused by a loose nut on the head, allowing a spray of diesel into the bilge. Both were fixed by Jeremy, ably assisted by Jamie.

Shortly after leaving Paris at 0900 on Thursday 5th August we left the Haute Seine, having been advised to turn to port into the Marne at Alfortville, with a 48-km passage to Meaux. We negotiated seven locks, arriving at Meaux at 1730, stopping for lunch and a swim on the way, so we were moving for three hours at an average speed (including locks) 6 km/hour which proved to be the wisdom for the rest of the passage.

After the Seine the Marne appears relatively small, but is more beautiful, and more interesting along the way. From Meaux to Chateau Thierry was one of our longest days at 83 km, taking ten hours of motoring, but we were kept busy by the six locks. On arrival diesel was only available at a local garage, and using our carrying tanks, a human chain of crew brought 71 litres back to *Emma*; both the main and the spare tanks were now all full.

Epernay is the centre of the Champagne district, and after a further six locks and 50 km we arrived at what proved to be one of the nicest stops of the passage. The Port de Plaisance D'Epernay is associated with the local tennis club, and is run by Monsieur Jacqmar who is both friendly and helpful, greeting you with a free kir. There were excellent facilities, with help to make a barbeque for dinner in the evening. The girls went off to a supermarket, getting a taxi back with all the goodies, including enough chicken for the barbecue. We were sad not to stay longer, but had to reach Chalons en Champagne by lunchtime on Sunday, to enable Rebecca and family to catch a train for Paris and Charles de Gaulle; they finally got home to Bristol around midnight.

One of the few hiccoughs on the trip occurred on leaving Epernay, because we had not done our homework. To get to Epernay you have to pass the lock at the entrance to the Canal Lateral a la Marne, consequently retracing your steps on leaving.

PASSAGE TO THE MEDITERRANEAN I: RYE – ST JEAN DE LOSNE 1999

We did this and waited for the lock to open. As nothing appeared to be happening after 15 minutes, Jeremy went ashore and found out that the lock was *automatique*, and that on approaching it from the direction of Chateau Thierry it is necessary to activate the lock by rotating a pole hanging over the water about 100 gards away. This starts the process, the lock gates open, and on entering there is a further simple procedure to fill the lock, open the gates and let you out. We got used to this and it proved very successful; this short delay did not prevent us from reaching Chalons in good time for the family to get their train.

Locks

Night falling at Villeguisen

297

FAMILY SAILING IN EUROPEAN WATERS

Orconte – mending the bilge pump

Chalons is a delightful town and, back on our original itinerary, it was nice to have a lay day and enjoy a Sunday afternoon and Monday with good food and wine. Work too, in cleaning ship and making ready for the arrival of our next crew, two of which failed to arrive, leaving only Bill Crawforth to hold the fort! It was found that the three of us were able to cope with all the locks for the following week. Diana became an expert lockmaster, working out a simple system for dealing with the locks, the central cleat being the key to its success; with the skipper steering the boat, and Diana and Bill dealing with the ropes.

Chalons en Champagne – Chaumont, 10th – 15th August

Tuesday 10th August saw us leave soon after 0800 for Vitry le Francois, where the Navicarte suggests specialist barge repairs and maintenance. As Vitry was not the most interesting of towns and we were unable to get diesel, said to be available a few kilometres further at Orconte we decided to carry on ... in the end there was no diesel there either, but it was a delightful stop, and a good place to watch the eclipse of the sun the following day. There was also a *bar typique* in the village, sadly lacking in many of the villages we passed.

A *peniche* or 120-foot long French barge was parked alongside, and talking to the English family on board, they told us that they had hired it for two weeks as a gite, or holiday home. The barge had been bought by the owner for £10,000 in poor condition, and he was doing it up, having so far spent £20,000, to complete the accommodation for one family in half the barge; by next year he hoped to complete the second half. One of the attractions was that during the two-week holiday he arranged for a skipper to take the *peniche* for a 40-km cruise along the canals.

Our perennial problem: the bilge pump had failed, and it seemed a good moment to service it during the morning, while waiting for the eclipse. To remove it means one person getting into the rear lazaret whilst a second has an equally uncomfortable job undoing the holding bolts below the cockpit seat. So while exciting things were happening in the sky, the crew, in the form of Diana and Bill, was busy. The pump was removed, a spring which had come dislodged was replaced and all returned to position. Right! Wrong! It failed again a few days later ... the skipper hates bilge pumps.

The problem has now been put down to dirty bilges, allowing extraneous matter to be sucked up through the strum box, fouling the bilge pump input value. Any suggestions gratefully received! We did see the eclipse through rather a lot of cloud, and were all tucked away and ready to go by lunchtime when we left for the short trip to St Dizier, 16 km and eight locks (mainly automatic) by 1300, arriving four hours later. St Dizier is a nice friendly place, and although we had to carry the diesel from the local garage, there was excellent mooring, and a well-stocked ship chandler. The town itself is not the most exciting, but has a nice church, a covered market, and a good central shopping area, about a mile from the moorings.

We left the mooring at St Dizier for the lock at La Noue around the corner, en route to Joinville, having seen the lock keeper (*eclusier*) and arranged a 0900 time of departure. When we found the gate to the lock open we entered. Mistake! Once in, we found that the *eclusier* had disappeared for half an hour, and we were left with water pouring in the forward gate and getting us stuck across the lock, unable to move further in or out. But this was the only time we were let down by the *eclusiers*, who were most courteous and efficient, travelling with us on their motorbikes, opening each lock in turn as we arrived.

For the passage to Joinville we motored in company with a small barge, the *Redquest*, owned by two elderly English people who had been travelling the French canals for over four years – cheaper than paying the Council Tax in the UK, other expenses being equal. We nicknamed them Nellie and Noah, as they were terribly houseproud, with Nellie polishing up the windows and brasswork. At Joinville, 34 km and 16 locks later, we used our spikes for the first time to moor to the bank. Our original plan was to leave for Froncles at 0900 the following day, but we woke up to find the river shrouded in a heavy mist – it was difficult to see the opposite side of the canal. We walked into town to find it was delightful, with traditional houses along the side of an interior canal, not unlike Holland.

Finally we left at 11 a.m. accompanied by a lady *eclusier* who was with us all day. She told us that her husband, the original *eclusier*, had died many years ago and she had now been doing the job for 30 years. She and her four children were well looked after, with the motorcycle and house all provided. We found all this out as she was ready to chat, and Bill wanted to practise his French; he helped by opening one-half of the gates on leaving the locks. We arranged with 'our' lady to leave for Froncles the following morning. She helped us all the way. It surprised us that there were so few other boats using the canal system: on most days we saw perhaps one other boat all day, and wondered how it could be economic for the UNF to keep the elaborate network of canals and operatives going. The canals of the Haute Marne are a delight, with beautiful scenery along the way, and full of birdlife – many herons, and a few kingfishers, apart from the usual ducks and water birds. The canals at this point are relatively shallow, only about 2 metres depth, so that it was necessary to keep the depth-sounder on at all times, and be very careful on tying up for the night.

We reached Chaumont on Saturday 14th August where there was a change of crew. Sunday was a lay day so that we could enjoy the town, some lovely old streets with fine mansions and corbelled turrets. Bill left to catch the TGV and Eurostar to the UK, arriving back in Guildford by the afternoon, and the Christie family arrived by car, Amelia and Cedric with Poppy and Noah.

Chaumont – Langres – Cusey, 16th – 22nd August

While Florence and Jamie had been old enough to enjoy the passage and to amuse themselves along the way, drawing pictures and playing Monopoly, it had been clear that Poppy and Noah were too young, so they would travel by car during the day, joining *Emma* in the evening, a system which worked well.

Monday 16th August saw us leave Chaumont for Rolampont with Cedric being shown by Diana how to deal with the locks; he became an expert and could soon do them on his own. Cedric also sorted out the water pump which had failed to operate, due to the wheel for the belt getting loose; he did a temporary repair, which lasted all the way. (A new wheel was really required, and the skipper picked one up from the Yanmar stand at the Southampton Boat Show later in the year.)

We arrived at the walled town of Langres the following day. Wednesday being a lay day we went by car to a garage and filled all the carry-tanks with diesel. We visited the town later in the day and had one of our few poor meals at the Moulon restaurant in the square. Langres is however a beautiful town, well worth a visit.

The following day, 19th August, found us negotiating the long tunnel at Balesmes-sur-Marne south of the town. The skipper had insisted that Diana and Amelia took the kids in the car, so that Cedric could help with the tunnel. It was a good thing he had, as half way through the tunnel the water pump belt broke, so red lights and screaming!

Fortunately Bob Read had provided a spare belt, and Cedric had the old bits off and the new belt fixed in about half an hour.

There were no other boats following us, the tunnel is lit all the way, and so that was no problem; but it was rather eerie, now that the engine was silent, with no sound but the drip of water from the roof. Despite its length the canal is quite straight, and it is therefore possible to make out 'the daylight at the end of the tunnel' – this helps to lessen the claustrophobic feeling.

The family had had a great day, with a visit to a lake and swimming. We all met in a bar in Villeguisen, where some friends (Jason and Shelly) who had travelled from Brussels met us. Diana provided a great meal for all on board. The next day Jason arrived with bread and croissants for breakfast, before we left for the little village of Cusey. Here there was nothing, no shop, no bar and only expensive cars and farm machinery – it appears that the farmers, enriched by the EC, run the countryside. Cedric discovered a camp site where the owner, a nice English lady, allowed us all to have showers, but without a car it would have been difficult as the nearest shop was at Fontaine Francaise, 15 miles away.

Cusey – Hugonne – St Jean de Losne, 22nd – 27th August

We were joined at Cusey by Jean Thornley, the wife of the skipper's old wartime pilot, an astonishing lady, older than Diana, who skis in the Swiss Alps and treks in Nepal. Jean had come from Switzerland, and stopped off to do a little sightseeing in France en route. We were parked under a bridge in Cusey, having gone aground close to the lock (pulled off by rope from the other bank) and it was lucky that we were walking down towards the lock to find her, when we saw her arriving by taxi. No water at Cusey, and water now very low, so we were having to buy bottled water.

We were now going downhill and all went well until lock 31 (Fontaine Francaise) where the *automatique* did not open. We returned to lock 30 at Lalau, and due to a misunderstanding Jean fell in attempting to go ashore to telephone for help. Scarcely was she in before she had climbed out, no worse for wear, helped by a stiff whisky. The telephone call was successful, with the arrival of an *eclusier* who escorted us back through the lock at Fontaine Francaise, where we parked by the lock for the night.

The Christie family had departed to see friends in Geneva and on their way back discovered us walking into town. Diana, whose bump of locality is rather suspect (she tends to get lost), had managed to walk away from the boat in the opposite direction, finally being picked up by a nice French couple and brought back to town. We all forgathered at the local Hotel de Tour for dinner. Dinner was served in the outside courtyard on a balmy evening, children playing outside; highly recommended.

It is unusual for the lock system not to operate, but the next day the lock at Reneve (no. 39) also failed. We found just enough depth of water to go close to the shore where this time Diana clambered ashore. This lock is not *automatique* and there was no *eclusier*, but Diana persuaded the man at the *eclusier*'s house to open the lock.

Our original plan had been to go only as far as Reneve, but as better facilities were promised at Pontailler-sur-Soane, we decided to go the extra 14 km and this was a good decision, with a well-protected *port de plaisance*, water and all the necessary; it is also a very charming town.

We had now entered the River Saone, and experienced the tremendous difference after the constriction of the canal system. The Saone is wide and majestic with tree-lined banks; not surprisingly this was the first time we encountered a large number of boats, mostly hire craft from St Jean de Losne, enjoying the holiday weather. There being only one lock before Auxonne, we did the 17 km in two hours, arriving in time for a swim from the pontoon where we had parked. The river is beautiful and we all swam several times.

Auxonne is the town where Napoleon Bonaparte is well loved and remembered; his career as Lieutenant Bonaparte really started here, and there is a fine statue of him in the square. (Wellington doesn't get a mention.) The town is full of interest and we were glad to spend a further lay day there. We all agreed to eat out in the main square with a 110-franc menu which was quite excellent. (The skipper had his favourite *escargots*.) Nearly at the end of our passage towards the Mediterranean, we left for St Jean de Losne the following morning, arriving at lunchtime to find an excellent port facility, with good mooring, engineering, and the best chandlery we had found in France.

Entrance to the tunnel at Langres

Our original plan had been to make a diversion from our route south, into the Canal de Bourgogne, leaving *Emma* at Dijon. This meant 20 locks up, and 20 locks back, so on reflection we decided to take a train up to Dijon, to see whether it was worth it. It wasn't: the facilities in the *port de plaisance* in Dijon are minimal, with an absence of security.

Jean travelled with us by train to Dijon, and then took the TGV on to Lausanne, and back to her flat in Anzere. Dijon is a large city, and rather intimidating. We booked a night in a hotel for the following day, and returned to St Jean de Losne, where all necessary arrangements were made at the H20 Marina to leave *Emma* for the winter. So on Saturday 28th August we tidied everything away, and left for the night at Dijon, catching the 7.59 TGV the following morning, to Lille where we boarded Eurostar, and found ourselves back in our home in Bovingdon soon after lunch: the easiest part of the passage plan.

We had made no clear plans for the future, but the likely scenario was that we would move *Emma* down the Rhone to Marseilles in the early spring of the next year, then it would be anyone's guess!

The H20 Marina at St Jean de Losne

Financial information

Income for the passage

From the skipper	8960 francs	(£927.00)
From the crew	6600 francs	(£683.00)
Total		£1610.00

Note: Each member of the crew paid £80 per week, children free.

Costs for the passage

Preparatory costs (excluding charts and engineering work)

Diesel (filled before the start), 18 gals @ £ 1.06/gal	£19.20
Vignette for 1 month on the canals paid to French UNF	£88.30
Provisioning ship	£80.00
	£187.50

Boat costs en route

Diesel	£124.00
Berthing (16 nights where payment was required)	£158.00
Dismasting *Emma* in Honfleur	£ 67.00
	£349.00

Food etc on board (excluding meals ashore) approx. £225.00 per week	£1133.00
Total costs for the passage	£1669.00

Note: Total costs do not include the Vodaphone mobile bill of £299.00

Total distances

Rye – Dieppe	64 naut. miles
Dieppe – Fecamp	30 naut. miles
Fecamp – Honfleur	37 naut. miles
	131 naut. miles (242 km)

Honfleur – Rouen	115 km
Rouen – Paris	235 km
Paris – Chalons en Champagne	218 km
Chalons – Chaumont	139 km
Chaumont – St Jean de Losne	151 km
Total	858 km (or 1100 km incl. sea passage)

Diesel purchased on passage

Total   247 litres
Total cost   1200 francs (£124.00)
Ave. Cost of diesel 4.85 francs/litre (£2.25 per gallon)

Diesel economics: 858 km in 133 engine hours = ave. 6.45 km/hour.
Distance per litre 3.73 km (or 16.8 km/gallon)

Number of locks

From Rouen to St Jean de Losne: 161 locks (no locks before Rouen)

Estimating time for passages

A useful calculation was found to be the distance divided by a speed of 6 km/hour, no allowance being made for the time at each lock.
e.g. Epernay – Chalons 37 km, seven locks: allow 37 ÷ 6 hours, actual time 6 hours
Whilst the time taken at each lock varied, it was generally about 10 minutes per lock. Speed on GPS read 5.3 knots (10km/hour).

14

*Passage to the Mediterranean II:
St Jean de Losne – Port St Louis 2000*

Sigi

Wolfgang

Elan and Sue

Jane

Introduction

Our passage plan had been to try to get as far as Naples this year, having realised that Malta would have been too far; however in the event it wasn't Naples we reached, but only as far as Marseilles. The first part of the journey down the canals of the Soane and the Rhone went according to plan, but in attempting to have the mast raised ready for sailing in the Mediterranean, it all went badly wrong. *Emma* had to be left in a port near Marseilles, at Port St Louis, and there she would have to wait until the next year.

St Jean de Losne – Lyon

17th June, Saturday

Diana and Derek left Bovingdon and caught Eurostar from Waterloo, arriving Paris in good time to get across from Gare de Nord to the Gare de Lyon, but the taxi driver was useless and took one and a half hours. We missed the train for Dijon, and had to catch a later one, which arrived too late to take the little train for St Jean. We spent the night in the same cheap hotel as last year (Hotel de Paris).

18th June, Sunday

We were up early to catch the first train to St Jean at 1006, arriving 1041 where the good Auberge de Marin had arranged a taxi to meet us. We arrived at the boatyard, finding *Emma* in good nick, and slept on board after an excellent meal at the auberge – 12 snails, so we knew we were in France.

19th June, Monday

Up early and managed to catch Philippe, the marina engineer, who sorted out one or two queries, allowing us to leave at 1345 to continue our passage south down the Soane. We did 59 km the first day, getting as far as Verdun sur le Doubs (50 francs the night) at 1800.

20th June, Tuesday

A problem: no water coming out of the taps, although the water tanks were full. This was sorted out by a local engineer for nothing. We purchased approximately 38 gallons of diesel, and left for Chalons sur Soane at 1130 (25 km) arriving 1410, two hours and 49 minutes later. A strong wind blowing up the Soane made progress slow down to Chalons (69.50 francs the night). We checked out the new electric bilge pump, which worked fine, but were conscious that the pump was pumping out a lot of diesel with the water.

21st June, Wednesday

We left Chalons at 0815, as berth was said to be required by the harbour-master. The decision was made to go only as far as Tournous, arriving at noon (30 km). Tournous is a delightful little town, with a music festival in the main square; we sat and listened, while having some wine.

22nd June, Thursday

We left Tournous at 0930, arriving in Macon at 1230 (39 km), and stopped at the *port de plaisance*. No facilities at the marina, but they were good enough to organise an engineer to come to inspect the engine. The engineer spotted the fault on the side of the engine casing, where diesel was being thrown out, and corrected it quickly for 50 francs. We found we had used up 14 gallons of diesel in 19 hours of engining due to this fault (1.4 gallons per hour); normal use is 1 gallon in two and a half hours. We had no problem with diesel spillage after this and the bilge pump was pumping out clean water from the bilge.

23rd June, Friday

We spent a little time in the morning in Macon, sampling the local Beaujolais, then left for Villefranche sur Soane, but found this rather unfriendly, and decided to continue on to Trevous, a lovely little town, where two young lads helped us to moor along the side of the river. They were clearly refugees, one from Bosnia and the other from Bulgaria. Both refused any remuneration, even a bar of chocolate – really nice youngsters. They were pleased when Diana took their photograph, but we decided to continue on to Neuville sur Soane, a total of 69 km for the day.

TO THE MEDITERRANEAN II: ST JEAN DE LOSNE – PORT ST LOUIS 2000

The two helpers in Trevous

24th June, Saturday

Leaving Neuville sur Soane in the morning, the engine failed to start. An engineer from a local garage called and found the fault was a faulty joint in the wiring to the engine; this was corrected and all well (cost 200 francs). It does seem that we have had our share of minor faults, but all were quickly rectified. There were very few other boats on the river, but a lot of wildlife, herons in large numbers, swans and a few kites.

Lyon – Avignon

We finally left Neuville at 1930, arriving at the historic marina in Lyon by 1259. Despite having written to book a berth for a couple of nights here no one seemed interested – the place seems to be sewn up by the locals, and consists mainly of a very expensive chandlery. We went upriver, parking beyond the three bridges ready for Jane Priestman to arrive the following day.

We spent the day sightseeing in Lyon, and in the evening went to the Place Terreaux for photography. The European Football

Cup was being played between Italy and Bulgaria, with a huge TV screen set up in the square; the place was crowded with happy sightseers and fans. It was great to be there but difficult to photograph the Bartholdi Fountain and to obtain good pictures of the square. We ate at a restaurant in the square.

25th June, Sunday

Sunday was a lay day in Lyon. Derek was up early to catch the morning market along the banks of the Soane – a market to die for, it had everything, Diana joined later and we spent the entire morning drooling over all the fantastic goodies. Cheeses, fruit and bread, meat and everything else. Derek had purchased 2 kilos of olives of all kinds for £2.09 in the morning.

Jane arrived about 4 p.m., her TGV having been delayed for an hour in Marseilles. We all walked into the centre of town in the evening, walking to the other side of the island washed by the grand Rhone, drank beer and then went back to boat for a splendid dinner, with masses of raspberries bought at the market in the morning. We were invited by friends in a neighbouring boat for drinks, getting to bed about 11.30.

26th June, Monday

We left Lyon for Condrieu at 1000 (42 km) arriving 1450. Jane had won £100 at roulette the night before when staying in Casis and decided to host a delightful meal in a restaurant overlooking the Rhone, with wonderful food. We sat out in the cockpit until midnight nattering and drinking; it was very warm.

27th June, Tuesday

We left at 1000 to get diesel (48 litres at 6.1 francs per litre, total 244 francs, less expensive than in the UK). We were held up at the lock at Ecluse de Sablons, apparently a lock keepers strike, but it didn't last long and we were moving again after an hour's delay, arriving in Tournon by 1600 (50 km) due to long waits at two locks. *Emma* was parked in the centre of town in a well-protected spot (50 francs). After a lie-in till 1800 we took a walk along the river bank and discovered a rock face sculptured into a war memorial, with an excellent system of floodlighting. Derek took pictures which came out reasonably well, and will be used in his next book on exterior lighting.

28th June, Wednesday

We left for Valence at 1110, arriving at 1330 at the very smart marina, with a good chandlery. This was fortunate as our second battery was beginning to fail, and it was felt that it might he unreliable for starting; the decision was made to have it changed. An engineer arrived about 1800 with a new battery, but as it was slightly larger than our old one he had a major job in installing it; having to cut away the old box to make room for it (1,280 francs). All was complete by 1900 and we were ready for the off.

29th June, Thursday

A long day of large locks, but very easy to operate, due to the 'floating bollards': you just have to hook on, and then as the boat descends, the bollard descends with you, a great system. We left Valence at 0945, not arriving in Vivier till 1750 (54 km), taking eight hours and 15 minutes. The lock keepers are now insisting that anyone on deck whilst in a lock has to put on a life jacket. There was a drama trying to enter a tiny marina where we hit bottom, and happily were pulled off by a large power boat. We spent some time in the town, which has delightful medieval streets, took photographs, and did some food shopping.

30th June, Friday

The day of the largest lock, 23 metres between Vivier and St Etienne des Sorts. We had left Vivier at 0945 and reached the Ecluse de Bollene by 1130. Told by the Eclusier that a large barge was coming and we would have to wait until 1230, this we did, leaving the lock at 1245.

We arrived at St Etienne de Sorts by 1350 (38 km) and went ashore for a 60-franc menu at an excellent little restaurant, the only one in the town, so returned there for dinner later (189 francs) having had a sleep in the afternoon, followed by a swim, then sat in the town square and played cards.

1st July, Saturday

St Etienne to Avignon, only two locks, so a fast passage past the locks at Caderousse and Avignon, berthing in Avignon at a marina close to the Pont de St Denezet, where there were showers, water and diesel. This is the famous Pont D'Avignon, 'On y danse', etcetera. The bridge was never finished, and spans only half of the river, for which you are now charged to walk across.

2nd July, Sunday

A lay day in Avignon, a lovely town. We took pictures of the palace of the Popes, both during the day and at night, and did shopping in the market, along the riverside like in Lyon. Jane left in the morning to catch the TGV back to Marseilles, and we did a walkabout in the town ending up in a cafe for coffees. Avignon was the meeting point for the next set of crew, Wolfgang and Sigi from Austria, together with Elan and Sue from Israel; we met in the afternoon, ending up in a little restaurant in the Place d'Horloge, the town square, to watch 'The Game' – the final of the European Cup between France and Italy! The town went mad when France won, with cars going round the town hooting till four o'clock in the morning!

Bridge over the Rhone

TO THE MEDITERRANEAN II: ST JEAN DE LOSNE – PORT ST LOUIS 2000

Vallabregues

Vivier

Locks on the Rhone

317

FAMILY SAILING IN EUROPEAN WATERS

Vallabregues

Those huge locks on the Rhone    Elan rescuing the rope around the prop

TO THE MEDITERRANEAN II: ST JEAN DE LOSNE – PORT ST LOUIS 2000

3rd July, Monday

We would have liked to stop in Tarascon, but there were no moorings, so we decided to go only as far as Vallabregues. Leaving Avignon was a performance, as we had to back out of the marina against a fast-flowing tide downstream; in doing so Elan contrived to get a mooring rope around the propellor (more of which anon). The engine stopped, and we got pulled back into the berth. Elan dived over and released the rope, so that we could get started again by 1400. It appeared that all was well, and we proceeded on to Vallabregues (20 km) where we arrived at 1600. There was no one about, and it appeared that it was just a camp site, albeit with a nice little town.

4th – 6th July, Tuesday – Thursday

There was a tremendous thunderstorm in the night, but it cleared the air, and was less oppressively hot the next day. We left for Arles, passing Tarascon where, as we had surmised, there was nowhere to tie up, but it looked an interesting rock-town with a castle. We arrived at Arles at 1300, and found an excellent mooring close to the new bridge, but moored three boats out from the bank. The boat next to us was called *Tin Fish* with a young couple (David and Jane) who were returning from sailing around the world. As they were going up the canals, it was decided to give them the plywood shutter boards which we had used for *Emma* all the way from Honfleur last year, but would no longer need in the one or two locks left before reaching the Mediterranean.

Arles is a town full of interest. Diana and Derek went to the 'bull fight' in the 'colosseum' in the town – rather like the one in Rome only rather smaller – and Derek took day and night pictures of the floodlighting for the new book. In France the bulls are not killed, but chase about ten men around the ring, whilst they in turn get points for touching the bull's head. I don't think we would have enjoyed seeing the bulls killed, but here the bulls had quite an opportunity to toss one or two of the men and often jumped right out of the ring and chased the officials!

FAMILY SAILING IN EUROPEAN WATERS

On the Thursday we took *Emma* up the Petit Rhone, imagining that this would make a nice diversion from the main river, but it was rather disappointing. We only saw two other boats, and a lot of lonely river without very much wildlife. In all it took two and a half hours down to St Giles and the same time back.

The bullfight in Arles

Van Gogh spent most of his life in Arles, and we visited the famous 'Cafe le Soir', place du Forum, which he had painted in 1888. Elan did a painting of the day view, Derek took some photographs, and it may he useful to contrast these night views with the artist's impression at night. It is difficult to see how modern lighting methods would have improved it, always bearing in mind that Van Gogh's view is somewhat idealised.

7th July, Friday

We finally left Arles for Port St Louis, with some regret, on Friday. The port is off the port side of the Rhone, and it is not possible to continue down the Rhone at this point, having to lock in to Port St Louis in order to proceed into the Bay de Fos, and finally the Mediterranean. We arrived in Port St Louis by 1500, where we telephoned Port Napoleon to arrange for the mast to be erected the following day ... however, this was not to be!

8th July, Saturday

We left Port St Louis for Port Napoleon at 0800, where the mast was to be erected. At 0830 approximately came an engine transmission failure, and loss of power. The anchor was thrown over but was not enough to stop the heavy mistral wind from pushing *Emma* onto the rocks at the side of the channel. Helped by two fishermen, efforts were made to keep the boat from breaking up. The lifeboat was called, but it took nearly an hour for them to arrive. Efforts by the crew and helpers were mainly successful, with damage confined to the rudder, which took most of the impact. A few scratches on the hull, but these were not serious.

The lifeboat arrived at 0945, and towed *Emma* back to Port St Louis, arriving at 1030. The lifeboat charge was 1,090 francs.

We arranged for the harbour-master to send an engineer from M3 at Navy Service to assess the damage, and agreed that the boat be towed to Navy Service on Monday (no work being done on Sundays) where it would be lifted out.

Approaching Lyon

'On the rocks'

Towed by lifeboat

9th – 10th July, Sunday – Monday

The harbour-master towed *Emma* around to M3 at Navy Service at 10 a.m., where she was lifted out for inspection, and necessary repairs (shown as 'Chantier' at Bassin des Tellines). *Emma* was placed on props, where she remained. The damage to the transmission was assessed by Marc Rhin of M3 who estimated the need for an engineer for three days (at 220 francs per hour) to repair the clutch bearing. The repair to the rudder would be in addition, depending upon how much work and materials were required.

It was only now that the real cause of the problem was determined: this had been due to the 'mooring rope round the propellor' problem back in Avignon. This had loosened the coupling between the clutch and the propshaft, which had finally given way. We had in fact been very lucky to get so far, seeing that the problem had occurred five days before.

11th – 12th July, Tuesday – Wednesday

We lived on *Emma* at Navy Service, watching the repairs, then returned to the UK on 12th July.

Our problem had been to stop the remaining crew from joining, as we had planned crew to join at Port Napoleon, San Remo, Civitavecchio and Naples. Much use of mobile telephones, and all was well except for contacting Bill Crawforth at his pad in France; finally by a mixture of phone and fax this was accomplished in the nick of time, the day before he was due to leave. Jonathan Woodhouse had already left and had the dubious honour of arriving just in time to help out at Port St Louis, and then coming home with us by TGV!

Financial information

Due to the passage ending in Marseilles, the usual system broke down. This is a fair assessment of the finances for the passage.

Income (four weeks only)

From the skipper	6000 francs	£ 600
From the crew	4600 francs	£ 460
Total	10600 francs	£1060

Costs for the passage: St Jean de Losne – Marseilles (Port St Louis)

Preparatory costs

	Francs	Sterling
Charts (to include Mediterranean)	1350	135.00
Diesel: 18 gals @ £1.10/gal.	198	19.80
Incidental/St Jean	900	90.00
Vignette for canals	312	31.20
	2760	£276.00

Passage costs: berthing/diesel/food/new battery

	Francs	Sterling
	8019	£801.90
Lifeboat rescue	1090	£109.00
	9109	£910.90
Total	11869	£1177.90

(Shortfall, paid by skipper, £126.90)

Other expenses not included:

Cost of repairs to transmission and rudder Port St Louis
                                                        4200   £420.00

3.12.08

Whilst cruising in Emma *along the French coast, nearing Honfleur, we had a very interesting discussion about the GPS systems. There were various opinions about the accuracy of them. Some thought that there was a variation of a few centimetres, some said metres. One person thought perhaps even more. (It is interesting how some think in inches and some in feet.) This set a feeling of challenge.*

From the chart a course was laid to the next buoy. The accuracy was proved to be spot on. So much so that with the strong tide we nearly rammed the buoy. All hands had to rapidly take up positions to fend off with feet and boat hooks.

We were all impressed by this demonstration.

Fred Wills

15

Barcelona – Marseilles 2003

Farewell to *Emma*

Introduction

This is to be the last log that I shall write, as this passage has been the last that I shall make as skipper. I believe that I have reached the age where it will be best for me to hand Emma *over to my son Adam, who will in future be the new owner and skipper.*

I am writing therefore to thank you all for the help and assistance you have given me since 1980, when we bought our first boat Midley Belle *in Rye, and took her to Brittany and Holland, and when in 1988 we invested in* Emma, *the second of the new Cornish Crabber Pilot Cutter 30s, and took her to Ireland.*

Since then we have sailed Emma *together to many places in Europe, ending up in 2001 in the Mediterranean, the Baleriacs and Spain. This year* Emma *had been berthed at Port Vell in Barcelona for the winter; we picked her up from there, and sailed her to Marseilles, where Adam and his new crew took over, to sail her to Italy, and her new home in Pescara on the east coast. So it's bye-bye* Emma, *and good luck to Adam and his crew ... and thanks to you!*

There's talk of a 'wrinklys' cruise next year ... interested?

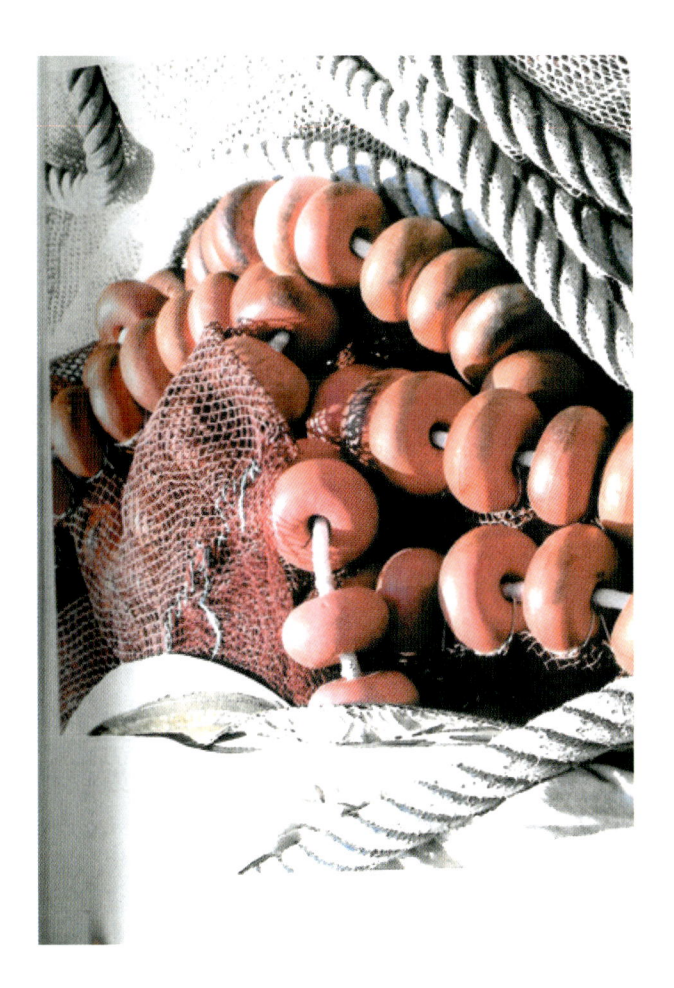

BARCELONA – MARSEILLES 2003

CREW

The Skipper and mate

Skipper and Diana

Michael Stower

Colin Day

The two Janes: Priestman and Fulton

The guests

Barcelona – Cadaques, 21st – 26th July

All the crew gathered at Port Vell by the Monday, and Tuesday was spent in preparing *Emma* for sea. Last year Starkie, Amelia, Wolfgang and Sian had left her in good order, covering the mainsail with white sheet covered by clear plastic, to protect against the UV and rain. The solar panel we had installed in 2002 had worked well, keeping the batteries in good shape throughout the winter; we have never relied on a shore line for an electric supply. Once removed the solar panel was not reinstalled until *Emma* was berthed in Marseilles for a week later. We installed tallow on the mast to ease the sail uphaul, after the dry winter.

After an early start at 0800, it was a disappointing first day as there was no wind, so we used the motor all day, arriving at Arensy del Mar at lunchtime. The cost for the night was 27 euros, which we thought expensive, but later proved to be par for the course (£18 – £19) a figure we paid throughout the passage, except at Filieu where it was even higher!

Arenys has a beautiful swimming pool and the crew luxuriated in this for the afternoon. In the evening we found the beautiful restaurant that Jane Priestman had discovered last time we were there, but instead of eating below the stars, the restarant had placed a cover over itself – it didn't seem the same, and the place seemed almost deserted. Perhaps it's always a pity to try to retrace the past ... no, it isn't!

The next day, Thursday, we went on to Saint Filieu de Guixols; this is where we had had *Emma*'s transmission repaired in 2001. They had lifted the ship out of the water after lunch, repaired the transmission – which had meant removing the rudder – and had it back in the water by the evening, a fantastic performance. I had at one time even thought of leaving *Emma* here for the winter. But this year we got the impression that times had changed; the engineering workshop seemed to have disappeared and been replaced by a pretty useless chandlery. We still spent a pleasant enough lay day at Filieu, but it was expensive (68 euros for the two nights).

Saturday saw us reach the destination for the first week, Cadaques, the home of Salvador Dali. We managed to sail some

BARCELONA – MARSEILLES 2003

Children's merry-go-round

Salvador Dali statue

of the way in light winds. This set the sort of pattern for the passage: the wind was either non-existent, or heavy and on the nose. We picked up a mooring which said 'For Rent' and sure enough a lad appeared asking for 12 euros a night. We were glad to pay this rather than be told to move in the middle of the night when an owner might return. The wind had picked up, making it uncomfortable in the dinghy.

We had planned to stay a couple of nights in Cadaques, where we had enjoyed the town before, and did so again. The mountain wind or *tremontana* was present and made journeys to and from the shore in our dinghy unpleasant – wet bums all round. The skipper hosted a dinner for all the crew at the El Barroco restaurant, designed by Dali, which we had enjoyed in 2001; it was as good as ever.

We had intended to leave the following day but 'events, dear boy, events' made this impossible.

Cadaques – Marseilles, 29th July – 2nd August

Our first attempt to leave Cadaques met with failure: we set off on Tuesday 29th July, after an early morning call at 0700, but the wind was strong and once outside the bay we had raised our sails, but there must have been a weakness in the jib, and it split across a seam. Once that was taken down a decision was made to return to our mooring in the bay, so we had another lay day, with good swimming. The following day was rather more successful, but after an early morning start we ran over the mooring rope, and the engine stopped with rope in the prop. It took the efforts of all the crew going over the side with knives to free it, with Michael as the hero who finally emerged with the evidence.

So, setting off again at 0930, we achieved the 3 – 6 miles to Bacarres in six hours on engine, the wind heavy on the nose. Bacarres has been described as the Milton Keynes of the Spanish coast, which is perhaps unkind to Milton Keynes; not a place to linger. We purchased 40 litres of diesel to fill the tank and left the following morning (the 31st) for the 47-mile haul up to Sete, berthing 'stern to' assisted by a helpful harbour crew by 1630.

Sete is a great place, an old fishing harbour: it is the entrance to the Etang de Thau and the Canal de Midi to take one across France to Bordeaux though this was not for us. Dining out in one of the many restaurants close to the fishing boats was a delight in perfect Mediterranean weather. A place to return to, in other circumstances.

Here we were faced with two alternatives: to go the short hop to Sainte Marie, with the longer hop to Marseilles the following day, or to make the long hop to Port St Louis, leaving the shorter trip to Marseilles for the next day. We chose the latter, but it did have consequences! I don't know what it is about *Emma* and Port St Louis, but it never seems to be good news.

Leaving for Port St Louis on 1st August at 0730 we made good progress motor-sailing, but the wind died in the afternoon, and the motor was increased to ensure our arrival at a reasonable hour. Turning the corner toward Port St Louis at 1700, the helmsman reported broken water ahead, and before we could take

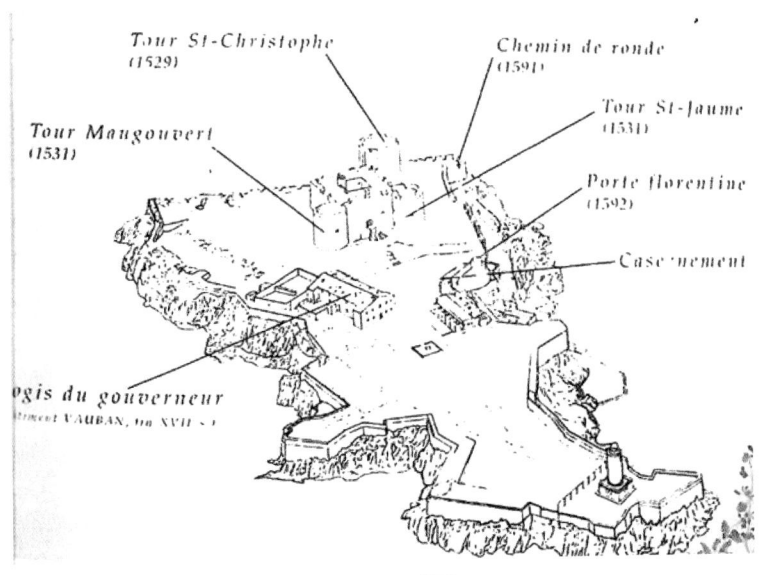

Château d'If

Restaurant on Château d'If

evasive action we hit the bottom, and despite efforts with the engine to back off we were aground on a sandbank. Taking the sails down helped, but not sufficiently to get us off. Surprise surprise! A fishing boat appeared within minutes – were they waiting for this to happen on a regular basis? At first they asked for the ship's papers, but as this smelt of salvage we resisted and finally made a deal to be pulled off for 600 euros. They had us over a barrel, and there was nothing for it but to pay up, using all the French and English currency we had on board.

We arrived at Port St Louis at 2030, going out for a meal in the little restaurant we know so well!

The following morning, keeping well clear of the shoal water, we made course for the shorter passage to Marseilles, motoring all day with not a breath of wind. We arrived in the Vieux Port where we had arranged a berth by telephone. We ended up on a pier owned by the Society Nautique de Marseilles (Club Prive) and booked in until Monday 11th August when Adam was due to take over. It should be noted that all the berths in the Vieux Port seem to be owned by different societies, and our booking with the harbour-master was worse than useless. All was well however, it was an excellent berth and enabled us to enjoy the delights of Marseilles for our final week.

Berthed in Marseilles

We were met in Marseilles with the news that Jhing, Starkie's wife, had produced a bouncing baby girl (8 lbs 15 oz), so it was champagne all round to celebrate our 12th grandchild.

As suggested in the proposed cruise schedule the final week in Marseilles was to be unplanned, after achieving the Vieux Port. There were three main aims: first, to go through all the systems on *Emma* and make necessary repairs; then to visit and enjoy Marseilles; and finally to look after Florence and her friends, who would be using *Emma* as a caravan for a week's holiday.

First, then, the needs of *Emma*. We had checked all the systems

A square in Aix en Provence

of both *Emma* and the dinghy and its outboard, and were left with the following problems:

1. The split jibsail in Cadaques.
2. The useless radio.
3. Out-of-date flares.
4. The forward starboard. fairlead missing.

Action:

1. We were lucky to find a sailmaker who had not yet closed for the August holiday, and he made an excellent repair to the jibsail.
2. We replaced the radio with a new one at a cost of 300 euros.
3. We purchased three new flares to supplement the out-of-date flares on board.
4. We purchased a new fairlead.

One further problem occurred in Marseilles: the sea loo became blocked, and despite efforts to correct it it was left to Adam –

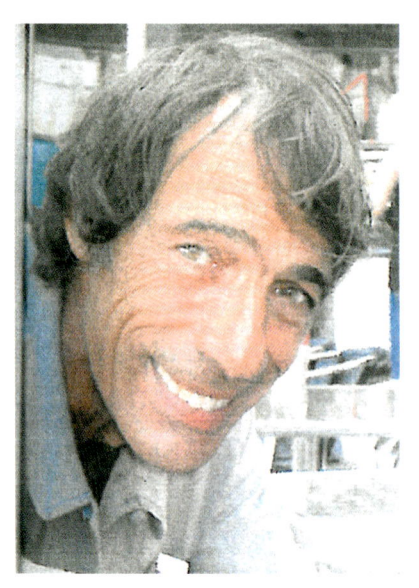

Lothar

a 'bucket and chuckit job' perhaps! (Later note: Adam replaced it.)

Next to enjoy Marseilles. It is a fascinating city, and the area around the Vieux Port is of particular interest. It is surrounded by restaurants, one of which is a three-masted schooner; we tried this but hadn't booked and had no chance to get in. We ate out at different restaurants every evening. On one occasion the skipper tried the obligatory dish of the Marsellaise, bouillabaisse, deciding that actually the standard *soupe de poisson* available all over France was to be preferred.

Emma was berthed 'bow to', to the pontoon, with the bowsprit overhanging, using our ladder to get on board. Diana contrived to fall off, injuring herself, and was saved by the skipper of the neighbouring boat!

Our favourite watering hole close to *Emma* was the Exit Cafe where we met an interesting Corsican who now lived in Marseilles. The skipper had noticed him sailing what looked like a dragon (actually a French boat) without engine in the harbour, with great expertise, each evening. For swimming we visited the village of

The Three Master Restaurant

FAMILY SAILING IN EUROPEAN WATERS

Cassis, and also one of the town beaches, and took the ferry to visit Château D'If, the setting for Dumas's *Count of Monte Christo*.

The girls explored the shops of Marseilles, and also visited the chateau; they were very self-sufficient and we only met up with them to take them out for dinner each evening; I think the 'caravan' idea worked well for them.

After the girls had left on the Friday, Diana and the skipper decided to have a night ashore right away from the sea and to visit the town of Aix en Provence, travelling by train. We had booked into a hotel for the night, called the Comfort Hotel in a place called Les Milles, described as a village! This proved to be 8 miles away from Aix, in a 'village' like the industrial estate in Hemel Hempstead! So we took a taxi into Aix the following day, and had a lovely walk around the old town, with its beautiful squares.

Adam and crew arrived at *Emma* late on the Saturday, with the unwelcome news of the floorboards floating, so water inside the ship. Adam spotted the problem – a broken pipe to the inlet water

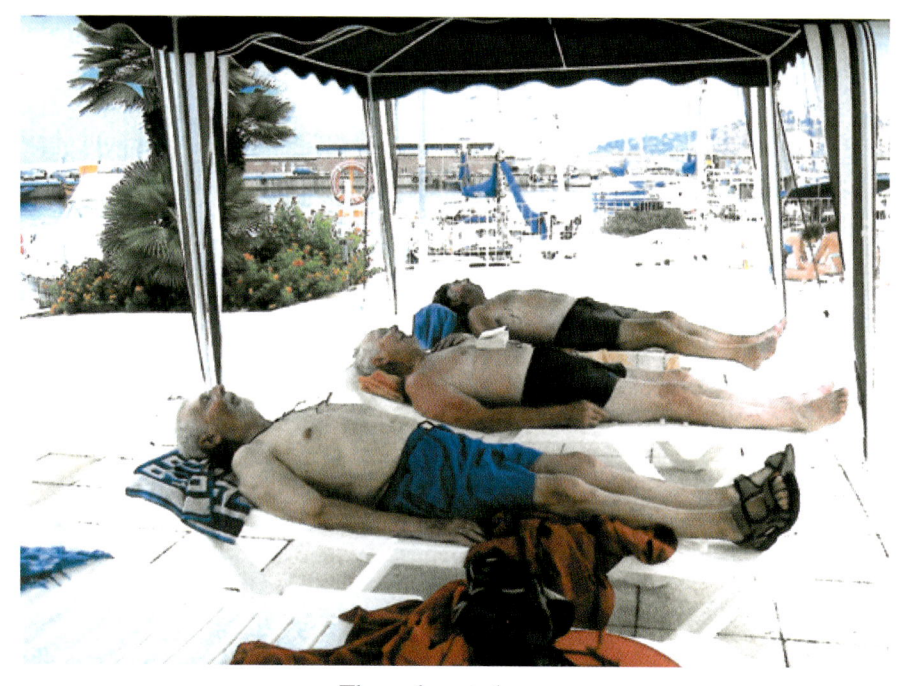

The exhausted crew

BARCELONA – MARSEILLES 2003

Skipper and Jane Fulton

Skipper and Adam

– and soon had it sorted. The new skipper now took over, and Derek and Diana left on Monday for the UK.

A minor hiccup on leaving the Sainte Charles Gare in Marseilles, a security alert which delayed the TGV for Lille, led us to miss the Eurostar and having to take a later one, arriving home at 11 pm. Exhausted – but then what are holidays for? Especially when we were arriving home to two daughters, and six grandchildren.

Finances

Credits

From skipper	2262 euros (1000 for boat)
From crew & passengers	1260 euros
For 3 weeks	3522 euros

Debits

Boat expenses	
Being pulled off sandbank	600 euros
Diesel	40 euros
Berthing	420 euros
Repairs: sail, pump etc	430 euros
	1490 euros
Food and meals ashore	2100 euros
	3590 euros
Credit	3522 euros
Debit	3590 euros

Apart from the 600 euros, paid by the skipper, the passage would have worked out well.

Emma *(from Jane Priestman)*

My first encounter occurred when I joined Emma *at Port Solaire, Majorca on her intended voyage around the island. Arriving in the late afternoon, I was ferried to join the crew in a not too inflatable rubber dinghy, which had wintered on deck, had a leaky bottom and took water on board. I was advised to take my shoes off at the start. Following an excellent meal and wine with the skipper and crew, I turned in. In the early hours of daylight I awoke to go to the heads, put my feet on the floor to find water up to my ankles. It was all hands to the buckets. An interesting first twelve hours aboard and baptism, albeit feet-wise, for the new crew member.* Emma *had wintered in Palma. It was the first voyage of the season. The fault was that a hose clip had been too tightly screwed during the pre-voyage service and had fractured. We sailed back to Palma, where Derek had acquired an excellent mooring alongside the swimming pool at the Royal Palma Yacht club. We had two days there whilst repairs were affected before taking off again.*

My second adventure with Emma *was at the invitation of Derek, to join him and his young bride of many years Diana, to take* Emma *from Barcelona, where she had wintered, to Marseilles. An entertaining, eventful and very enjoyable trip.* Emma *was my first experience of sailing with a long bowsprit. I often wondered what the advantages of a bowsprit were. It was only after a while that I found the skipper, once inside a port, was not in the least bit interested in the workings of marinas or berths. He had mastered the ploy of charging into the harbour rather like a bull at the start of a fight. The bowsprit had the effect of terrifying all and sundry to the extent that dinghies, launches and every Tom, Dick and Harry very quickly came to assist. The result was that berthing was remarkably easy. This ploy may well have been gained from some previous experience. The skipper had, however, recognised that the bowsprit left out could be usefully turned to advantage.*

Colin Day

Twice, I have joined Derek and Diana in Cadaques, both times having travelled via friends in Spain.

Cadaques must be the most magical of habours in the Med – and for that reason very crowded – meaning that Emma *was not visible from the waterfront fishy restaurant's viewpoint.*

On principle, I have no mobile phone – I prefer adventures – so on both occasions I had no idea whether Emma *had arrived or not. So – ask the fishermen!*

Yes – they had seen Emma *way beyond (she has a way of being recognised) and a handsome hunk would take me to her (at a price).*

But crew on Emma*? No! All out roistering and not a scrap to be found on board (except gin).*

Much later, in the dark and after midnight – noises that only an Emma *crew can make! I won't, of course, mention the rope-wrapped rudder, the Mistral, and other delights that kept us happy for another day or two?*

Why, I wonder, do I like adventures?

Jane Priestman

Dear Derek (from Jane Fulton)

Thank you for your letter, I would be only too happy to give you my memories from our sailing trip.

I received an invitation from Derek to join him and Diana on what was to be Derek's last voyage as skipper. I'd received many invitations before but was reluctant to go as I'm not a good sailor – ha! But seeing as it was Derek's last one as skipper, how could I refuse?

As the weeks got nearer I got more excited. The day finally came, I left home with my suitcase on wheels heading for Barcelona – I was to arrive a day before Derek and Diana. Derek told me that two crew members, namely Colin and Michael, would meet me.

Firstly, I didn't know there were two marinas in Barcelona. I of course went to the wrong one. After speaking to two Americans they too were in the wrong place. So between the three of us plus suitcase we hailed a taxi to take us to the port where Emma *awaited us.*

Bidding farewell to the Yanks, I strode along the array of boats and sailing vessels until I spotted Emma. *My excitement was growing with every breath. Sure as day becomes night, Colin and Michael welcomed me on board.*

With the niceties done with, I was asked to don my bathing suit as we were going to the beach for a swim. My heart was sinking fast as I can swim, but I just don't like what's in the sea. Diana will confirm this as she experienced my tantrums when I was little on a visit to Rye.

Once at the beach Michael and Colin went for a swim, I told them I would join them soon (I lied) but good old Colin came back for me. With a fake smile I entered the water; before long I was diving under the huge waves. I couldn't believe how brave I was, it was either that or cry in front of two grown men, ha! I actually enjoyed myself, I took in some sunbathing for good measure.

The three of us got aboard Emma *and the men prepared an evening meal all washed down with a nice bottle of red. Later that evening we went for a walk, by now I was ready for my first night in my bunk.*

The next afternoon Diana and Derek arrived. I was so looking forward to this trip with Derek the skipper and his three and a half crew members – me being the half.

Every day we moored up at different locations, it was just so beautiful being at sea with the shoreline merely a swim away.

Diana told me beforehand that it was compulsory for the ladies to have their toenails painted, which the two of us did. Mine were shocking red.

I remember eating in a famous restaurant with no roof. Jane Priestman had joined us by this time. Lunchtimes I always remember too, as Diana and I took turns inventing salads with new things added, like nectarines. God, they were delicious (yummy).

I remember always of an evening (Derek) you always sat and filled in the log (what a clever man you are) it looked quite impressive to me anyway (a non-sailor). If I remember correctly, Jhing was due to give birth. I remember me and Diana trying to find a phonebox that worked. Talking of phones, I remember of an evening teaching Di Di how to text.

A funny story I remember about you, Derek. You, me, Diana and Colin went to a beachside cafe, you decided there and then to don your bathers – right in front of a packed cafe you stripped from the waist down. I remember thinking he can't do that in here, but yes, you did. You were oblivious to the stares you were getting, ha! (Good on ya, me ol' hearty.)

I also remember Michael having to climb up to retrieve our washing as it had tangled in the mast.

One of the fun things for me was climbing down from Emma *into the dinghy. I was OK at light but when darkness came and we had to board* Emma *from a late dinner somewhere, I don't mind admitting I was scared.*

When Jane Priestman joined us she and I shared my bunk, topping and tailing. It was good fun though, each telling different stories before bedtime.

One time Colin and myself went in the dinghy to get some supplies. I can't remember exactly what happened but the dinghy got damaged. It was dark before she finally got put back in the water. I remember having to wait for a part to come in, I think we communicated back to you via the mobile phone, ha! Or it was sabotage on Colin's half, ha! He knew I was vulnerable – only kidding.

Oh what fun I had. I think my voyage came to an end in St Filoux. Colin, bless him, escorted me to the bus station and waited till I was on my way, he stayed and waved me a big farewell. I must add he slipped his card into my coat pocket.

I have spoken to him a few times since. So very different from Michael but both so very nice (Gentlemen). I helped out on deck, I even got a few blisters along the way, a far cry from my first two nights when Diana gave me her magic pills to stop the sickness.

I do hope that Adam gets his arse in gear and gets Emma *seaworthy again. When's my next adventure at sea?!*

Come on Adam – I'll even scrub the deck – walk the plank too.

One more thing comes to mind. The second day everyone went swimming off the boat – IN THE SEA. I stood on the side thinking I'll just watch. The water was so clear and inviting – Derek you and Diana were shouting at me: 'Come on, Jane. Just jump in.'

Without even thinking I didn't jump in, I DIVED in, yes, head first. That night I got out of the washing up for being brave ha! ha! ha! No sooner was I in the water, I thought of Jaws and got back out a bit rapid – not so brave after all.

Jane Fulton

Glossary of Sailing Terms

AGLOMERATOR
Attached to the engine to control the flow of fuel.

AUTOTILLER
An automatic pilot. Attached to the tiller enabling the boat to be steered automatically.

BAGGYWRINKLE
Attached to a shroud to avoid chafing of the sail.

BEARING
The direction in which the boat is heading.

BILGE PUMP
Pump used for removing water from the bilges (the lowest part of the hull).

BOBSTAY
Cable to hold down the bowsprit.

BOWSPRIT
A spar attached to the bow for securing head sails.

BROAD REACH
A point of sail with wind on the side; allows excellent sailing.

BURGEE
A small flag at the top of the mast for identification, also for checking the direction of the wind.

CLEAT
A metal or timber fitting for tying ropes.

CENTRE BOARD
An extension to the keel, can be raised or lowered.

CHANDLER
Shop selling items for a boat.

CARDINAL BUOY
A navigational buoy indicating points of the compass, an indicator for navigation.

COURSE
The heading of the boat.

COURTESY FLAG
A small flag used to acknowledge the country visited.

DEAD RECKONING (DR)
A method of navigation based on chart work.

DECCA
An electronic method of navigation.

ETA
Estimated time of arrival.

FURL
To roll up a sail to reduce its area.

GARMIN
An electronic method of navigation.

GAFF
A type of sailing pattern, eg gaff rigged, gaff jaws, metal end to gaff spar, allowing the spar to raise and lower against the mast.

GPS
Global positioning system, satellite based, also used on land.

GULL-WINGING
A method of sailing using the two foresails, one on each side of the mast, sometimes called goose-winging.

GLOSSARY OF SAILING TERMS

HEAD
A ship's toilet.

HYPOTHERMIA
Loss of body heat.

IRON TOPSAIL
Slang used to depict use of the engine.

JIB
A triangular foresail.

KEDGE
A method of pulling a boat off an obstruction.

KEEL
The extension to the bottom of the boat, can be removable, eg drop keel.

LAZARETTE
A compartment at the stern for storage.

LAZYJACK
A method of controlling the sails.

LOG
A method of measuring the ship's speed.

LAY DAY
A holiday.

MAINMAST
The tallest mast on the ship (on a Cornish Cutter, the only mast).

MAINSAIL
The most important sail.

MAKE & MEND
A holiday often used for correcting small errors of rigging or engine.

MOORING
A method of securing a boat to a buoy or quay.

NAUTICAL MILE
A minute of latitude, one-eighth longer than a statute mile.

OLD SALT
An experienced sailor.

PREVENTOR
A line designed to limit the movement of a spar, usually the boom.

PORT TACK
Sailing with the wind from the port (left) side.

QUAY
Wharf used for discharging cargo.

REEFING
Reducing sail generally by furling the sail.

RIGGING
Lines used for the control of the sails, running or standing.

RIDDLE OF THE SANDS
The fictional book by Erskine Childers about the plot for the invasion of the east coast of England, using barges designed to navigate in Dutch waters of the Friesian Isles south of Vlieland and Terschelling.

SHACKLE
An adjustable metal link.

STARBOARD
The right side facing forward, eg starboard tack is wind from starboard side.

STANDING RIGGING
Shroud and other stays which remain in place.

STAWFING GLAND (Stuffing Gland)
A device associated with the propellor shaft, which prevents water from entering the ship.

STRUM BOX
A device in the bilge to allow water to be pumped out.

GLOSSARY OF SAILING TERMS

STERN GEAR
The propellor and shaft for the boat's propulsion.

TENDER
Dinghy or small boat, used when moored off shore.

TABERNACLE
A wooden or metal base fixed to the deck to support the main mast.

TIDE
Rise and fall of water level over time, associated with the moon.

TOP SAIL
Triangular sail filling in between the main and the top of the mast (or Jackyard topsail).

TR
Radio message to give position and time of arrival at a port.

VHF
Very High Frequency radio. Usually used for ship to ship or shore communication.

WAYPOINT
Position to head for.

WETGEAR
Gear for wet weather, eg oilskins (Oilies).

YELLOW
The flag flown to indicate that you require Customs clearance.

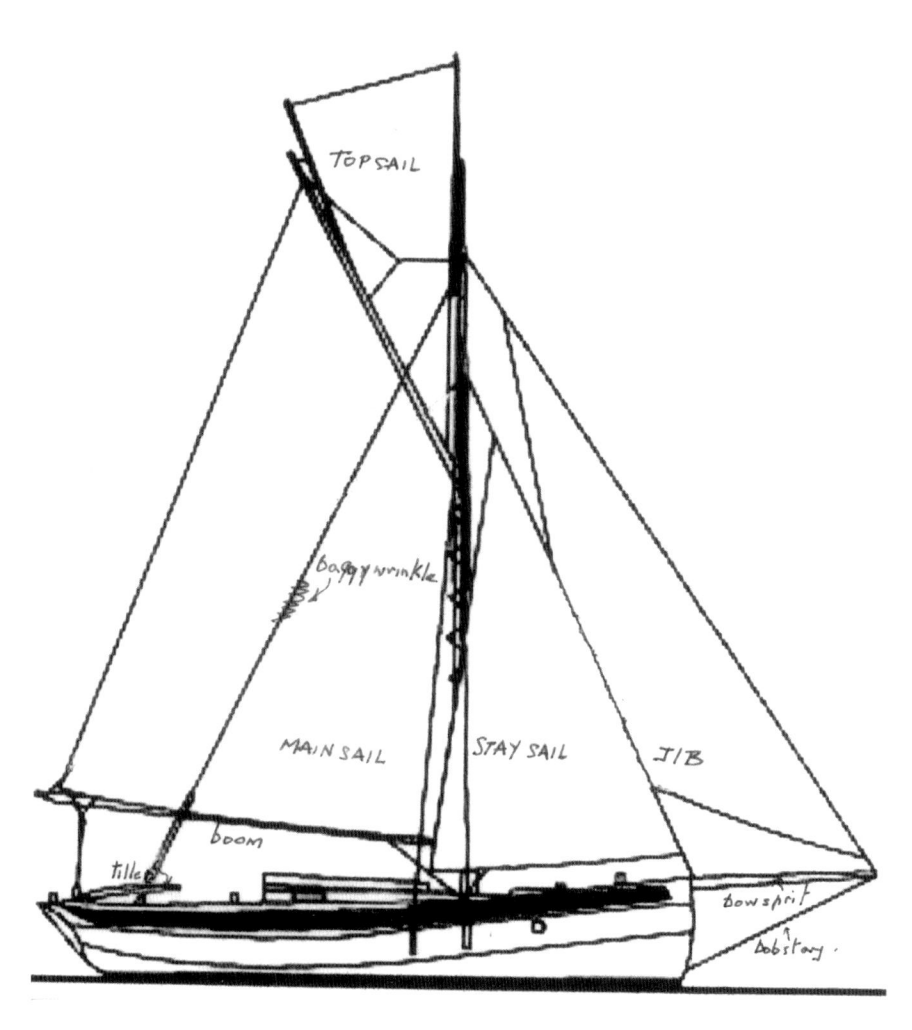

Sail plan for gaff rig